EXPERIENCING DEWEY

Insights for Today's Classroom

Second Edition

*Edited by Donna Adair Breault
and Rick Breault*

KAPPA DELTA PI
INTERNATIONAL HONOR SOCIETY IN EDUCATION

Routledge
Taylor & Francis Group

NEW YORK AND LONDON

Second edition published 2014
by Routledge
711 Third Avenue, New York, NY 10017

and by Routledge
2 Park Square, Milton Park, Abingdon, Oxon OX14 4RN

Routledge is an imprint of the Taylor & Francis Group, an informa business

© 2014 Kappa Delta Pi

First published 2005 Kappa Delta Pi

Library of Congress Cataloging-in-Publication Data

Experiencing Dewey: insights for today's classrooms / edited by Donna
    Adair Breault, Rick Breault, Kappa Delta Pi, International Honor
    Society in Education, Indianapolis, Indiana — Second edition.
        pages cm
    Includes bibliographical references and index.
  1. Dewey, John, 1859–1952.   2. Education—Philosophy.
  3. Education—Experimental methods.   I. Breault, Donna Adair.
  II. Breault, Rick.
    LB875.D5E96 2013
    370.1—dc23
    2013015715

ISBN: 978-0-415-84163-4 (hbk)
ISBN: 978-0-415-84159-7 (pbk)
ISBN: 978-0-203-76508-1 (ebk)

Typeset in Bembo
by Apex CoVantage, LLC

Portraits, photos, and Dewey's personal correspondence that appear in this
volume are from the Special Collections Research Center, Morris Library,
Southern Illinois University Carbondale. Used with permission.

The photo of Dewey surrounded by children and the postcards are
courtesy of Craig Kridel.

Printed and bound in the United States of America by Sheridan Books, Inc. (a Sheridan Group Company).

EXPERIENCING DEWEY

Experiencing Dewey: Insights for Today's Classroom offers an inspiring introduction to one of the most seminal figures in the field of education. In this collection of essays, contemporary authors consider their favorite quotations from Dewey's bountiful works and share how Dewey has impacted their teaching practices. Responses are organized around the themes introduced in the first edition: active learning, the educative experience, critical thinking, inquiry and education, and democratic citizenship, plus a new section on accountability added for the second edition. Quotes and responses are kept deliberately brief as an effective way of inviting readers to reflect on and experience Dewey.

Co-published with Kappa Delta Pi, International Honor Society in Education, *Experiencing Dewey* remains a powerful resource for current and aspiring teachers. This thoroughly updated edition also includes online resources for teacher educators to help facilitate the book's use in higher education courses.

Donna Adair Breault is department head of Childhood Education and Family Studies at Missouri State University.

Rick Breault is director of the Southwest Regional Professional Development Center at Missouri State University.

CONTENTS

PART III
Critical Thinking

The "Varied and Unusual" Abuses of Critical Thinking   87
Donna Adair Breault

FIGURES

SOURCES FOR DEWEY QUOTES

Dewey, J. (1972). My pedagogic creed. In J. A. Boydston (Ed.), *John Dewey: The early works, 1882–1898: Vol. 5. 1895–1898* (pp. 81–95). Carbondale: Southern Illinois University Press. (Original work published 1897)

Dewey, J. (1972). The significance of the problem of knowledge. In J. A. Boydston (Ed.), *John Dewey: The early works, 1882–1898: Vol. 5. 1882–1898* (pp. 3–24). Carbondale: Southern Illinois University Press. (Original work published 1897)

Dewey, J. (1976). The school and society. In J. A. Boydston (Ed.), *John Dewey: The middle works, 1899–1924: Vol. 1. 1899–1901* (pp. 5–112). Carbondale: Southern Illinois University Press. (Original work published 1899)

Dewey, J. (1976). The child and the curriculum. In J. A. Boydston (Ed.), *John Dewey: The middle works, 1899–1924: Vol. 2. 1902–1903* (pp. 271–292). Carbondale: Southern Illinois University Press. (Original work published 1902)

Dewey, J. (1977). The relation of theory to practice in education. In J. A. Boydston (Ed.), *John Dewey: The middle works, 1899–1924: Vol. 3. 1903–1906* (pp. 249–272). Carbondale: Southern Illinois University Press. (Original work published 1904)

Dewey, J. (1977). Experience and objective idealism. In J. A. Boydston (Ed.), *John Dewey: The middle works, 1899–1924: Vol. 3. 1903–1906* (pp. 128–144). Carbondale: Southern Illinois University Press. (Original work published 1906)

Dewey, J. (1978). Valid knowledge and the "subjectivity of experience." In J. A. Boydston (Ed.), *John Dewey: The middle works, 1899–1924: Vol. 6. 1910–1911* (pp. 70–79). Carbondale: Southern Illinois University Press. (Original work published 1910)

Dewey, J. (1978). How we think. In J. A. Boydston (Ed.), *John Dewey: The middle works: 1899–1924: Vol. 6. 1910–1911* (pp. 177–356). Carbondale: Southern Illinois University Press. (Original work published 1910)

Dewey, J. (1980). Democracy and education. In J. A. Boydston (Ed.), *John Dewey: The middle works, 1899–1924: Vol. 9. 1916* (pp. 1–370). Carbondale: Southern Illinois University Press. (Original work published 1916)

Dewey, J. (1983). The classroom teacher. In J. A. Boydston (Ed.), *John Dewey: The middle works, 1899–1924: Vol. 15. 1923–1924* (pp. 180–189). Carbondale: Southern Illinois University Press. (Original work published 1924)

Dewey, J. (1981). Experience and nature. In J. A. Boydston (Ed.), *John Dewey: The later works, 1925–1953: Vol. 1. 1925* (pp. 1–326). Carbondale: Southern Illinois University Press. (Original work published 1925)

Dewey, J. (1984). The public and its problems. In J. A. Boydston (Ed.), *John Dewey: The later works, 1925–1953: Vol. 2. 1925–1927* (pp. 235–372). Carbondale: Southern Illinois University Press. (Original work published 1927)

Dewey, J. (1984). The quest for certainty. In J. A. Boydston (Ed.), *John Dewey: The later works, 1925–1953: Vol. 4. 1929* (pp. 1–250). Carbondale: Southern Illinois University Press. (Original work published 1929)

Dewey, J. (1984). The sources of a science of education. In J. A. Boydston (Ed.), *John Dewey: The later works, 1925–1953: Vol. 5. 1929–1930* (pp. 1–40). Carbondale: Southern Illinois University Press. (Original work published 1929)

Dewey, J. (1986). A common faith. In J. A. Boydston (Ed.), *John Dewey: The later works, 1925–1953: Vol. 9. 1933–1934* (pp. 1–58). Carbondale: Southern Illinois University Press. (Original work published 1933)

Dewey, J. (1987). Art as experience. In J. A. Boydston (Ed.), *John Dewey: The later works, 1925–1953: Vol. 10. 1934* (pp. 1–352). Carbondale: Southern Illinois University Press. (Original work published 1934)

Dewey, J. (1987). Democracy and educational administration. In J. A. Boydston (Ed.), *John Dewey: The later works, 1925–1953: Vol. 11. 1935–1937* (pp. 217–225). Carbondale: Southern Illinois University Press. (Original work published 1937)

Dewey, J. (1987). Education and social change. In J. A. Boydston (Ed.), *John Dewey: The later works, 1925–1953: Vol. 11. 1935–1937* (pp. 408–418). Carbondale: Southern Illinois University Press. (Original work published 1937)

Dewey, J. (1986). Logic: The theory of inquiry. In J. A. Boydston (Ed.), *John Dewey: The later works, 1925–1953: Vol. 12. 1938* (pp. 7–528). Carbondale: Southern Illinois University Press. (Original work published 1938)

Dewey, J. (1988). Experience and education. In J. A. Boydston (Ed.), *John Dewey: The later works, 1925–1953: Vol. 13. 1938–1939* (pp. 1–62). Carbondale: Southern Illinois University Press. (Original work published 1938)

Dewey, J. (1988). Freedom and culture. In J. A. Boydston (Ed.), *John Dewey: The later works, 1925–1953: Vol. 13. 1938–1939* (pp. 63–252). Carbondale: Southern Illinois University Press. (Original work published 1939)

Dewey, J. (1988). Creative democracy: The task before us. In J. A. Boydston (Ed.), *John Dewey: The later works, 1925–1953: Vol. 14. 1939–1941* (pp. 224–230). Carbondale: Southern Illinois University Press. (Original work published 1939)

Dewey, J. (1952). Introduction. In E. R. Clapp, *The use of resources in education* (pp. vii–xi). New York, NY: Harper & Row.

Dewey, J., & Tufts, J. H. (1985). *The moral self*. In J. A. Boydston (Ed.), *John Dewey: The later works, 1925–1953: Vol. 7. 1932* (pp. 286–310). Carbondale: Southern Illinois University Press. (Original work published 1932))

FOREWORD

In a discussion about college teaching nearly 20 years ago, I recall an administrator lamenting those courses that relied on texts and their interpretation. His concern was that anybody could interpret anything from what, say, Jane Addams or John Dewey wrote a hundred years ago. The primary objection, it seemed to me, was to interpreting others' ideas. I found the comment odd, if not anti-intellectual, because we navigate text (and images, etc.) in interpretive ways all the time. Or do we? Increasingly, I worry that people, particularly students, are adept at following instructions but largely fail at making meaning of ideas and arguments. This book illustrates interpretation and meaning making in at least two productive ways: (a) the authors' interpretations of Dewey quotes and (b) the readers' interpretation of the interpretations.

The authors' interpretations are important, but what this book offers is the excitement of and engagement with readers. To best understand whether the authors' interpretations have merit, the reader should read more than the selected quotes. The quotes are but temptations for a larger inquiry—one that begins with the experts' ideas but then opens those ideas for further scrutiny and investigation on the part of readers and others. In this way, the book is an extended invitation. Readers are invited to understand key snippets in the hope that agreement *and* disagreement lead to broader and deeper readings of more of Dewey's vast oeuvre. The vastness of Dewey's writings, in fact, are part of the reason this book is such an important contribution to the study of American philosophy. By parsing significant elements of Dewey's philosophy and opening these parts to critical interpretation, the editors are providing pathways of meaning making. What thoughtful person wouldn't find this appealing and interesting?

As I noted, experts are on display here. But as the editors rightly point out, expertise is not restricted to the dusty offices of my scholarly colleagues whose professional affiliations typically situate them in colleges and universities. Part of the appeal of this volume is that the editors have included a variety of voices, including practitioners in P–12 schools, administrators, and students, in order to show how important it still is to interpret Dewey's ideas. Indeed, the book is Deweyan not only because it examines Dewey's ideas but also because it includes a broad community of interested thinkers—a community that is both divergent and diverse. Agreement or single-minded approval is not the goal of this work. Instead, the authors and readers are encouraged to consider and reconsider the objects of the quest in inquiry without reifying the objects themselves. Said differently, interpretations continue to grow and change in light of continuing organic inquiry—something to which Dewey was deeply dedicated. There are facts about Dewey's claims, but these facts are not part of what Dewey critiqued as "the dead wood of the past" but, rather, vital clues to understanding both Dewey's point and the changing contexts in which we find ourselves navigating.

With all of this in mind, I invite readers to engage with the quotes, the interpretations, and the larger works from which this book draws. It will be productive, in a Deweyan sense, when readers continue thinking about the ideas they confront, understand, and make meaningful.

Deron Boyles
President, The John Dewey Society
Georgia State University
Atlanta, March 26, 2013

ACKNOWLEDGMENTS

Executive Director
Faye Snodgress

Director of Publications
Kathie-Jo Arnoff

Art Director
Chuck Jarrell

Assistant Editor
Laurie Quay

The editors and publisher thank the following educational professionals, all leaders in Kappa Delta Pi, for reading and critically analyzing early drafts of chapters.

Lisa Goeken-Galliart
Illinois State University
Normal, Illinois

Valeri R. Helterbran
Indiana University of Pennsylvania
Indiana, Pennsylvania

J. Wesley Null
The University of Texas–Austin
Austin, Texas

Maria Stallions
Barry University
Miami Shores, Florida

INTRODUCTION

Rick Breault and Donna Adair Breault

John Dewey is more than a scholarly influence in our household. In fact, you might say that he always has been, to borrow from Dewey, part of our day-to-day living—and not just a part of our preparation for some future life. Rick's first publication was a short piece reflecting on the 70th anniversary of *Democracy and Education* (1916/1980). We first met at a conference when each of us went to hear the other's paper on Dewey and Freire. Some of our friends might even recall the holiday greeting cards that featured J. D. wearing a Santa Claus cap and expressing the hope that the receiver would "*experience* a happy holiday." If you were to talk to any of Donna's graduate students, they likely would recount the missionary zeal with which they were introduced to *How We Think* (1910/1978) and might still wonder whether we based our wedding vows on "My Pedagogic Creed" (1897/1972). In a way, you could say that the idea for this collection was conceived as a sort of evangelical effort.

Over the years, as we have introduced Dewey's writings to both undergraduate and graduate students, we have tried to elicit reactions on the scale of Oliver Wendell Holmes's (1941) famous remark about Dewey's writing:

> It seemed to me ... to have a feeling of intimacy with the inside of the cosmos that I found unequaled. So methought God would have spoken had he been inarticulate but keenly desirous to tell you how it was. (p. 287)

Our students wade through the often dense sentence structure and are confused as to whether Dewey is describing a position with which he disagrees or one that he espouses. Then, every once in a while, they come to a few sentences that knock them off their pedagogical feet, and they can never look at their own teaching the same way again. Time after time, when students have been ready to quit, we have encouraged them to continue reading just a few more paragraphs so that they might find that it somehow all comes together. And usually it does.

That approach has worked well, as far as it goes. However, for the reader who has not yet become a true believer and may not be reading in a class setting, that type of mentally exhausting and sometimes frustrating initial exposure to Dewey's writing may not be the spark that sends that individual into the rest of the philosopher's enormous body of work. Moreover, we are not sure that the best way to win converts to Dewey's thought is to send readers diving head-long and unassisted into *Experience and Nature* (1925/1981) or *Logic: The Theory of Inquiry* (1938/1986). Still, there are gems to be mined even from the most difficult volumes.

Beyond the intellectual challenges and rewards of reading Dewey, there is another dimension. It is difficult to walk away from his work unmoved—especially his writing about schools and teaching. To engage seriously with Dewey's work is to be motivated, encouraged, reenergized, and overwhelmed with the possibilities of an active, inquiring classroom. If you truly have entered his world, you cannot avoid making a decision. Either you can ignore what you found there and con-tinue teaching like you always have, or you can live with the knowledge that you are somehow less of a teacher than you can and should be.

Dewey, the Person

One last dimension of Dewey has come to be more important in our own teach-ing and reading in recent years. That has to do with Dewey, the person. Several years ago, we were fortunate enough to see Craig Kridel's slides of Dewey playing at the beach and just having fun with children. Knowing about that part of his life, his practical work with schools, and his commitment to a lived philosophy, we doubt that he would have been happy knowing that the discussion of his work more often than not is limited to scholarly circles, theoretical debates, or simplistic historical overviews of the progressive movement in foundations textbooks. We would like to believe that Dewey would feel more honored and perhaps even more excited by the story of a teacher who began teaching based on his work than by news of another class or American Educational Research Association panel *about* his work.

Our notions about Dewey as a person came together as an outgrowth of what was originally a humorous aside during a conversation about popularizing Dewey. One of us suggested that what Deweyan disciples needed was the sort of daily devotion book common in various Christian traditions. Typically, those books offer a passage from scripture followed by a short written reflection or meditation on the ideas in the scripture. Because we often had joked about quoting from the writings of "St. John," the suggestion was in keeping with our common faith in progressive education. But soon, the discussion turned serious. Maybe a book like that really could be a meaningful and useful way to embody our desire to more effectively introduce educators to the broad scope of Dewey's works and to do so in a personal and practical way. Furthermore, maybe such a collection also could prove valuable to experienced Deweyan readers and thinkers by rekindling the personal and pedagogical engagement that led to their initial attachment to the philosopher.

About the Collection of Essays

The process of actually constructing this volume, now in this second edition, has been a truly enjoyable and fulfilling one. In this new edition, several of the original contributors have reconsidered or updated their essays. Eighteen new authors have been integrated into the book to include prominent Dewey scholars who were unable to contribute the first time or who have risen to prominence in recent years.

Though we anticipated that bringing this dream to fruition would be rewarding, the task was even more meaningful in that we learned so much and enjoyed the help of so many friends. In identifying quotations for possible inclusion, we unearthed some Deweyan gems that we had never noticed before and were reminded once again of the enormous breadth of Dewey's genius. Then, after selecting hundreds of quotations, we began the process of inviting potential authors, asking them to select a quotation (or suggest one of their own) and reflect on its importance to them. The response we received was encouraging in many ways. Of course, we truly were honored to be able to include contributions from scholars whose reputations in our field are without question. We also were thankful for the words of encouragement and support we received from those same people, who saw this as a labor of love and an opportunity to revisit familiar quotations from a new perspective. More than one contributor mentioned that this short piece was the most difficult one they had written in a long time, for we had asked all the contributors to step away from their traditional roles of scholars and interpreters of Dewey. Instead, we asked them to draw from their personal and emotional encounter with Dewey's work—an exercise that is often difficult for those of us trained in and rewarded for traditional scholarship.

Although you will find many of the names in this collection familiar, some you will not. It was important to us to include the voices of teachers, administrators, and students who probably would not consider themselves to be Deweyan scholars but who have nonetheless been affected by Dewey's writing. That is the spirit in which we hope this book will be read. Despite Dewey's obviously formidable intellect and his sometimes heated engagement with the scholars of his day, ultimately we believe that Dewey wanted his philosophy to be lived by those who work in schools. He wanted his ideas to be used to create humane, vibrant classrooms. This aspect of his work, we envisioned, could be represented best by those who have been revitalized through their introduction to some aspect of his philosophy and are still immersed in the day-to-day work of the classroom teacher.

How to Use This Book

The approach taken in this book is not, however, without its risks. Whenever words are taken out of context, something important can be lost or, worse yet, misinterpreted. All the authors have made an attempt to recontextualize the quotes to the extent possible, and we deem all the contributions to be true to the intent and content of the original sources. The other risk, which is even more difficult to avoid, is that some readers—especially those previously unfamiliar with Dewey—could come away thinking that they have gained a sense of Dewey's work and are ready to either reject it or use it in their teaching in a way that captures only the most superficial essence of his thought. It is not our intention to promote the kind of simplistic "learning by doing" misuse of progressive educational philosophy that led to so many attacks on the movement and to the need for Dewey to disavow some aspects of the movement and defend his own ideas in his later work. Therefore, we strongly encourage those of you who are new to Dewey's work to read the full works from which the quotations are drawn.

In response to readers who have used the book in classes, we have created supplemental instructional materials and suggestions for the second edition. These supplements are intended especially for those readers who are new to Dewey's work and, we hope, have been designed in a way that honors Dewey's thoughts and would meet with his approval.

How This Book Is Organized

The first edition of *Experiencing Dewey* was organized into what are arguably five of the central ideas in Dewey's educational thought. We have retained those five themes in the present edition and have added a new section of essays, on accountability in public education, at the beginning of the volume.

Although Dewey did not write directly to the theme of Part I, "Accountability," at least not in the ways in which the concept is currently being used, we felt that it is now such a pervasive part of school life that Dewey certainly *would* have had some powerful things to say about it. Besides, the very fact that Dewey did not write in response to current, narrowly defined notions of accountability meant that we and the other authors could explore broader notions of accountability implied by his work. In turn, we hope that those contributions will help you broaden your own ideas of accountability and more effectively respond to those who would define your effectiveness solely by your students' scores.

In Part II, "Active Learning," the authors reflect on what might be the most commonly misunderstood or oversimplified aspect of Dewey's work. You will find that Dewey, who never actually used the phrase "learning by doing," intended something very challenging and substantive when he encouraged teachers to get their students actively engaged in their own learning.

"Critical Thinking" is the theme of Part III. It also might be considered central to all aspects of a Deweyan education—and maybe to Deweyan thought in general. As Dewey (1910/1978) reminds us:

> Genuine freedom . . . rests in the trained power of thought, in the ability to 'turn things over,' to look at matters deliberately. . . . If a man's actions are not guided by thoughtful conclusions, then they are guided by inconsiderate impulse, unbalanced appetite . . . or the circumstances of the moment. To cultivate unhindered, unreflective external activity is to foster enslavement. . . . There is probably no more crucial task before teachers than to nurture critical thinking in their students in the face of anti-intellectualism and what often seems to be an overwhelming emphasis on simple recall. (p. 232)

Too often, however, critical thinking has been misconceived as a set of discrete, teachable skills. Witness the various "critical thinking curricula."

Ultimately, to understand and find the full meaning of Dewey's work, you must place it in the context of implications for living as a citizen in a democracy. If your only exposure to John Dewey was a few paragraphs in an undergraduate educational foundations text or those ever-popular references to "learning by doing" in a methods course, you might be quite surprised by what you read in Part IV, "Democratic Citizenship." Yes, Dewey is concerned with the development of the individual, the mind, and the more meaningful learning of subject matter. But, in the end, what mattered for Dewey is how an individual would live in community with other individuals. In Dewey's (1933/1986) words: "The things in civilization we most prize are not of ourselves. They exist by grace of the doings and sufferings of the continuous human community in which we are a link" (p. 57).

Part V, titled "The Educative Experience," uses Dewey's words and our contributors' reflections to reemphasize the fact that not every experience had by a learner can be considered meaningful and productive.

In Part VI, "Inquiry and Education," contributors attempt to recapture the breadth and complexity of the process of critical thinking by resituating it in the process of inquiry. We think that you will find the quotations they have chosen to be especially inspirational. In reading both Dewey's words and the reflections on those words, you will be able to sense some of the excitement that the teachers in Dewey's lab school must have felt as they and their students carried out inquiry that was simultaneously artistic, challenging, freeing, and maybe even a little utopian in its feel.

We hope that Dewey would look favorably on this collection and its potential to forge another link in that human community. We also hope that you will read it in that spirit—the spirit of connection. We feel that we have done our part by linking the works of Dewey with teacher-scholars who have formed their own meaningful connections to the philosopher. They, in turn, have acted as the connection through which you may develop a closer link with Dewey. Finally, it will be up to you to translate these ideas into a new set of beliefs, reformed pedagogy, and enlivened conversations with colleagues that might create the connection Dewey would have liked best of all—the connection that brings to fruition the kind of meaningful educational experience he desired for all children.

References

Dewey, J. (1972). My pedagogic creed. In J. A. Boydston (Ed.), *John Dewey: The early works, 1882–1898: Vol. 5. 1895–1898* (pp. 81–95). Carbondale: Southern Illinois University Press. (Original work published 1897)

Dewey, J. (1978). How we think. In J. A. Boydston (Ed.), *John Dewey: The middle works, 1899–1924: Vol. 6. 1910–1911* (pp. 177–356). Carbondale: Southern Illinois University Press. (Original work published 1910)

Dewey, J. (1980). Democracy and education. In J. A. Boydston (Ed.), *John Dewey: The middle works, 1899–1924: Vol. 9. 1916* (pp. 1–370). Carbondale: Southern Illinois University Press. (Original work published 1916)

Dewey, J. (1981). Experience and nature. In J. A. Boydston (Ed.), *John Dewey: The later works, 1925–1953: Vol. 1. 1925* (pp. 1–326). Carbondale: Southern Illinois University Press. (Original work published 1925)

Dewey, J. (1986). A common faith. In J. A. Boydston (Ed.), *John Dewey: The later works, 1925–1953: Vol. 9. 1933–1934* (pp. 1–58). Carbondale: Southern Illinois University Press. (Original work published 1933)

Dewey, J. (1986). Logic: The theory of inquiry. In J. A. Boydston (Ed.), *John Dewey: The later works, 1925–1953: Vol. 12. 1938* (pp. 7–528). Carbondale: Southern Illinois University Press. (Original work published 1938)

Holmes, O. W. (1941). Letter to Frederick Pollock, 15 May 1931. In M. D. Howe (Ed.), *Holmes–Pollock letters: The correspondence of Mr. Justice Holmes and Sir Frederick Pollock 1874–1932* (Vol. 2, p. 287). Cambridge, MA: Harvard University Press.

PART I

Accountability

ACCOUNTABILITY: TO WHOM, FOR WHOM, AND BY WHOM?

Rick Breault

Most avid followers of Dewey have probably speculated as to how he would be responding to the testing and accountability movement if he were alive today. Given that Dewey's last writings were produced more than 30 years before *A Nation at Risk* (National Commission on Excellence in Education, 1983) and its fallout, we can only speculate as to the exact nature of his critique and response. In light of everything he did write and the language of growth, experience, and educative experiences that permeates his educational philosophy, we can be pretty sure that he would find little to support in the ways that learning and accountability are determined in present-day schools. On the other hand, I think Dewey would be greatly concerned about teacher accountability . . . just not in the limited way it is currently being discussed.

In *Democracy and Education* (1916/1980), he writes passionately about the accountability (not his word) the philosophy of education has to the social necessity of the curriculum: "As formal teaching and training grow in extent, there is the danger of creating an undesirable split between the experience gained in more direct associations and what is acquired in school" (p. 10). Dewey also writes repeatedly about our accountability to the individuals in our charge.

> Education, therefore, must begin with a psychological insight into the child's capacities, interests, and habits. It must be controlled at every point by reference to these same considerations. These powers, interests, and habits must be continually interpreted—we must know what they mean. (Dewey, 1897/1972, p. 86)

In addition to our accountability to the society and the individual, Dewey reminds us that we who teach are accountable to the methods and insights of science. His words are especially relevant at a time when masses of scientific findings related to issues like global warming or the teaching of evolution are ignored or manipulated in the name of ideology, politics, or religion.

> If ever we are to be governed by intelligence, not by things and by words, science must have something to say about what we do, and not merely about how we may do it most easily and economically. And if this consummation is achieved, the transformation must occur through education, by bringing home to men's habitual inclination and attitude the significance of genuine knowledge and the full import of the conditions requisite for its attainment. (Dewey, 1910/1978, p. 78)

Or in another place, he wrote:

> There is but one sure road of access to truth—the road of patient, cooperative inquiry operating by means of observation, experiment, record and controlled reflection. (Dewey, 1933/1986, p. 23)

Most important, in terms of the educational project, Dewey reminds teachers in *The Sources of a Science of Education* (1929/1984) that if they do not consider their accountability to the processes and findings of science, instead seeing themselves as "mainly channels of reception and transmission" of scientific conclusions, those conclusions "will be badly deflected and distorted before they get into the minds of pupils" (p. 24). What results is teachers who want only recipes and not the "illumination and liberation" (p. 7) that could come from the proper use of science.

Additional reading of Dewey's work would also find an accountability to the democratic structure of society, to our own need for growth, to the consideration of "a plurality of ideas" (1938/1988, p. 131), and more. In this section we have tried to capture this broad sense of what it means to be held accountable in Deweyan terms. To do that, however, it might be helpful to think more in terms of responsibility than of accountability. The term *accountability* carries with it images of a narrowly focused bottom line or an assumption of failure. When you search a thesaurus for synonyms for *accountability*, you find words like *answerability, liability,* and *culpability*. All of these speak of punitive consequences and the need to force compliance to policies with no inherent value or larger significance. *Responsibility,* at least as is used throughout the contributions that follow, speaks more to the obligation we have to our young people, our profession, our craft, and our future. It speaks to what we might think of as a higher calling, a more noble cause.

In *Democracy and Education* (Dewey, 1916/1980), we are reminded that the purpose of formal education is indeed a noble and, perhaps, irreplaceable one.

> As a society becomes more enlightened, it realizes that it is responsible not to transmit and conserve the whole of its existing achievements, but only such as

make for a better future society. The school is its chief agency for the accomplishment of this end. . . . The inclination to learn from life itself and to make the conditions of life such that all will learn in the process of living is the finest product of schooling. (p. 24)

When we take this role seriously we see that we are responsible for far more than any single battery of tests can measure. Considered in light of the rest of Dewey's writing, we know that we are responsible for a young person's growth as a moral being; an aesthetic being; a political being; an intellectual being; and, of course, as a being who lives in democratic community with other beings. He knew well, however, how easy it was for schools—even before *A Nation at Risk* or No Child Left Behind—to lapse into a narrow focus on what is easiest to teach and test but most distant from the child's lived experience.

There is the standing danger that the material of formal instruction will be merely the subject matter of the schools, isolated from the subject matter of life-experience. The permanent social interests are likely to be lost from view. Those which have not been carried over into the structure of social life, but which remain largely matters of technical information expressed in symbols, are made conspicuous in schools. (Dewey, 1916/1980, p. 325)

More than 20 years after writing those ideas, as Dewey considers the threats to a new education based on the experiences of young people, he makes what I have found to be his most explicit statement about the accountability of individual teachers. He believes that if the newer education ideas he advocates eventually fail, it would be due to the "failure of educators who professedly adopt them to be faithful to them in practice" (Dewey, 1938/1988, p. 61). In 1938, Dewey could not have foreseen the extent to which federal and state governments and even private business and foundations would eventually take top-down control of public education, leaving individual teachers relatively powerless and educational philosophers relegated to the academic margins. Still, his speculation has always left me with a nagging question. If we had taken his caution seriously, if professional educators—teachers, researchers, teacher educators, union leaders—had indeed devoted "ourselves to finding out just what education is and what conditions have to be satisfied in order that education may be a reality and not a name or a slogan" (Dewey, 1938/1988, p. 62), when we had the chance, maybe we would still have control over our own accountability.

References

Dewey, J. (1972). My pedagogic creed. In J. A. Boydston (Ed.), *John Dewey: The early works, 1882–1898: Vol. 5. 1895–1898* (pp. 81–95). Carbondale: Southern Illinois University Press. (Original work published 1897)

Dewey, J. (1978). "Valid knowledge and the "subjectivity of experience." In J. A. Boydston (Ed.), *John Dewey: The middle works, 1899–1924: Vol. 6. 1910–1911* (pp. 70–79). Carbondale: Southern Illinois University Press. (Original work published 1910)

Dewey, J. (1980). Democracy and education. In J. A. Boydston (Ed.), *John Dewey: The middle works, 1899–1924: Vol. 9. 1916* (pp. 1–370). Carbondale: Southern Illinois University Press. (Original work published 1916)

Dewey, J. (1984). The sources of a science of education. In J. A. Boydston (Ed.), *John Dewey: The later works, 1925–1953: Vol. 5. 1929–1930* (pp. 1–40). Carbondale: Southern Illinois University Press. (Original work published 1929)

Dewey, J. (1986). A common faith. In J. A. Boydston (Ed.), *John Dewey: The later works, 1925–1953: Vol. 9. 1933–1934* (pp. 1–58). Carbondale: Southern Illinois University Press. (Original work published 1933)

Dewey, J. (1988). Experience and education. In J. A. Boydston (Ed.), *John Dewey: The later works, 1925–1953: Vol. 13. 1938–1939* (pp. 1–62). Carbondale: Southern Illinois University Press. (Original work published 1938)

Dewey, J. (1988). Freedom and culture. In J. A. Boydston (Ed.), *John Dewey: The later works, 1925–1953: Vol. 13. 1938–1939* (pp. 63–252). Carbondale: Southern Illinois University Press. (Original work published 1939)

National Commission on Excellence in Education. (1983). *A nation at risk: The imperative for educational reform.* Washington, DC: U.S. Department of Education.

1

A CALL FOR CREATIVITY AND FREEDOM IN THE MIDST OF ACCOUNTABILITY

A Teachable Moment

Maggie Allison

> *Finally, I saw how inconsistent it was to expect this greater amount of creative, inde-*
> *pendent work from the student when the teachers were still unemancipated; when the*
> *teachers were still shackled by too many rules and prescriptions and too much of a*
> *desire for uniformity of method and subject matter.*
> —*The Classroom Teacher*, Middle Works 15: 187

Recently, my 9-year-old daughter, who is in third grade, brought home a social studies quiz on a unit about communities. The quiz was a single paper among many in a folder labeled "Graded Papers." The quiz appeared to be a typical, book-generated quiz: 10 fill-in-the-blank questions where students had to circle the "correct" answer. At the top of her quiz, the teacher had written, "9/10 B." In usual fashion, my daughter and I proceeded to review the question she got "wrong" to be sure she understood why. The question she got wrong read:

Citizens / Laws help keep order in a community.

My daughter circled *Citizens* and the "correct" answer was *Laws*. When I asked her about her thinking on this question, she offered a very plausible response. She said that people such as policemen and firemen help keep order and that's why she circled *Citizens*.

I rarely choose to interfere in school matters mostly because my daughter loves school and she experiences much success; however, it just didn't seem right to me that there was necessarily a right and wrong answer in this case. After all, citizens *can* help keep order in a community, as can laws. So I wrote a note to the teacher. In my note I pointed out the problematic nature of a "correct" answer given that both laws and citizens can and do, in fact, help keep order in a community. I asked the teacher whether the aim of the quiz was to assess learning or whether it was to trick students. I attached the note to the quiz and sent it back to school in the "Graded Papers" folder. When my daughter arrived home, I checked the folder anticipating the teacher's response to my note. To my dismay, I received a one-sentence reply: "Sorry, I went with the book's answer key."

It strikes me that this scenario in my daughter's third-grade class illustrates the very essence of Dewey's quote. Dewey believes that teaching is an *art,* requiring much freedom. To carry out the art of teaching, Dewey advocates that teachers ought to be in charge of their own work. They ought to have the freedom to think for themselves about subject matter rather than resorting to carrying out recipes that are prescribed by others. However, with freedom comes much responsibility. As educators, we cannot hope to inspire creativity in our students unless we approach our craft creatively, and we need to be empowered in order to do so.

The teacher's response to my inquiry about the social studies quiz violated both the need for creativity and freedom within the classroom. The problematic quiz question might have provided a "teachable moment" for students to discuss how both laws and citizens help to maintain order within a community. Or better yet, in lieu of the quiz on the concept of communities, the teacher might have found a more creative means of assessing student understanding. For example, why not allow students to write their own laws to be followed within the classroom to show how members of the school community share ownership in maintaining order within the school? Either one of these assessment methods might have demonstrated a mindful effort on the part of the teacher to design an educative experience that allowed for greater potential for creativity. Based on the teacher's decision to strictly adhere to the answer key, my conclusion is that for this teacher, there is either little freedom of method or little sense of responsibility, or possibly both.

The teacher's lack of freedom and responsibility in the aforementioned educative experience is precisely what Dewey warns about when he makes his claim in an address to teachers at the Massachusetts State Conference of Normal School Teachers in 1922. In fact, Dewey might acknowledge the social studies quiz as a "mis-educative experience" in that it served to stunt the intellectual growth of the student. For Dewey, the responsibility of determining subject matter and method ought to be in the hands of the teachers who do the work. And for Dewey, the work of teachers is to create rich, educative experiences for students. Dewey defines the *method* of an educative experience as being critical thinking (Dewey, 1916/1980). When teachers are thoughtful and creative in designing learning experiences for their students, students will consequently have a better opportunity to become creative and thoughtful members of the learning community and, eventually, society. Conversely, when creativity and freedom are lacking in the design of educative experiences, the ability of students to think creatively and critically is stifled.

Although Dewey's words were spoken nearly a century ago, they are arguably just as relevant today. Academic standards and other legislated accountability measures demand action on the part of the classroom teacher, but this action ought not to be to make all teaching look the same. Although academic standards might provide a framework for school curricula, they should not undermine the creativity and freedom of the teacher. Might the teacher use the academic standards to inspire creatively designed educative experiences to prepare students to think and contribute responsibly and productively in society? This, Dewey might say, is the ultimate responsibility of teachers in ushering students on their way to reaching their fullest potential.

References

Dewey, J. (1980). Democracy and education. In J. A. Boydston (Ed.), *John Dewey: The middle works, 1899–1924: Vol. 9. 1916* (pp. 1–370). Carbondale: Southern Illinois University Press. (Original work published 1916)

Dewey, J. (1983). The classroom teacher. In J. A. Boydston (Ed.), *John Dewey: The middle works, 1899–1924: Vol. 15. 1923–1924* (pp. 180–189). Carbondale: Southern Illinois University Press. (Original work published 1924)

2

TRACING ANEW THE PROCESS OF LEARNING

A. G. Rud

> *Learning is active. It involves reaching out of the mind. It involves organic assimilation starting from within.*
> —*The Child and the Curriculum*, Middle Works 2: 276

This quote contains a kernel of truth, albeit one-sided. These are words that Dewey imagines a child-centered romantic theorist would say about learning. He was recounting the dispute between those who see teaching and learning as child-centered versus those who see it as subject-centered. For Dewey, neither view is completely true, because each is only an artificial half-truth of a holistic and organic process. To the child-centered advocate, Dewey would say, yes, learning is active and involves reaching out of the mind, but it is not simply something that starts from within, and what you say is only part of the story.

For Dewey, this movement toward the inner and personal goes too far toward the subjective and connotes a separation from the subject matter that is then seen as "outside." Rather, for Dewey, the learner psychologizes subject matter, tracing anew the process many have made to learn it and imagine it further. Subject matter can be seen as a series of logical connections but also as a psychologized whole that we have learned or could learn. Otherwise, subject matter becomes inert if not psychologized. Just as the child-centered advocate can become wrapped in inner-directed subjectivity, so too can the subject-matter advocate describe "disciplinary knowledge" absent from psychological attention and energy, leading to discussion of why anyone would find any particular bit of knowledge interesting.

Take a map—Dewey's own example from the text. In and of itself, a map is not a psychological journey. We could recreate and thus psychologize an existing map, as William Least Heat-Moon did in *Blue Highways* (1982), but the simple accreted logic of a map we pull up on the web or unfold from our pocket is meant chiefly to save steps of toil. We don't have to delve further if we choose to use that map to find a way to get from A to B. Logical presentation saves time because the human or psychological connection is set aside in favor of organization. It remains possible to invigorate, and thus psychologize, any subject matter, and any map can be emended with a singular quest by a new traveler. However, in much teaching and learning, the logical trumps the psychological. A standard-issue textbook is easier and cheaper than a journey in psychologized subject matter. It is easier to rest in what Dewey (1902/1976) calls the "prejudicial notion that there is some gap in kind (as distinct from degree) between the child's experience and the various forms of subject-matter that make up the course of study" (pp. 277–278).

If Dewey were alive today, I have no doubt that he would still assert the connected wholeness of child and curriculum. But I think he might want to stress the child-centered aspect a bit more strongly. There is little child-centered education in mainstream schooling in the United States, and I am not blaming anyone for this. It is difficult and expensive to accommodate the needs and interests of each child and to help each child on his or her own unique psychologized journey with subject matter. Granted, there are robust progressive teaching advocates for individualized and psychologized instruction, but the mainstream is not so. The inner psychological drive and yearning for knowledge is not even acknowledged in the common information-processing view of education.

Unfortunately, in too many places much of what Dewey decries in *The Child and the Curriculum* (1902/1976) is still, almost exactly, how we teach and learn today. In all but the most privileged schools, instruction is teacher-directed, and the curriculum is driven by standardized assessments. Students might be awake, but they are not often active and involved. My state recently approved the establishment of charter schools. Perhaps predictably, the public discussion was not about what would be taught in these schools (in our terms here, ways we can allow subject matter to be psychologized) but whether a particular kind of instruction, or school management, will yield higher test scores. In our schools today, innovative teaching can be simply different ways to package and finesse curricular materials. We need to be reminded of the organic connection of child and curriculum that Dewey describes and the interaction of child and curriculum in a psychologized and dynamic whole.

References

Dewey, J. (1976). The child and the curriculum. In J. A. Boydston (Ed.), *John Dewey: The middle works, 1899–1924: (Vol. 2. 1902–1903* (pp. 271–292). Carbondale: Southern Illinois University Press. (Original work published 1902)

Heat-Moon, W. L. (1982). *Blue highways: A journey into America.* Boston, MA: Little, Brown.

3

RESPONSIBILITY, NOT ACCOUNTABILITY

The Experiential Artistry of Teaching

Walter S. Gershon

> *If education is going to live up to its profession, it must be seen as a work of art which requires the same qualities of personal enthusiasm and imagination as are required by the musician, painter or artist. Each one of these artists needs a technique which is more or less mechanical, but in the degree to which he [sic] loses his personal vision to become subordinate to the formal rules of the technique he falls below the level and grade of the artist. He becomes reduced again to the level of the artisan who follows the blue prints, drawings, and plans that are made by other people.*
> —*The Classroom Teacher*, Middle Works 15: 187

This quote can be read as a call not for educational accountability, the measurable checking of boxes and filling of pails, but instead for educational responsibility, the adoption of ideas and ideals in response to educational experiences and inquiry. Responsibility shifts the practice of teaching from fulfilling sets of prescribed knowledge to the adaptation of frameworks to fit the necessary ebb and flow of learning. Presenting education as responsibility also moves teaching and learning from predetermined closed sets of knowledge to emergent open sets of possibility. Where accountability is fair, responsibility is just. Accountability can be fulfilled by checking off the correct steps in someone else's plan that can mask equity in a measureable veneer of satisfied requirements. Being responsible requires involvement in educational processes that respond to lived experiences, a move that creates the space for the artistry of teaching and learning, the dignity for teachers and learners to make sense in their own ways and time, and the trust in both teachers and students in their ability to make such connections.

What might such an orientation mean for an educational system where, in the name of equity and access, student success in public schools across the nation is now measured according to scores on standardized assessments, tests that tend to reduce possible avenues of knowledge and inquiry to questions to which there are prescribed singular correct answers? Similarly, conflating teaching and learning—an assumption that strong teaching necessarily leads to learning and that learning can always occur according to a prescribed timetable—teacher, school, and student successes are now measured according to students' scores on their annual standardized assessments. However, as many have experienced at some point in their schooling, one can have difficulty grasping a concept or idea although it was well taught, and one can learn something in spite of, rather than resulting from, a teacher's pedagogy. These measurable tendencies in formal curriculum are also present at a more local level in the classroom. For example, many elementary school language arts textbooks are still constructed with literal scripts for teachers to follow so that teachers might increase their success at fostering future student success on their future assessments.

In our contemporary educational moment, teachers face ever-increasing pressures for students to score well on standardized assessments, and the moral obligation teachers feel to help students test well is not to be overlooked. It continues to be the case that ZIP code remains one of the most determining factors in students' test scores and related measurements of teacher and school success—the more wealthy the community, the greater the likelihood that the students, their teachers, and schools will be successful as measured by annual standardized assessments. Should this seem like hyperbole, it is important to remember that discussions of increasing economic gaps in student success tend to focus solely on public schools and in so doing perhaps underrepresent the degree to which money buys educational success—an argument not unlike the one Dewey (1934/1987) makes about relationships between wealth, art, and "esthetic experience" (p. 15). Additionally, amid all the public accounting of schools, far less documented is financial information about school communities, districts, or the amount of additional monetary subsidies parents are asked to contribute to a given school.

However, such educational possibilities are built on a tendency toward formulas and static plans that are evident throughout the past 100 years of teaching and teacher education in the United States (Bobbit, 1918; Tyler, 1949; U.S. Department of Education, 2012). The lesson plans that teachers are taught to create and use are but one example. They begin at the ending, with what students are to learn before they start learning, then build forward so that the teacher leads students to the answer that the teacher already has in mind. Questions are therefore often asked to herd students toward a singular predetermined correct answer, and success for both student and teacher is measured by the degree to which students can arrive at the prescribed answer. In this fashion, educational experiences tend to be reduced to measurable procedures and teacher-created objectives that often replace the space for student-driven inquiry. Instead of artistic interpreters of curriculum, teachers are often curricular literalists, seeking the best practices through which they can deliver the prescribed content.

Additionally, there is a tendency for teachers and teacher educators to either actively resist or try to get ahead of the latest educational trends and possibilities, a movement that strongly contributes to the pendulum-swinging impression that many have of education and educators. Although resistance to or proactive adoption of a seemingly never-ending series of educational trends may appear to be contradictory movements, both trajectories can create a kind of self-censorship where the adoption of others' pedagogical suggestions can trump one's own pedagogical tendencies. This is not to say that such suggestions and trends are necessarily unfounded or cannot facilitate strong teaching and learning. Rather, the pressure and clamor to keep abreast of educational trends can result in the creation of a teacherly habit of accepting others' blueprints over their own experiences.

How is one to have an educational experience if the parameters for that possibility are prescribed and its possible trajectories controlled? Of equal importance, following Dewey's arguments that education is experiential (1938/1988), that arts are experiences (1934/1987), and that a person's intuition and affect give rise to what and how he or she learns (1925/1981), where is the necessary wiggle room for artistic expressions of teaching and learning when answers precede questions and educational practices are most often sets of procedures? Why do students even need to attend school when what they are to know and how they are to gain those understandings move forward according to a curriculum map rather than student need? Why is their presence necessary other than on testing days when what counts as knowledge is decided regardless of what students already do or do not know and both the questions and answers about that knowledge are determined in relation to an educational blueprint rather than students' actual educational needs?

Furthermore, what might Dewey's argument in this quotation mean for students whose roles are in many ways defined by their teachers' approaches to pedagogy? If teachers are reduced in role and capacity by accepting others' "blueprints," are not students similarly reduced by accepting their teacher's blueprints? What does it mean to be a student when those who have the authority to shape your educational ways of being and knowing are in turn following "plans that are made by other people"? As arts programs are systematically dismantled in favor of "core subjects" and "foundational skills," how will future teachers develop a non-mechanistic pedagogical artistry when they have little to no experience in the arts in their lives as students? Although no one answer is a silver bullet, perhaps a move toward responsibility and away from accountability might facilitate the kinds of educational artistry in which Dewey so strongly believes.

References

Bobbit, F. (1918). *The curriculum.* Boston, MA: Houghton Mifflin.

Dewey, J. (1983). The classroom teacher. In J. A. Boydston (Ed.), *John Dewey: The middle works, 1899–1924: Vol. 15. 1923–1924* (pp. 180–189). Carbondale: Southern Illinois University Press. (Original work published 1924)

Dewey, J. (1981). Experience and nature. In J. A. Boydston (Ed.), *John Dewey: The later works, 1925–1953: Vol. 1. 1925* (pp. 1–326). Carbondale: Southern Illinois University Press. (Original work published 1925)

Dewey, J. (1987). Art as experience. In J. A. Boydston (Ed.), *John Dewey: The later works, 1925–1953: Vol. 10. 1934* (pp. 1–352). Carbondale: Southern Illinois University Press. (Original work published 1934)

Dewey, J. (1988). Experience and education. In J. A. Boydston (Ed.), *John Dewey: The later works, 1925–1953: Vol. 13. 1938–1939* (pp. 1–62). Carbondale: Southern Illinois University Press. (Original work published 1938)

Tyler, R. W. (1949). *Basic principles of curriculum and instruction.* Chicago, IL: The University of Chicago Press.

U.S. Department of Education. (2012). *Education department invites districts to apply for $400 million Race to the Top competition to support classroom-level reform efforts.* Retrieved from http://www.ed.gov/news/press-releases/education-department-invites-districts-apply-400-million-race-top-competition-su

4

AN ALTERNATIVE IMAGE OF DATA

Not *What* but *Where*

Sebastián Díaz

> *Many, perhaps most, errors in physical inference arise from taking as data things that are not data for the problem in hand; they undoubtedly exist, but they are not the evidence that is demanded.*
>
> —*The Quest for Certainty*, Later Works 4: 144

In the charming, expensively renovated building where the central administration of my colleagues' for-profit university resides, we liberated ourselves last week through dialogue and reached a simple insight that somehow had evaded me for the 26 years I've worked as an educator. That insight, I believe, resonates with Dewey's notion that sometimes, data we use is not the evidence that is demanded.

Here was our insight: What if we simply stop viewing evaluative "data" (i.e., examinations, course evaluations, assessments) as something that informs teaching and instead view them as that which informs student learning?

In other words, let's ignore for a moment debates surrounding *what* are valid measures of student growth and instead focus on *where* that feedback is directed. This may sound innocuous, yet there is a challenging implicit assumption at play here. Our insight assumes that teachers are not necessarily the pivotal focus of the feedback loop.

As my colleagues and I explored this idea, we became more aware of how our approaches to evaluation in both K–12 and postsecondary education are instructor-centric. For example, we bemoan how state standards, and the respective norm-referenced tests created, impact *teachers*. Yet, have we really systematically asked students how the tests impact *them*? For the life of me, I can hardly remember a public school teacher *not* complaining about standardized tests. It's the exact opposite for students, who never seem to mention them. And when you ask students what's wrong with education, rarely do they mention "testing." As my psychotherapist friends often say, "There's some rich stuff worth exploring there."

Here's how we envisioned our model. End-of-course evaluations employing the Community of Inquiry framework survey (Arbaugh, et al., 2008) are administered instead midway through the online course. Whereas our original intent for this instrument was to inform instructor efficacy, we remove for the moment a focus on faculty. We instead ask the students to reflect on their own responses to the survey and compare theirs with aggregate measures for the class. And we design courses so students are asked to incorporate this feedback into their reflections as well as how they subsequently participate. We certainly won't prevent faculty from viewing anonymous aggregate results. But to be honest, we're much more confident in the student's ability to act on the data than we are in the instructor's.

We envision that this approach eventually will desensitize the student, thus removing shame and anxiety from the process of feedback. Outside the confines of the contrived educational experiences we design for our students, they seem to function rather well with feedback that occurs on an hourly basis, much of it comparative (i.e., norm-referenced). Mortgage lenders provide them feedback about their suitability for a loan. Potential lovers provide them feedback about their suitability for a committed relationship. Coaches provide them feedback about their ability to be on the football team, and glee club directors provide them evaluative feedback about their suitability for being a singer. Parents provide feedback on how adequately clean a room is (or isn't). Racists provide feedback about why they are not accepted into a circle of friends or a country club. And in addition to desensitizing students to feedback that they are bound to receive throughout their lives, we envision helping students develop a belief that the most valuable feedback is that which they receive from themselves as they quietly contemplate their own goals, dreams, and aspirations.

When we liberate ourselves from viewing evaluative data and information as being central to measuring an instructor's worth and instead view them as one cog in a complex process of introspection for the student, we can remove, in one fell swoop, much of the shame, anxiety, and anger surrounding testing. Let's be honest with ourselves. Many educators collectively abhor testing not because we don't know how to measure student intellectual growth but instead because we don't exactly know how to measure faculty worth. If we did know how to measure our worth, we would practice our profession more confidently. So why not empower students to make sense of their state proficiency exam scores, ACT scores, SAT scores, GPAs, and so on? By doing so, we may find that students themselves, whether as sixth graders or as college juniors, will ask for more holistic measures of growth and innate characteristics that provide them a better sense of their own uniqueness. Students, not teachers, will be the catalysts for adoption of more progressive forms of accountability. And because these measures are designed to serve their needs, they will pick and choose a variety of feedback mechanisms that go beyond simplistic measures of cognitive ability to more complex and subjective measures of multiple intelligences.

As educators in public schools and universities, we should be more careful about not burdening our students with our collective insecurity, especially because our students have to deal with enough insecurities already. And it behooves us to explore, much more candidly, exactly what those insecurities are. One tremendously valuable insight that online learning has provided us is the revelation that not all aspects of traditional instruction add value to the educational enterprise. Change is therefore imminent, and that's scary.

Had Dewey lived another few decades and ventured a few steps further on the creaking revisionist branch of his writings, he may have come to realize eventually that in addition to the possibility that standardized testing has become irrelevant, so too has the entire educational industrial complex around which we build our own professional, personal, and economic identities. I find it contradictory, almost hypocritical, that those who often rail against any proscription whatsoever of either curriculum or accountability are the very educators who hold on to the proscription that teaching and learning *have* to occur either in a conventional K–12 school or within the confines of a conventional brick and mortar university.

If we say our raison d'être is to facilitate a student's holistic growth, then why do we insist that such learning occur in stodgy, antiquated buildings that employ schedules for industrial production, replete with bells and whistles that resemble a Ford automobile factory? Why do we insist that youth spend the majority of their lives in classrooms that are designed to serve primarily the needs of individuals who run these systems? There are few norm-referenced, quantitative tests out there that can even begin to approach the level of incongruity found in the very design of our public K–12 school systems.

Yet this essay does not call for such an immediate revolution. A more realistic adjacent possibility (Johnson, 2010) is to revolutionize how we manage feedback loops within the schools and the academy. My personal dream is that someday, students will be able to process evaluative feedback in a school environment in every bit as emotionally uncomplicated a manner as they process feedback for just about every other aspect of their lives. We may benefit greatly from recognizing that it isn't so much that the data we have are not *what* is demanded, but instead that the data are not going *where* they are demanded.

References

Arbaugh, J. B., Cleveland-Innes, M., Diaz, S. R., Garrison, D. R., Ice, P., Richardson, J. C., & Swan, K. P. (2008). Developing a community of inquiry instrument: Testing a measure of the Community of Inquiry framework using a multi-institutional sample. *The Internet and Higher Education, 11,* 133–136.

Dewey, J. (1984). The quest for certainty. In J. A. Boydston (Ed.), *John Dewey: The later works, 1925–1953: Vol. 4. 1929* (pp. 1–250). Carbondale: Southern Illinois University Press. (Original work published 1929)

Johnson, S. (2010). *Where good ideas come from: The natural history of innovation.* New York, NY: Riverhead Books.

5

WHO IS ACCOUNTABLE?

Alexander David Tuel

> *A human being is held accountable in order that he may learn; in order that he may learn not theoretically and academically but in such a way as to modify and—to some extent—remake his prior self.*
>
> —*Ethics,* Later Works 7: 304

What is accountability? Romzek (2000) believed it to be the "answerability for performance" (p. 22), and with the passage of No Child Left Behind Act (NCLB) in 2001, the "answerability" mentioned by Romzek focuses on student performance, with teachers given the enormous responsibility to be the agents of improvement. Although teachers have always been change agents, schools are now more widely subjected to public reporting of achievement (good or bad) with consequences for continuous low student performance.

As mentioned, the main thrust behind NCLB is student performance and improvement, with teachers being the ones held accountable for the outcome of their respective classes. Dewey and Tufts (1932/1985) argue that "one is held responsible in order that he may *become* responsible, that is, responsive to the needs and claims of others" (p. 304). Individuals in positions of responsibility, such as teachers, must learn from past mistakes or experiences and, in turn, adjust their actions. For Dewey, it does not necessarily matter how a person acts at a particular moment, but "whether he is capable of acting differently *next* time" (p. 304). In this frame of mind, Dewey believes that "we cannot undo the past; we can affect the future" (p. 304).

Should teachers be the only ones accountable? Should not students bear the burden of learning as well? There is an unfortunate trend in American society of blaming educators for all the woes in our educational system, but no sense of responsibility is placed on students. Is it taboo in our society to point fingers at students and the idea that teachers and schools need to place a sense of responsibility on students? Are we not setting up students for future failure if we do not hold them accountable now? The ability to study on their own in college or the capability for critical thinking on the job—is this not what Dewey and Tufts (1932/1985) are referring to when an individual is "held accountable in order that he may learn" (p. 304)?

The issue of accountability in American education has become volatile in recent years. For example, as recent as September 2012, school districts in Los Angeles and Boston implemented performance evaluations based in part on how well students succeed. The same direction is taking place in Chicago, the nation's third largest district, but with dramatic consequences. For the first time in 25 years, 25,000 Chicago teachers went on strike, in part due to performance evaluations.

In college and the workplace, individuals are responsible for their own learning, but rarely in K–12 education do we properly prepare students to assume that responsibility. While in school, how should students be held accountable? What is their job? It can be argued that their occupation is to learn. However, our society usually places the burden of student performance solely on teachers. Teachers should be evaluated by how well they teach. Do they deliver their content appropriately? Do they provide help and timely feedback? Are concepts demonstrated well? Do teachers match student knowledge with what they are to accomplish? If so, then the teachers have done their jobs, and that is where they should be held accountable. However, it is then up to the students to take responsibility for their own actions and learning. The ability to empower students with the ability to study well and learn what works best for them is an invaluable tool to prepare them for future schoolwork and employment, and as students progress through school, "there develops a larger degree of accountability" (Dewey & Tufts, 1932/1985, p. 304).

Although the theme of my essay revolves around teachers and students, it should not be overlooked that, in the end, for change to occur we must hold policymakers accountable. Accountability in our society has been given a negative connotation, evoking a sense of blame, with policymakers seizing control of the true purpose of accountability—growth. Dewey is consumed by the sense of continuous improvement, believing "the closest to an all-inclusive educational end was the principle of growth" (Hook, 1959, p. 12). Teachers and students alike can grow and value the educational experience, if we use accountability measures for their original purpose. It is through accountability that teachers can learn from their mistakes and new experiences to help foster their growth. Similarly, students need to better understand themselves as productive students and hold themselves responsible for their education. However, until policymakers see accountability the same way Dewey does—as a means through which we grow and change— then our system of accountability is nothing more than a system of blame.

References

Dewey, J., & Tufts, J. H. (1985). *The moral self.* In J. A. Boydston (Ed.), *John Dewey: The later works, 1925–1953: Vol. 7. 1932* (pp. 286–310). Carbondale: Southern Illinois University Press. (Original work published 1932)

Hook, S. (1959). John Dewey: Philosopher of growth. *Journal of Philosophy, 56*(26), 9–17.

No Child Left Behind Act of 2001, Pub. L. No. 107–110, § 115, Stat. 1425 (2002)

Romzek, B. S. (2000). Dynamics of public sector accountability in an era of reform. *International Review of Administrative Sciences, 66,* 21–44.

6

ART AND ACCOUNTABILITY

Kyle Greenwalt

> *Common things, a flower, a gleam of moonlight, the song of a bird, not things rare and remote, are means with which the deeper levels of life are touched so that they spring up as desire and thought. This process is art. . . . Artists have always been the real purveyors of news, for it is not the outward happening in itself which is new, but the kindling by it of emotion, perception and appreciation.*
> —*The Public and Its Problems*, Later Works 2: 350

Teaching, as Maxine Greene (1973) reminded us through her many writings, is an art.

Recently, I was rewatching the film *Être et avoir* (2002) by the French director Nicolas Philibert. In the film, a scene ripe with the emotional labor that artful teachers must undertake most every day of their careers unfolds between two young boys, Olivier and Julien, and their teacher, Mr. Lopez. Mr. Lopez, as he does throughout the film, speaks in a voice that is simultaneously warm, reticent, and authoritative.

In the scene, we see Mr. Lopez tactfully navigating Olivier through a range of difficult emotions—alienation, fear, anger, and despair. Not without hesitations and missteps, Mr. Lopez nonetheless works Olivier through this incident. Masterfully mobilizing both the nostalgia for times past and the apprehension of things yet to come, Mr. Lopez reminds us of the embodied wisdom that can help teachers navigate the most delicate of circumstances. Mr. Lopez restores Olivier to the sense of community that is necessary if meaningful learning is to ever take place.

The Role of Criticism and Policy

What role might works like *Être et avoir* play in improving the lives of teachers and students in the current educational landscape? Put more broadly, what do art and accountability, criticism and policy, have to do with one another? For Dewey, the answer is pretty clear: they are all forms of inquiry that seek to enrich the life of individuals.

Over the past 25 years in the United States, we seem to have built a whole system of schooling around failure: its constant detection and punishment for it. There continue to be beautiful things happening in schools across North America, but those things happen in spite of, not because of, recent educational policy.

Dewey would have shuddered at this. Today's educational bureaucrats would do well to heed his statements on policy. He writes:

> Policies and proposals for social action [should] be treated as working hypotheses, not as programs to be rigidly adhered to and executed. They will be experimental in the sense that they will be entertained subject to constant and well-equipped observation of the consequences they entail when acted upon, and subject to ready and flexible revision in the light of observed consequences. (Dewey, 1927/1984, p. 362)

The key here is the notion of revision in light of *observed consequences*. Any program for education reform—indeed, any action undertaken by a human being—will set into action a series of desired *and* undesirable consequences. The world is a web of interdependency. It is amenable to our interventions, but never completely so.

The critic, Dewey says, is that person who, through long experience and training, brings herself to the point where she is quite good at noticing things. She puts this noticing to good use, by evoking for her contemporaries some of the same things she notices. She reeducates the perception of the community.

Teachers as Artists

How does society improve? How will schooling be made better? The answer, says Dewey, is through shared inquiry *and* communication—through the socialization of intelligence.

Films like *Être et avoir* help educate the public on the intimate, complicated, and multifaceted work of the teacher. Scenes like those between Mr. Lopez, Olivier, and Julien help us rediscover the tact and acumen that the skilled teacher needs to possess. They remind us that education is a matter of the heart as well as the head and hand. We need more films, more novels, and more television programs like this to broaden the way the public thinks about schoolteachers and the importance of their work.

But as teachers, we might undertake this work more directly by inviting the public into the very conditions of our work. An outstanding classroom teacher is every bit a creative genius as any Mozart or Brontë. But if the conditions for our work are to improve, our work needs to be more effectively communicated to the public. We are in desperate need of a forum wherein parents and politicians can not only observe but also join in tactful pedagogical work. In this way, we might hope to kindle the type of "emotion, perception and appreciation" that will make of everyone a connoisseur of teaching.

References

Dewey, J. (1984). The public and its problems. In J. A. Boydston (Ed.), *John Dewey: The later works, 1925–1953: Vol. 2. 1925–1927* (pp. 235–372). Carbondale: Southern Illinois University Press. (Original work published 1927)

Greene, M. (1973). *Teacher as stranger.* Belmont, CA: Wadsworth.

Philibert, N. (Director). (2002). *Être et avoir* [Motion picture]. France: Maïa Films.

7

ON DEMOCRATIC ACCOUNTABILITY AND THE EDUCATIVE EXPERIENCE

Patrick M. Jenlink

> *The belief that all genuine education comes about through experience does not mean that all experiences are genuinely or equally educative. . . . Any experience is mis-educative that has the effect of arresting or distorting the growth of further experience. . . . A given experience may increase a person's automatic skill in a particular direction and yet tend to land him in a groove or rut; the effect again is to narrow the field of further experience.*
>
> —*Experience and Education*, Later Works 13: 11

I believe that John Dewey embraces a philosophical position wherein questions about democracy are in no small way questions about education, and vice versa. It is important to understand that for Dewey, democracy is a result of schools and the larger society. The person who experiences democracy both shapes and is shaped by the democratic form of life (Biesta, 2004). This extends into schools as a context for preparing our young for the role of citizen and the work aligned with civic responsibility. Simply stated, the educative process of school is critical to Dewey's philosophy of democratic education. This principle extends Dewey's philosophy of democratic education by focusing on quality of experience, the educative versus mis-educative nature of experience, as formative in shaping the democratic form of life.

However, a question of transcendent importance, as Dewey (1937/1987) argues, is whether this educative process is carried on in a predominantly democratic or nondemocratic way, which translates into the final effect on all the interests and activities of a society that is committed to the democratic way of life. Parallel in importance to this question is whether experience is educative or mis-educative. In an era of competency-based accountability when technical standards and high-stakes testing have eroded the foundation of progressive thought about democratic education, I believe it is important to advance democratic accountability in both schools and the larger society. We must reexamine whether what we define as the school processes, based on current standards and accountability, meet the democratic commitment set forth in Dewey's philosophy of democratic education. More specifically, we might ask, "What are the principals of educative experience that are also principles of experiencing democracy?" and "Where does democratic accountability reside?"

Principles of Experience

For Dewey, faith in experience is inseparable from faith in democracy. Dewey identifies two primary dimensions along which the educative value of experiences can be measured. The first is the principle of *continuity* (1938/1988, p. 13). This refers to the impact that an experience has on future experiences. All experiences have an impact, an element of continuity, so the question becomes what *kind* of impact? Dewey argues that experiences in traditional education have largely negative influences on future experiences; for instance, students experiencing traditional education are often "rendered callous to ideas" and lose "the impetus to learn" (1938/1988, p. 12). Experiences with such continuity Dewey refers to as *mis-educative*. In this sense, the mis-educative experience fails to meet the commitment to an educative process that is democratic. Experiences that promote callousness toward learning include those that place a student in a "groove or rut" (Dewey, 1938/1988, p. 11) or those that lead to carelessness. The kinds of experiences that are dictated by high-stakes testing in a culture of standards; experiences that are rote, habitual, or engaged in only begrudgingly and without investment; and experiences that are individually pleasant but disconnected such that they lead to an inability to make sense of future experiences are all what Dewey would call mis-educative.

In contrast, *educative* experiences promote the growth and desire of the student toward further experiences. The cultivation of a "desire to go on learning" is one of the most important benchmarks of educative experiences (Dewey, 1938/1988, p. 29). The educative experience "arouses curiosity, strengthens initiative, and sets up desires and purposes that are sufficiently intense to carry a person over the dead places" (Dewey, 1938/1988, pp. 20–21).

The second dimension relating to the value of experience is that of *interaction* (Dewey, 1938/1988, p. 24). Is there a balance between the objective factors (the content or subject matter) and the internal factors (the learner's wants, needs, and abilities) of experience? Traditional education is significantly askew in the direction of the objective (Dewey, 1938/1988, p. 24). To extend the principle of interaction to the realization of educative experiences that are democratic requires that we understand the necessity of interacting in democratic processes as a form of educative experience. Interaction that is democratic is necessary to experience the freedom of intelligence that Dewey (1938/1988) emphasizes—the importance of intellectual freedom as the "freedom of observation and of judgment exercised in behalf of purposes that are intrinsically worth while" (p. 39).

If the principles of continuity and interaction form a basis for evaluating experience and the democratic nature of the educative experience, the question still remains of the educational ends toward which the experiences should aim. Dewey answers this in several ways. First, with respect to subject matter, Dewey believes fundamentally in connecting the subject matter to the student's experience as a starting point, but he also writes that the organized (logical) subject matter "represents the goal toward which education should continuously move" (1938/1988, p. 56). Second, he feels that a positive attitude toward further learning is more than just one end of the experiential continuum and should be a primary goal of education as well (1938/1988, p. 29). Third, Dewey writes that the "ideal aim of education is creation of power and self-control" (1938/1988, p. 41). Here Dewey is referring primarily to the ability of an individual to direct his or her thoughts and actions, to master his or her impulses, via reflection and judgment. In these three points we also find the essential elements of an educative experience that is at the same time democratic in nature.

Democratic Accountability

In the end, what we do to ensure that students have educative experiences that are democratic rests, in large part, on the level of accountability we have to democracy and to the foundation of Dewey's philosophy of democratic education and his belief in the importance of "educative experience." Dewey places a strong emphasis on the subjective quality of a student's experience. He also stresses that the teacher needs to understand the student's past experiences to effectively design a sequence of liberating educational experiences that will allow the student to fulfill his or her potential as a member of democratic society.

The culture of accountability currently in place is denoted by technical standards and is focused on performance. This is manifest in the rhetoric of improvement and raising standards, of efficiency gains and best practice, of respect for students and teachers. Beneath this admirable rhetoric, the real focus is on performance indicators chosen for ease of measurement and control rather than because they measure accurately what the quality of performance is, rather than assuring educative experiences for students that are democratic.

Democratic accountability requires that we ask the question: Whither democracy in our educative processes, in our curricula and pedagogy, in our school life as democratic life? The answer lies, in part, in democratization of accountability that necessarily involves communication and negotiation between teachers and other constituencies of schools, including (perhaps especially) students. Importantly, democratization must involve processes for the recognition of difference (including differences in power) and for dealing with conflict in constructive ways. Democratic accountability requires that we pay particular attention to continuity and interaction as the principles essential to fostering democracy in schools.

References

Biesta, G. J. J. (2004). Education, accountability, and the ethical demand: Can the democratic potential of accountability be regained? *Educational Theory, 54,* 233–250.

Dewey, J. (1987). Democracy and educational administration. In J. A. Boydston (Ed.), *John Dewey: The later works, 1925–1953: Vol. 11. 1935–1937* (pp. 217–225). Carbondale: Southern Illinois University Press. (Original work published 1937)

Dewey, J. (1988). Experience and education. In J. A. Boydston (Ed.), *John Dewey: The later works, 1925–1953: Vol. 13. 1938–1939* (pp. 1–62). Carbondale: Southern Illinois University Press. (Original work published 1938)

8

HOW MECHANIZATION LEADS TO CONTEMPT FOR THE TEACHING AND LEARNING PROCESS

Louise Anderson Allen

> *Familiarity breeds contempt, but it also breeds something like affection. We get used to the chains we wear, and we miss them when they are removed. . . . It is possible for the mind to develop interest in a routine or mechanical procedure if conditions are continually supplied which demand that mode of operation and preclude any other sort.*
> —*The Child and the Curriculum*, Middle Works 2: 289

What chains impede teachers in creating learning environments? We may readily identify restrictions on a continuum of enforcement from those imposed by dictatorial administrators to the ones now mandated by the federal No Child Left Behind legislation. Most teachers are well aware of how they are tied by both federal and state accountability requirements through the chains of the mechanical procedures of a standardized curriculum or a standard course of study. Other chains, however, are equally binding and far more insidious.

Indeed, most teachers are used to, comfortable with, and perhaps complacent about what has become the most common of all chains that bind them to the standard operating procedure in many American classrooms—canned curricula that are pervasive and that demand a highly mechanized approach to the teaching and learning process. How do teachers come to know and accept these chains they are first forced to wear and eventually may embrace as well-loved friends?

Canned Curricula

These curricula—used in nearly every subject matter and discipline—have bound teachers and their students to others' thoughts, methods, and teachings. Teachers have developed such an overreliance on them that they do not seek freedom from mindlessness or the freedom found in the flexibility in planning, creating, and participating in learning experiences. In fact, many teachers voice much affection for the canned curricula that help them make it through the day with students who seem unmotivated and uninterested in classroom lessons. Canned curricula represent the strongest and tightest links in the chains that bind education to standardization and mechanization.

If education is to provide educative experience as Dewey intends, then teachers first must recognize the chains beyond the state and federal mandates that are immediate to their environment. Teachers use canned curricula that have little or no relationship or relevance for students who sit in classrooms day after day participating in a routine that fosters thoughtlessness. These curricula are a part of the mechanization that places teachers in the position of being merely deliverers of information that is perceived by students as meaningless. How can we change this situation? What conditions must be in place in schools that will encourage a nonmechanistic view of the teaching and learning process? Whose role is it to ensure that teachers and students do not develop contempt for school but through a respect for education learn to understand and desire the reciprocity of the teaching and learning process?

Breaking Out of the Mechanistic Routine

These are the challenges faced by all educators today in our public schools. Principals and superintendents are under tremendous pressure for schools to meet state and federal guidelines on standardized tests. They, in turn, place an equal amount of pressure on teachers and students, who then must perform to someone else's standards. In each instance, educators become part of a mechanistic routine that breeds familiarity and contempt for the teaching and learning process. Students are no longer performing to their own best ability but to someone else's definition of what is standard for some mythical average student somewhere in the middle of Nowhere, USA.

Although this situation may seem hopeless, teachers can reclaim their role by breaking these chains. One of the greatest joys and most profound responsibilities of being a teacher is creating new ideas, new learning situations, and new materials in response to the needs of students. Teachers are role models for students as learners. If teachers are enchained to a mechanistic view of learning, then students never will have role models in their classrooms to teach them how to be thinkers and analyzers. In this mechanization of the curricula, chains develop and familiarity sets in, leading to contempt for the teaching and learning process. But if teachers are urged by school leaders and officials to move away from learning experiences that numb the mind and limit student learning, then they will serve as the kind of role models we claim we want for students.

Creating Critical Thinkers

If we want students to think and analyze critically, then we must want that for teachers as well. Accordingly, teachers should not be chained to canned curricula but provided with opportunities to learn how to develop curricula appropriate for their students. Furthermore, school leaders and teachers should create learning opportunities for students to experience learning from one another and teaching one another, including opportunities for teachers and school leaders to serve in the student role. In this way, the teacher–student relationship will be shown not simply as one situated in a power relationship but in the love of learning. This approach should provide all participants with evidence that the teaching and learning process is one that does not have to lead to standardization but one that is constantly being reinvented and reinvigorated by the participants—the teachers and the students.

Reference

Dewey, J. (1976). The child and the curriculum. In J. A. Boydston (Ed.), *John Dewey: The middle works, 1899–1924: Vol. 2. 1902–1903* (pp. 271–292). Carbondale: Southern Illinois University Press. (Original work published 1902)

9

TEACHING OUR LEGISLATORS A BIG IDEA IN 52 WORDS OR LESS

Peter S. Hlebowitsh

> It is the office of the school environment to balance the various elements in the social environment, and to see to it that each individual gets an opportunity to escape from the limitations of the social group in which he was born, and to come into living contact with a broader environment.
>
> —*Democracy and Education*, Middle Works 9: 24–25

Bipartisan support for No Child Left Behind (NCLB) has left many of us in the profession of schooling shaking our heads over yet another small-minded school reform strategy. NCLB has some lively ideas in it, such as referring to the act of reading as a civil right, but its relation to school reform is largely procedural and represents little more than a demand to teach to the test. And its logic is straight out of a Pavlovian experiment gone bad: The public schools either answer the bell by meeting various state-established cut scores on proficiency exams in reading, math, and science or get zapped with a punishment equal to the effect of an electric prod.

Parents who send their kids to neighborhood schools should remember that if one statistically valid subgroup in the school (say, students with disabilities) fails to meet the state cut scores for 5 consecutive years, the school could become dissolved by NCLB. At that point, the school would be required to recast itself in the form of a charter school or to offer itself over to a private management corporation or a state takeover. And in such a case, almost everyone associated with the school likely would be fired. Even a school's aggregate scores in the 99th percentile (as high as they can be) don't influence this fate. One subgroup out of compliance for 5 consecutive years, and the school is done in.

The Refrain: Raise the Test Scores

Just think about what our legislators have done here. They finally have found a way to define what a good school does, and they came up with a whopper: Good schools raise test scores. The progressive idea of fashioning the school as a comprehensive experience dedicated to socio-civic, academic, vocational, and socio-personal goals (most of which are not easily measured) is largely a lost cause. "Raise the test scores" is the refrain. And just try to criticize the law as unreasonable, and you're likely to hear someone ask you which child *you* would like to leave behind.

So how did we get such legislation? Some educators, those who lean farthest to the political left, are certain that a right-wing conspiracy is at hand. They believe that a right-wing faction is prepared to dismantle the public schools as we know them, using the annual yearly progress (AYP) data in the NCLB legislation to swing a wrecking ball through the neighborhood school and clear out a spot for privatization efforts. Their case is straightforward. Good neighborhood schools eventually get dissolved, and look who moves into town—the private management corporation rubbing its hands over the prospect of getting schools' access to the public purse.

What a School Does

I, however, am not among the conspiracy theorists. The fact that NCLB is the handiwork of bipartisan cooperation and the states always could tell the feds to get lost makes me think that the law is not moved by anything other than a base misunderstanding of what schools are and what schools do. My theory is that if you can get the legislators to understand the comprehensive agenda of the school, you stand a better chance of getting a comprehensive legislative strategy for its improvement.

Ideally, we could send our legislators back to elementary school, where they could find object lessons in the disconnect between what good teachers do with children and what NCLB tests. But if wishes were horses, beggars would ride. So I propose something more modest. I'd simply like to ask our legislators to read the 52 words penned by John Dewey in 1916, which precede this essay, and to think about their meaning in the light of NCLB efforts. The intention is to convey a big idea that might encourage a bigger and better view of reform. Here is the quote again:

> It is the office of the school environment to balance the various elements in the social environment, and to see to it that each individual gets an opportunity to escape from the limitations of the social group in which he was born, and to come into living contact with a broader environment. (Dewey, 1916/1980, pp. 24–25)

To say, as Dewey does, that school provides an experience through which children can escape from the limitations imposed by family and community is quite a mouthful and is quite impolitic today. One could imagine the reflexive criticism from those who might be inclined to portray such a view as antifamily or as going against the core of individuality that makes American democracy so special. I could almost hear it—a Fox news analyst declaring, "And look who the liberals are quoting now: John Dewey, a liberal philosopher who wanted to impose the will of the government on the people and separate them from the very things that the family cherishes most."

So here is a point that must be confronted. Is Dewey's view antifamily? Most reasonable people will acknowledge that the family is not always a benevolent institution. Ask any teacher, social worker, police officer, or medical doctor, and you're likely to learn a few horror stories about families. Fortunately, however, most parents love their children and take their responsibilities to socialize their children seriously. Parents try to reflect the forms of religion, language, culture, politics, ethics, and so forth that they believe are in the best interests of their children. But this would happen whether there was school in the child's life or not.

The school, on the other hand, doesn't fashion itself along the narrow dimensions of family or neighborhood life. It has a wider normative agenda to build a common experience across the differences that prevail among people, their families, and their neighborhoods. School has to transcend the differences, not by abusing them or ridiculing them, but by offering an expansion of experience that should have some effect in challenging or questioning the parochial.

Building a Common Experience

This is another way of saying that the school has some obligation to widen the margins of experience and to be sure that it finds a way to bring bright ideas about democracy; the problems of living; and history, literature, mathematics, and science into the hearts and minds of children. It also has to cultivate a wide range of skills, including a variety of thinking, inquiry, and communication skills.

Such a project balances the diversifying agenda with the unifying agenda of the school. We unify by teaching a common history, a common language, and common skills and values as well as by providing a common universe for discourse. We diversify by ensuring that our common experience makes appropriate and useful inclusions of multiple perspectives and by securing a place in the curriculum for individualizing opportunities. Teaching children to read, to do math, and to learn science (the three critical NCLB areas) obviously is important, but so much more needs to be done to ensure that children have the opportunity to escape from the limitations of the experiences into which they were born. And such a project will not get done with NCLB standing in its way.

In response to my argument, I imagine that Washington might aim to make NCLB even more pervasive in its testing reach. The logic would be on the scale of saying, "Let's test everything; this way we make everything important." The problem with such a tactic is that no tests designed in the state capitals of our nation could capture the full complement of things that local schools teach children. So, if anything, the approach should move away from a statewide testing accountability system and toward the design of local evaluation systems. If the concern is about accountability, more might be gained if we asked school systems to design comprehensive evaluation systems that were responsive to their articulated purposes and missions (which few schools take seriously today). These evaluations might include tests, but they also might include a variety of other methods or instruments.

This way, the evaluation—including the tests—is of the experience, rather than the reverse. The general idea is to remove the test as a barrier to the fulfillment of the all-inclusive mandate of the school. Doing so would show our legislators that, all things being equal, an idea-oriented school curriculum (even one that yields lower NCLB test scores) that provides cosmopolitan experiences to children is better than a school that provides an impoverished taught-to-the-test experience. That's a big idea—something we need more of in Washington.

Reference

Dewey, J. (1980). Democracy and education. In J. A. Boydston (Ed.), *John Dewey: The middle works, 1899–1924: Vol. 9. 1916* (pp. 1–370). Carbondale: Southern Illinois University Press. (Original work published 1916)

10

WHAT IMPOSED STANDARDS DO TO THE CHILD

M. Frances Klein

> *The source of whatever is dead, mechanical, and formal in schools is found precisely in the subordination of the life and experience of the child to the curriculum.*
> —*The Child and the Curriculum*, Middle Works 2: 277

This is a time when standards that set levels of expectations and define excellence in many areas are being established for American education. We have, for example, standards for students to meet in various content areas, high-stakes tests that set standards for achievement, textbooks that meet selection criteria, and specific learning expectations that direct how time is to be spent in the classroom. On the surface, finding fault with having high teacher and student standards is difficult. Who can oppose this drive for excellence in education? The issue of what educational standards to have must be carefully considered, however, because of the significant impact they can have on the lives of students. The issue is further complicated by the fact that not all standards are in agreement with one another.

In spite of numerous claims to the contrary, the impact of many of the current standards on student learning has not been positive. A large number of students are compliant about school requirements and work hard to meet these formal expectations. Others question expectations and sometimes seek other means of education that are not so rigidly controlled. Some students simply drop out of school because it no longer seems relevant to them. In light of Dewey's observation, we should carefully examine how these imposed standards affect student learning in at least three areas: the isolation of evaluation from the ongoing work of the classroom and the curriculum, the curriculum imbalance that results from the imposition of current standards, and the restriction of learning materials to the textbook. These conditions have led to excesses and bad educational practices.

Isolation of Evaluation

High-stakes tests are the dominant form of evaluation in most states. They have removed evaluation as an inherent component of teaching and learning processes.

The proper role of evaluation (in various forms)—as a means to determine what students have learned and to suggest what next steps might be warranted for particular students—is missing. It has been replaced by standards set far afield from the classroom. In the final analysis, standardized tests have become the dominant form of evaluation and the only one that counts.

Students in my own community, for example, are coached on how to take standardized tests, subjected to pep rallies to get them revved up to do their best on high-stakes tests, treated to breakfast at school on the day of testing, given sugar snacks just before testing, and presented with gift certificates to stores in the local mall when they do well on the state tests. Ongoing evaluations as a part of the educational process are ignored in favor of what must be done to get lagging or failing students up to grade level or beyond for the next round of high-stakes tests. Teachers feel a keen sense of what they must do to prepare students for the state tests because the rewards are dependent on scores the students make on the mandated tests.

Curriculum Imbalance

The curriculum students experience in the classroom has been seriously out of balance for many years. This phenomenon is a significant result of the student's role being severely diminished as the drive for high standards becomes more dominant. (Unfortunately, budgetary constraints also have been a factor.) Time spent in elementary schools to get students up to standards in reading and math has too often limited the curriculum to little else except those two areas. In the push to meet standards, the arts, social studies, and science have received short shrift or even have been eliminated from the curriculum, and the impact on the quality of schooling as described by Dewey has been eliminated from discussions about curriculum. Few of us would recognize this condition as a desirable feature of the education we want for our students.

Restricted Learning Materials

Though textbooks have been judged as severely limited by a variety of studies, the curriculum—planned and implemented to meet high standards—has strengthened the use of a single textbook in classrooms. Students whose interests may be beyond what is between the covers of the text are not encouraged to explore other topics, nor are teachers rewarded for trying to make the curriculum more responsive to students' needs and interests by using a variety of learning materials. Supplemental materials that might make the curriculum more interesting, understandable, and relevant to the lives of students are not found in many classrooms. The textbook that best matches the high-stakes tests becomes the only teaching and learning tool to be found. This situation severely restricts the curriculum and disregards the students' interests in the learning process.

Our schools must be able to give evidence of what is being taught by teachers and learned by students. New ways to foster excellence in American education— beyond the remotely and politically set standards that do not take into account students' needs and interests—are desperately needed. Though many teachers continue to do all they can to honor the lives and experiences of students beyond the classroom as they work within the designated curriculum, their work is severely handicapped by the drive to meet high external standards. We have overlooked a significant part of the equation for school success: the student and what he or she brings to school today. Dewey's reflection on "the source of whatever is dead, mechanical, and formal in schools" as stemming from "the subordination of the life and experience of the child to the curriculum" is just as applicable today as when he first penned it.

Reference

Dewey, J. (1976). The child and the curriculum. In J. A. Boydston (Ed.), *John Dewey: The middle works, 1899–1924: Vol. 2. 1902–1903* (pp. 271–292). Carbondale: Southern Illinois University Press. (Original work published 1902)

11

COLLECTING AND PRESERVING THE EDUCATIONAL PRESENT

Craig Kridel

> *The things in civilization we most prize are not of ourselves. They exist by grace of the doings and sufferings of the continuous human community in which we are a link. Ours is the responsibility of conserving, transmitting, rectifying, and expanding the heritage of values we have received that those who come after us may receive it more solid and secure, more widely accessible and more generously shared than we have received it.*
>
> —*A Common Faith*, Later Works 9: 58

I am touched by Dewey's selflessness and his reminder that we are indeed an important part of a larger entity—namely, the continuous human community. We often forget this exulted role as we cope with the constant and endless procession of students who pass through our classrooms. Yet, as Dewey reminds us in his characteristically gentle way, we must not overlook our responsibility to those who come after us.

That ours is to conserve and transmit the heritage of values has become a moral call to me. As a curator of a museum of education, my life is committed to conserving and transmitting the heritage of values that represents our educational system. I maintain that, in what certainly may be construed as an idiosyncratic interpretation of this passage, this same moral call goes out to all educators who live fruitful lives in schools today and who wish to pass on this rich heritage to future generations of teachers and students.

Material Culture and Life in Schools

Why do I raise this topic? Because while much is being written about education—newspaper editorials, professional journal articles, No Child Left Behind critiques, and charter school reports and descriptions—not enough of the material culture of schools is being preserved. *Material culture,* a term commonly used in the fields of archives and museums, refers to those artifacts, documents, and objects modified by humans, consciously or unconsciously, that define and reflect the beliefs and values of the larger society of which they are a part. Can we identify material culture that represents the beliefs and principles that we as educators hold dear for the schools? And, of this material, what is being conserved?

Perhaps various newspaper accounts and journal articles represent your values. Those documents are being saved in our libraries. Further, we can rest assured that federal records also are being kept. The federal government currently generates in a four-month period records equal in volume to those of the first 124 years of our government—from the Washington to Wilson presidencies—all cataloged and archived. Yet, do these federal reports and academic writings truly characterize the heritage of values for which we wish to be remembered?

While this abundant amount of material will survive, does it reflect our lives in schools? Does it embody the markings on a lesson plan (marginalia) for that day when a class finally "gets it"? Does it represent the newsletter clippings with accompanying notes posted by the proud teacher, or the troubled student's corrected worksheet saved by a concerned teacher aide? These are the items, the material culture, that reflect our values and serve to remind future educators that their struggles and their joys of teaching, different yet similar through the years, have been shared by others. The human community of educators is indeed continuous, and it is our responsibility to contemporary times to ensure that our lives in schools are fully documented, solid, secure, and accessible. To this end, I ask educators to accept a role of collecting school culture.

Collecting School Culture

Please do not groan at the thought of yet another educational duty. This role does not require committee meetings, agreed-upon goals and objectives, or even the knowledge of others. The profound gesture of collecting may be an active or sedentary activity with or without a public profile. Further, educators already collect school documents! Today's educational research is filled with the outgrowths of accumulating material culture: teacher portfolio (Bullough, 1989; Bullough & Baughman, 1997), teacher narrative and autobiography (Clandinin & Connelly, 2000; Connelly & Clandinin, 1999), portraiture (Lawrence-Lightfoot & Davis, 2002), local history (Butchart, 1986), and biographical research (Kridel, 1998). Teachers compose portfolios for National Board Certification, and students are asked regularly to compile exhibition portfolios of their work. Teacher memoir, narrative, and portraiture have improved staff development and teacher education and, when saved with accompanying artifacts, could transform the presentation and understanding of educational values for future generations.

Could not such school portfolios be prepared for future generations? A scrapbook here and there, a carton of clippings, or one mere filing cabinet drawer in a teacher's room filled with an array of documents and artifacts could more than portray school life for a 10- to 20-year period. The intent is not comprehensiveness; one need not rent storage space at the nearby mini-warehouse. With periodic donations to one's local historical society, a collage of material culture would be preserved. Certainly some teachers would leave such archival treasures, selected with care, as mementos of a rewarding life of teaching.

Preserving the Present

One still may ask whether this preservation is truly necessary. While educational historians talk about the importance of preserving the past, I question whether we are conserving the present. I have spent years assisting researchers who were able to obtain more information about certain classrooms in the 1890s than about educational practices from the 1970s. As I work on a progressive education school study from the 1930s, I find many period documents of students' work and teachers' thoughts and reflections of school life. For some of these same schools, similar materials cannot be located from the early 1980s. Other than a few brochures or yearbooks, little exists. Certain institutions have preserved a distinguished and distinctive past—yet the recent is lost.

Further, the present is being lost during this time that we assume to be an abundant information age. Actually, documents are becoming victims of the false sense of assurance that is suggested with each technological advancement. While paper lasts for decades and vertical files may be accessed by anyone, today's technological storing, arranging, and retrieving of information creates new complications. CD-ROM storage has a life of just 20 years. Audiotapes and videotapes are most likely nonfunctional after as few as 10 years. As computer technology advances, the danger of storing data in irretrievable, antiquated forms increases. I regularly receive e-mail from well-meaning archivists who have found buried material, such as Kaypro files, with no ability to retrieve the records.

Transferring electronic information from one medium to another has been termed *technology refreshing*. I find myself in too many conversations where administrators, far removed from the intricacies of archival retrieval, state how easily the information can be refreshed. However, I rarely hear that funds actually are set aside for such activities. Irreplaceable audiotape cassettes may be digitized and then further refreshed once the DAT (Digital Audio Tape) medium is replaced. But for now, the cassettes wait, playable only until a rewinding snaps and destroys the tape. Many of the Museum of Education's irreplaceable three-quarter-inch Betamax videotape interviews from the mid-1970s remain safe, solid, and secure, yet inaccessible. Perhaps I should be pleased that we were unable to transfer the content to a one-half inch VHS format because we now would be searching for funds to refresh to DVD. Regardless, the irreplaceable content is, in fact, irretrievable.

Even with technology refreshing, many samples of material culture, representing dimensions of school life and the individual lives of teachers, are not conserved. Too often, old technology leads not to refreshing but to dispensing. Many filmstrips and reel-to-reel tapes from the early 1970s are thrown away—not due to bureaucratic inefficiency or to administrative ineptness, but instead to the pretentiousness of living in a technological age where we assume copies abound and always will be preserved—by others.

Preserving with Foresight

Dewey's call, however, should not give carte blanche privileges to anyone to go out and start gathering artifacts. Contemporary materials must be preserved with some foresight. To restate the primordial caveat of archivists: "There is little virtue in mere acquisition if it is divorced from intelligent purpose." I have suffered through too many occasions where a donor has displayed a "willing suspension of significance" and has thrust upon my archives a batch of materials representing little purpose and importance. Material culture consists not of those piles of texts and unused workbooks.

Instead, teacher and student artifacts—corrected worksheets of a child's repeated attempt to complete an assignment, an exhibition poster representing students' work, teacher notes for next week's lessons, meeting agendas with the doodling of a bored staff member, a school newsletter with witticisms (and complaints) jotted in the margins about school policy—these are the items that display the richness of school life. Such perspectives manifest themselves in autobiographies and diaries; in personal narratives and class ethnographies from students' writings and projects; in school and institutional documents, newsletters, annuals, yearbooks, and audio and video documentaries; and in the professional portfolios of education that emerge from our offices as a result of neglecting to prune our filing cabinets. These are the materials, selected from vast unbridled accumulations with the care of a reflective teacher's eye, which must be preserved.

I will be the first to admit that I have interpreted Dewey's statement from *A Common Faith* in a rather peculiar and atypical manner. Yet, his plea to conserve finds its resonance for me in the quest to preserve the educational present and to transmit our educational heritage for those future members of our profession. By accepting an active role in the collection and preservation of educational material culture—*archival agency,* so to speak—today's educators rectify the limiting aspects of lost materials and technological refreshing and fulfill Dewey's plea to expand the heritage of values so that those teachers and students who come after us "may receive it more solid and secure, more widely accessible and more generously shared."

References

Bullough, R. V., Jr. (1989). *First-year teacher: A case study.* New York, NY: Teachers College Press.

Bullough, R. V., Jr., & Baughman, K. (1997). *"First-year teacher" eight years later.* New York, NY: Teachers College Press.

Butchart, R. E. (1986). *Local schools: Exploring their history.* Nashville, TN: American Association for State and Local History.

Clandinin, D. J., & Connelly, F. M. (2000). *Narrative inquiry: Experience and story in qualitative research.* San Francisco, CA: Jossey-Bass.

Connelly, F. M., & Clandinin, D. J. (Eds.). (1999). *Shaping a professional identity: Stories of educational practice.* New York, NY: Teachers College Press.

Dewey, J. (1986). A common faith. In J. A. Boydston (Ed.), *John Dewey: The later works, 1925–1953: Vol. 9. 1933–1934* (pp. 1–58). Carbondale: Southern Illinois University Press. (Original work published 1933)

Kridel, C. (Ed.). (1998). *Writing educational biography.* New York, NY: Garland.

Lawrence-Lightfoot, S., & Davis, J. H. (2002). *The art and science of portraiture.* San Francisco, CA: Jossey-Bass.

PART II

Active Learning

ACTIVE LEARNING: A GROWTH EXPERIENCE

Rick Breault

Few Deweyan concepts have been as misunderstood and misused as the notion of *active learning*. Dewey (1916/1980) conceives of active learning as natural to the child:

> We do not have to draw out or educe positive activities from a child. . . . Where there is life, there are already eager and impassioned activities. (p. 47)

Yet, many teachers and teacher educators fail to grasp the complexity and intention required to create learning opportunities that are educative as well as active. Active learning never was meant to let children do whatever they want and follow whatever grabs their attention at the moment. Instead, the task of the educator, as Dewey (1916/1980) explains, is to

> engage pupils in these activities in such ways that while manual skill and technical efficiency are gained and immediate satisfaction found in the work, together with preparation for later usefulness, these things shall be subordinated to *education* [author's emphasis]—that is, to intellectual results and the forming of a socialized disposition. (p. 204)

Beware of Quick-Fix Solutions

Educators today, as were those in Dewey's era, are susceptible to quick-fix solutions and techniques. We look around and see educational entrepreneurs (a.k.a. "consultants"), and even a few major professional organizations and journals, touting simplistic techniques based on "constructivism" or "multiple intelligences" that seem increasingly far removed from the theories on which they are based.

Well-intentioned teachers—and teacher educators—are excited to find such relatively easy theory-based teaching methods. Unfortunately, acting out a story from the reading book or coloring a picture about a history lesson is not teaching to multiple intelligences. Just because there is some sound theory behind the notion that we construct our own learning does not mean that students naturally construct anything meaningful or educative when left on their own.

In Dewey's lifetime, as now, the first casualty of such "active learning" was subject matter, which always leaves professional educators easy targets to a variety of critics. Teachers during the early and middle years of the last century grabbed onto terms like "progressive education" and "the project method" and made them into empty, albeit at times fun, classroom actions. In the case of progressive education, what Dewey articulates as a sophisticated and radical rethinking of existing education had become, by the late 1940s, associated with anything not related to the teaching of basic academic subjects. All bad teaching had become known as progressive education, and with some high schools providing classes in hypnotism and contract bridge in the name of progressive education, the critics might not have been far off (Cremin, 1961; Martin, 1951; Trillingham, 1951).

What Does Dewey Mean?

None of this, however, does much to say what Dewey *does* mean by active learning. Although the nature of this introduction does not allow for a careful treatment of this very important idea, there are four things you might keep in mind as you read the essays in this section.

First, Dewey never intends to set activity and subject matter against one another. Learning subject matter and learning through meaningful activity were not to be mutually exclusive. In fact, in *Experience and Education* (1938/1988), Dewey argues strongly against an either/or mentality toward traditional and progressive education and reframed the problem of subject matter as one in which we have to decide how to help the "young become acquainted with the past in such a way that the acquaintance is a potent agent in appreciation of the living present" (p. 10). Moreover, even subject matter was to be seen as something active, as something "fluent, embryonic, vital" (Dewey, 1902/1976, p. 278). To that end, Dewey (1938/1988) emphasizes that although "the organized subject matter of the adult and the specialist cannot provide the starting point . . . it represents the goal toward which education should continuously move" (p. 56). Subject matter is a means and not an end in active learning.

Second, active learning is concerned with more than subject matter; active learning also implies social engagement. Dewey believes that traditional schooling in his time had failed to prepare young people for their roles in society because it had "erected silence into one of its prime virtues" (Dewey, 1938/1988, p. 40) and had endeavored "to prepare future members of the social order in a medium in which the conditions of the social spirit" were "eminently wanting" (Dewey, 1899/1976,

p. 10). Those schools had wasted an educational opportunity by failing to allow students to utilize the experiences they got outside the school in any "complete and free way within the school itself"; students were unable to "apply in daily life" what they learned in school (Dewey, 1899/1976, p. 46). Active learning is most effective when it takes place in the context of an "embryonic community life, active with types of occupations that reflect the life of the larger society *and* [emphasis added] permeated throughout with the spirit of art, history, science" (Dewey, 1899/1976, p. 19). Within these embryonic communities, active learning would saturate the students in a spirit of service and provide them with the instruments of self-direction.

Third, although Dewey encourages a Copernican-like shift that would move the child to the center of the educational universe, active learning is not to be based on the child's impulsive and haphazard preferences. Instead, Dewey (1899/1976) suggests that valuable educational results come most likely "through direction, through organized use" (p. 25). The teacher has the responsibility to channel the students' naturally intense activity by directing their activities, "giving them exercise along certain lines" (Dewey, 1899/1976, p. 25). The teacher should indeed let students express their initial impulse; but then, the teacher's task is, "through criticism, question, and suggestion," to bring each student "to consciousness of what he has done and what he needs to do" (Dewey, 1899/1976, p. 28). In sum, active learning that is also educative and meaningful happens when the teacher helps the child "to realize his own impulse by recognizing the facts, materials, and conditions involved, and then to regulate his impulse through that recognition" (Dewey, 1899/1976, p. 27).

Finally, learning that is active takes place when viewed in the context of a continuum of individual intellectual development. Active learning that is educative, and not mis-educative, is characterized by continuity and growth. Continuity in education means that any learning experience that is organized for the student should take into consideration the experience the child brings to the learning activity and should prepare the child for future experiences. This criterion is *not* met, however, simply by helping students acquire skills they will need 6 years later in college. Rather, preparation for the future means helping the student get out of the present experience "all that there is in it for him at the time in which he has it" (Dewey, 1938/1988, p. 29). More specifically,

> We always live at the time we live and not at some other time, and only by extracting at each present time the full meaning of each present experience are we prepared for doing the same thing in the future. This is the only preparation which in the long run amounts to anything. (Dewey, 1938/1988, p. 29)

Reconsidering Hands-On Lessons

Another characteristic of meaningful active learning is growth. In *Experience and Education* (1938/1988), Dewey discusses growth as one aspect of continuity. I have chosen to treat it separately here for the sake of emphasizing its importance and our tendency to overlook its implications. Dewey warns that it is not sufficient to talk simply of growth as the result of activity. We must, instead, "specify the direction in which growth takes place":

> From the standpoint of growth as education and education as growth the question is whether growth in this direction promotes or retards growth in general. Does this form of growth create conditions for further growth, or does it set up conditions that shut off the person who has grown in this particular direction from the occasions, stimuli, and opportunities for continuing growth in new directions? (Dewey, 1938/1988, p. 19)

If teachers take this caution seriously, they will have to reconsider those "hands-on" activities in which they believe that students are constructing their own understandings. For it is possible that the understandings they construct could be undisciplined and even inaccurate. Moreover, because these activities are conducted with the teacher's approval, these understandings are assumed to be correct by the student, thus creating a false sense of certainty that might discourage future experimentation or openness and create barriers to new exploration.

Deweyan activity implies so much more than simple hands-on lessons and student movement around the room. Though active learning might be manifest in external movement, real active learning is cognitive and social. It is a process; it is communal; it is a growth experience; it is continuous. Most of all, it requires a rethinking of your role as a teacher and learner in the classroom. As you read the following selections, read them with the characteristics of active learning in mind. Think in terms of how their content relates to your own experiences. Share them with your colleagues and challenge one another to examine your own practice in relation to what they have to say. Read them in the context of where you want to go as a teacher and how they might help you get there. Read them for all you can get out of them both for the teacher you are today and the teacher you hope to be tomorrow.

References

Cremin, L. (1961). *The transformation of the school: Progressivism in American education, 1876–1957*. New York, NY: Vintage Books.

Dewey, J. (1976). The school and society. In J. A. Boydston (Ed.), *John Dewey: The middle works, 1899–1924: Vol. 1. 1899–1901* (pp. 5–112). Carbondale: Southern Illinois University Press. (Original work published 1899)

Dewey, J. (1976). The child and the curriculum. In J. A. Boydston (Ed.), *John Dewey: The middle works, 1899–1924: Vol. 2. 1902–1903* (pp. 271–292). Carbondale: Southern Illinois University Press. (Original work published 1902)

Dewey, J. (1980). Democracy and education. In J. A. Boydston (Ed.), *John Dewey: The middle works, 1899–1924: Vol. 9. 1916* (pp. 1–370). Carbondale: Southern Illinois University Press. (Original work published 1916)

Dewey, J. (1988). Experience and education. In J. A. Boydston (Ed.), *John Dewey: The later works, 1925–1953: Vol. 13. 1938–1939* (pp. 1–62). Carbondale: Southern Illinois University Press. (Original work published 1938)

Martin, L. (1951, September 8). Denver, Colorado. *Saturday Review of Literature,* pp. 6–13.

Trillingham, C. C. (1951). What's right with public education? *The School Executive, 70,* 39–42.

12

A SPECTATOR'S VERSION OF KNOWLEDGE

Deron Boyles

> *If we see that knowing is not the act of an outside spectator but of a participator inside the natural and social scene, then the true object of knowledge resides in the consequences of directed action.*
>
> —*The Quest for Certainty*, Later Works 4: 157

Armchair quarterbacks who complain about botched passes.

Well-meaning friends who suggest your child should play the violin.

Accountability-minded administrators who use checklists during classroom observations.

Each of these groups of people "knows" things. The armchair quarterback gets to see instant replays. The friend gets to project wishes onto a child he or she doesn't live with 24/7. The administrator gets to use a checklist to determine that a teacher needs better classroom management skills. Each group has knowledge. But the knowledge is not only limited, it also isn't that important. The armchair quarterback isn't actually on the field staring at an advancing defensive lineman and making immediate decisions about passing the football. The friend isn't around long enough to know whether the child is talented, disciplined, or even interested in music. The administrator isn't in the classroom with the various students long enough to understand the culture of a teacher's room.

Admittedly, teachers suffer from the same problem: They often treat their students as they are treated. Teachers become armchair quarterbacks, well-meaning friends, and administrators to their students. Covering material because of Iowa Tests of Basic Skills (ITBS) or other standardized testing constraints, assuming that they know what students need without first getting to know them, and imposing their own version of checklists in the form of worksheets and other busywork that are detached from students' lives—teachers fall into the same trap that Dewey warns us about.

We can't treat knowledge as a static entity. Knowledge isn't a series of discreet bits of information passed from a teacher to a student, even though that is a major assumption we carry with us. In fact, knowledge isn't really the point at all. *Knowing* is the point. And the risk in not understanding the difference is in turning students into the same kinds of spectators that armchair quarterbacks, well-meaning friends, accountability-minded administrators, and even teachers often represent.

The Relevance of the Spectator

Dewey's suggestion is twofold: (a) A statement about how things are may or may not correspond to how things actually are; (b) at the same time, it is not possible to treat this correspondence as if it were a matter of comparing the statement against reality. What we have to do is make judgments in "real time" about consequences of actions in solving actual problems. Correspondence, then, becomes a metaphor for Dewey, allowing him to argue that although a "spectator" version of knowledge is not always wrong, neither does it describe or explain how people actually use information from their lives to solve their problems. The relevance of the "spectator" is in the very detachment Dewey rejects. "Spectators" don't assert; they passively observe. "Spectators" are outside of experience—at least the kind of experience that is engaging of others.

Knowing, Knowledge, and Intelligence

Distinguishing between a few key concepts may be helpful to better understand the larger meaning and its relationship to classroom interaction. Knowing, knowledge, and intelligence are distinct for Dewey. Knowing is a process of inquiry (involving specific instances of applied problem solving); knowledge constitutes the stable outcomes of inquiry; and intelligence is the result of the development and accumulation of capabilities to act (i.e., inquire) in specific ways.

Organic and natural environments for learning impel knowing and the habits of intelligence. Detachment from natural environments for learning indulges "spectating" and habits of routine. When you participate in the "consequences of directed action," you side with active inquiry. That is, given Dewey's theory of knowledge/knowing, classrooms should be places where students make knowledge claims at the same time they are engaged in knowing (inquiry). The means and ends are not separable for Dewey.

Active engagement of the sort Dewey suggests means that students engage rather than observe. They are not in the business of "discovering" the "facts" as though there is some cosmic puzzle to solve once and for all. The point of inquiry is not to collect detached artifacts. Rather, active inquiry puts functionality above abstraction. Active inquiry means students identifying problems and actually solving them. As a result, a general pattern emerges when students use their own experiences (individual and joint) as a backdrop to solve other problems. Like an ever-expanding upward spiral, students develop and grow best when their interests are engaged and utilized.

Of course, not all inquiry is fruitful. That's why Dewey talks about "directed action." Some actions are whim and do not lead to educative experiences. Rather than "directing" students to be "spectators," the teacher directs students toward engaging activities—to active inquiry that leads to further inquiry (and knowing). Be clear: Directing students to prefabricated "learning centers" or "activity centers" to do busywork is not what Dewey is describing. Dewey advocates students becoming experimenters themselves.

The Quest for Certainty

Students, Dewey espouses, do not search for "the truth" or "the right answers." Instead, students make assertions to be judged by the bounds of their own experiences—bounds that already exist and that expand via inquiry and directed action. This approach not only represents a big shift in our understanding of the roles of teachers and students but also shifts the purpose of schooling away from "getting" answers, grades, diplomas, and jobs—which Dewey obliquely calls the "quest for certainty."

Such a "quest for certainty" may be largely to blame for the general lack of inquiry found within U.S. classrooms. Students as testable objects themselves, and whose role it is to gather discreet bits of data and information, are largely subjected to a classroom sphere where the only evidence of relation is between imposed artifacts and superimposed goals. Even good teachers are burdened by the perversion of the "quest for certainty" seen in most schools. Never mind that the reality is itself subjectively constructed—all the tests, the standards, the mission statements, the learning objectives. The reality makes little difference because the presentation of that reality is summed up as "the real world" or "the way it is." As a result, teacher-proof curricula, accountability policies, and the enormous focus on both standardization and competition arguably are examples of what Dewey would have considered misguided.

Of course, some teachers in some schools practice active inquiry, but they are few and far between. Preordained and prefabricated, the reality of most teacher and student roles in schools has been so long established that the task of changing the culture of schools is daunting. When education students begin their course work, they enter with ideas and experiences that inform what they want to do and how they want to do it. But these ideas are virtually unchanged from the culture from which they came. These students were reared as spectators (and often spectated in their college classes as well). Even when some education students say they want to "engage" their students in "active" learning, the result usually is a souped-up version of traditional schooling.

Dewey's position, however, is an offering. It's a possible "out." It represents one way students and teachers might develop relations in less contrived ways than what currently goes on in most schools. By shifting roles of teachers and students so that both groups are inquirers into problems they face, the "quest for certainty" goes out the window and the expectations for both the "quest" and the "certainty" are challenged. In place of certainty is inquiry—*knowing*—and it comes into being when the engagement between teachers and students (and students and students, parents and students, etc.) supports investigations and experiments, leading to directed action and to continual knowing.

Reference

Dewey, J. (1984). The quest for certainty. In J. A. Boydston (Ed.), *John Dewey: The later works, 1925–1953: Vol. 4. 1929* (pp. 1–250). Carbondale: Southern Illinois University Press. (Original work published 1929)

13

MAKING INFORMED JUDGMENTS

Dan Marshall

> *The essence of critical thinking is suspended judgment.*
> —*How We Think*, Middle Works 6: 238

Shortly after introducing an activity in class, I observed a more or less typical display of apparent student engagement, ranging from raised-voice discussion accompanied by waving arms and pointing fingers, to fluttering-eyed, head-dropping somnambulism. After scanning the room for several minutes from a fixed location, I began to wander, having decided that some of the students could use my help. Roaming the room, using physical proximity along with some calculated questions and comments to "encourage" select students to join in, I felt satisfied that all was well.

Teachers are, by definition, consummate judges and decision makers. This is, in large part, because our work is action-oriented and student-related. Day after day, we find ourselves identifying situations, weighing options, making choices, and taking actions. However, this routine creates its own problems. As Maxine Greene (1988) noted:

It is clear that choice and action both occur within and by means of ongoing transactions with objective conditions and with other human beings. They occur as well within the matrix of a culture, its prejudgments, and its symbol systems. (p. 4)

The Problem With Routine

This ever-present decision-making problematic for teachers has much to do with the judgmental aspect of our choices. Briefly, all decisions are choices typically made on the basis of habit or custom (it's the way we do things), external force or influence (it's the way the district or state wants things done), or deliberate (i.e., intelligent) choice among alternatives (it's what ought to happen, given the evidence).

In the worst cases, decisions can reflect little or no deliberate judgment at all; that is, we make them reflexively, without sufficient knowledge or careful comparison of our options. In the best cases, teachers recognize the inherent traps within what Greene (1988) called our *cultural matrix*, particularly its established prejudgments (e.g., some students are lazy), as well as the apparent external forces that impinge on our choices (e.g., high-stakes testing pressures). Skeptical of the preceding, we set out to gather whatever information is necessary for us to select the best option. The resulting decision is said to reflect an *informed judgment*.

Informed Judgment

When I had some time to reflect, I found myself cataloging the students I had "visited" during the activity. One student seemed frequently disengaged with the class as a whole, while a second often had difficulty keeping social chat separate from activity-based talk. One student probably hadn't done the requisite reading, while another may have felt inferior within his small group and tuned out as a protective measure.

Judgment involves the consideration of different options before arriving at a decision regarding their comparative merit or worth. To judge, therefore, is to form a value-oriented opinion or understanding—to find the *best* choice available. Decisions resulting from *informed judgments* represent the combination of efforts to bring our intellect (i.e., deliberation) into play with our value-grounded understandings and dispositions when choosing among different options. In contrast, many—perhaps most—of our teaching decisions are made "on the fly" and without the benefit of much informed judgment. Teachers' work is hectic, reflecting a kind of routine immediacy unlike almost any other professional work. Taking the time to consider the circumstances, the voracity of available information, and the options at hand seems impossible when we don't have the time in the first place.

Consequently, the intelligent or deliberative basis for judgment prior to our decision making often goes unattended. This happens too because we often seem to find ourselves making familiar, routine, almost habitual decisions based on our teaching situations and contexts. In my case, I looked around the room, determined that some students had decided to ignore their responsibilities, and chose to provide them with a little extrinsic motivation.

Prejudgment

The embarrassing part, for me, is that on reflection, my judgment, my action, and my subsequent reflection on both were merely habitual. I was not acting intelligently, nor later that day was I thinking intelligently. Mine were *prejudgments* stemming from my teaching cultures. I was not thinking much, and I certainly was not thinking critically about the situation before me. To do so, I would have had to suspend my judgment—to have looked over the room and decided *not* to make a decision about what I was seeing at that moment. For Dewey, suspended judgment is the essence of critical thinking.

Several days later, I was led to reflect on this same activity and, more important, my judgments about it and the students in class. What led me to this revisiting is another story entirely, but what I learned about myself remains deeply troubling.

In his dictionary of Dewey's thoughts, Ralph Winn (1959) reminded us that Dewey understands criticism as "discriminating judgment" and "careful appraisal" (p. 18) regarding value-laden choices. What makes serious thinking *critical* is the ability to bring "the possible" or "the ideal" to bear on what we take to be the situation at hand (Winn 1959, p. 138). That is, we carefully appraise the situation and imagine it, if only for a moment, as it could or should be in an ideal sense.

Suspended Judgment

Had I suspended my judgment momentarily, I might have doubted my matter-of-fact thinking processes. My take on the class activity had everything to do with off-task behavior and how to fix that problem. Thinking more critically, I might have wondered about the nature of the task itself (a single task with little individual flexibility), or my narrow-minded notion of on-task behavior (not to mention my ignoring of the purposes of the activity), or my choice to "police the area" rather than engage certain students in conversation about their impressions of the activity.

Ironically, I try my best to help undergraduate and graduate students value and develop what I call a "healthy skepticism" about their pedagogical decisions because what we think we know, feel, or can do underlies not only our judgments but our choices and actions as teachers. I routinely encourage my students to base their pedagogical decisions on informed judgment, as Henderson and Kesson (2004) reminded us: "If educators do not take on the responsibility of making informed judgments directed by intelligence, the profession will increasingly find itself subject to the decisions of others" (p. 45). This is, I tell them, not an easy responsibility. Even after teaching for more than 25 years, I continue to struggle with it.

References

Dewey, J. (1978). How we think. In J. A. Boydston (Ed.). *John Dewey: The middle works: 1899–1924: Vol. 6: 1910–1911* (pp. 177–356). Carbondale: Southern Illinois University Press. (Original work published 1910)

Greene, M. (1988). *The dialectic of freedom.* New York, NY: Teachers College Press.

Henderson, J. G., & Kesson, K. R. (2004). *Curriculum wisdom: Educational decisions in democratic societies.* Upper Saddle River, NJ: Pearson/Merrill/Prentice Hall.

Winn, R. B. (Ed.). (1959). *John Dewey: Dictionary of education.* New York, NY: Philosophical Library.

14

THE GROWTH OF FUTURE GENERATIONS STARTS TODAY

Jonathan T. Martin

> But the process of living is continuous; it possesses continuity because it is an everlastingly renewed process of acting upon the environment and being acted upon by it together with institution of relations between what is done and what is undergone.
> —*Art as Experience,* Later Works 10: 109

Each human travels through existence continuously interacting with his or her environment and surroundings in the experience we know as human life. As human beings, we each grow and expand our minds by learning from the experiences and interactions we have with the world around us. We build our understandings from these experiences we live each day and construct our thoughts from past knowledge and related experiences, thus continually expanding our own perceived view of the world. An individual witnesses the world through a lens intricately developed and refined by his or her life experiences and continual daily interactions with family, friends, environment, and society.

No two humans in existence are exactly the same. Life is too complex and intricate; no matter how many similarities and traits we share with others, we are still going to have at least a few differences. As well as differences in influence, no two humans walk the same path. The myriad of influences around us and the unique walks of life we each experience lead the human mind to continually grow and develop new thoughts and conceptions by connecting new experiences with past context and similar experiences, in turn creating in each of us a unique mental framework through which each individual perceives the world around himself or herself. Considering the infinite multitude of interactions and experiences humans live through each day, no one's life is exactly the same and no one processes information in the same manner.

In modern society, success is often measured in dollars and cents. Driven by free markets and capitalistic economic systems, we are continually inundated with advertisements, blind consumerism, competition, and a drive for monetary and personal gain. Our daily habits and routines can often constrict the limits of human thought and expression. Most individuals in society are preoccupied with a fight for survival, striving for personal security and enough money and resources to make it through life in a challenging world. The business world and free market societies are based largely on competition and the quest for the almighty dollar, far too often at the expense of the individual and greater good.

Unfortunately, these are the ideals and values that are so thoroughly ingrained in our society. As William Wordsworth (1845) stated during the rise of the industrial age, "The world is too much with us; late and soon, / Getting and spending, we lay waste our powers: / Little we see in nature that is ours; / We have given our hearts away, a sordid boon!" (p. 203). Continually in pursuit of personal gain, profits, and possessions, we find it difficult to perceive the world outside of our own conceptions and mental maps that are so largely influenced by modern society. By allowing your mind to shed these restrictions, you create a space for ingenuity and unlimited opportunity. I would like to challenge you to expand the depth and breadth of your imagination, to think about new ways to perceive outside the constraints of your current reality, and to open your mind to the possibility of a more compassionate and humanistic society.

As educators, it is important that we never forget either the varying complexities of the human experience or the strong influences imposed by society and environment that limit individual expression and thought. Far too often, we are quick to judge and group students on the basis of our previous experiences in the classroom and experiences with similar students. Although the demographics of students in a particular school may be similar, the life experiences that each student brings to the classroom will be unique to that individual. Furthermore, a teacher must bear in mind the innumerable sources of outside influence present in each student's life. The teacher has a responsibility to factor these experiences and influences into the execution of the school's curriculum. Once his or her teaching reflects this understanding, the students will, in turn, not only be able to understand the curriculum but also to see how this knowledge ties into what the student has done and will experience.

Students, especially adolescents, frequently complain that adults are too quick to brush off their concerns and often distance themselves from the purpose of traditional school curriculum. They are made to feel as though their current existence is secondary to the ever-looming "real world" and that the only goal of a traditional school curriculum is to prepare them for "adult life." However, a student's past is the only world he or she knows, and it is unfair to discredit all prior knowledge, passions, and interests of the students. Ask a student what makes a good teacher, and that student will most likely tell you his or her favorite teachers are the ones who listen, who understand the uniqueness of each class member.

Every effort should be made by educators to use this rich base to build a solid, relevant framework for instruction. One of the challenges lies in the typical class size. It is quite the task for a teacher to deeply understand the varying backgrounds of an entire class and integrate them all into the curriculum in a genuine and relevant way. This is why teachers usually gear lessons more toward the demographics of the entire class and less toward each individual's prior knowledge base. Although this approach may be the practical one, especially given how little time teachers have to create well-developed lesson plans and units, teachers should instead open their minds to possibility and creativity and try to think outside the normal constraints of the profession. Teachers should strive to create experiences in the classroom that embed opportunities for students to explore elements of the curriculum in their own context; teachers also should encourage students to expand the horizons and limits of their thoughts beyond the constraints and limits of their surroundings and past knowledge base.

Instead of viewing a curriculum as a list of "What do students need to know?" we should see it as a catalyst of "What will this allow them to be?" Each student's desires, goals, and needs are based on his or her unique past and life experience. By instructing in a way that allows students to connect their past with their education in a real way, students will respond with piqued interest and a passion for learning. Once teacher and student view the classroom as a place where the process of learning is continuous, where there "is an everlastingly renewed process of acting upon the environment and being acted upon," learning will become more relevant to the present and allow the learner to act and think critically in life. It is important for educators to connect curriculum and content to the array of experiences each student has lived. Through these enriching experiences and deep meaningful relationships, educators will be able to instill in students the infinite possibilities of imagination and a sense of purpose and compassion for future generations. Hence, educators should constantly reevaluate, reflect, and expand on their professional practices to make every effort to include instruction that allows students to continually grow and make connections to "what is done and what is undergone."

References

Dewey, J. (1987). Art as experience. In J. A. Boydston (Ed.), *John Dewey: The later works, 1925–1953: Vol. 10. 1934* (pp. 1–352). Carbondale: Southern Illinois University Press. (Original work published 1934)

Wordsworth, W. (1845). *The poems of William Wordsworth.* Oxford, England: E. Moxon Publishers.

15

EXPERIENCE, HEIGHTENED VITALITY, AND AESTHETIC ENGAGEMENT, OR WHY IS STICK MAN SMILING?

P. Bruce Uhrmacher and Christy M. Moroye

> *Experience in the degree in which it is experienced is heightened vitality. Instead of signifying being shut up within one's own private feelings and sensations, it signifies active and alert commerce with the world; at its height it signifies complete interpenetration of self and the world of objects and events.*
>
> —*Art as Experience*, Later Works 10: 25

Consider the following vignette—does it ring true for many students in schools today?

Maria slides into her seat two seconds before the bell rings and curses her alarm clock. She's already behind. Class starts practically before the bell rings because Mr. Alvera likes to cram the period full with as much information as possible. Maria glances over the handout waiting on her desk—it's a bullet-point recap of last night's reading. . . . Rob tugs a hand through his mussed dark red hair and pulls out a notebook as the chemistry teacher explains the formula for the thermodynamic behavior of a gas. He tries to focus on the scrawled chalk that says "$pV = nRT$"—and diligently copies it into his notebook, as though that will change the fact that he doesn't get it. (Christensen, Horn, & Johnson, 2008, p. 21)

Even in a livelier environment, today's classroom tends to focus on standards and cognition. We think about making assessments fair and matching learning objectives to standardized tests. We might also think about students' backgrounds, about their cultures, and about relating material to their lives; in short, we might make sure students understand the learning goals and help them achieve these. All of these objectives are good and reasonable, but in our view they are not enough. What tends to be ignored in today's educational environment is an expectation of joy, of meaning making, and of memorable experiences that will shape a lifetime.

We ask you, the reader, to think back on your K–12 experiences. Can you remember an activity that you might describe as a "wow experience"? There may very well be a continuum of such wow activities, from brief punctuated experiences to ones that last for hours or days. Allow us to describe one that Bruce remembers:

It is first grade in 1963. My teacher, Mrs. Goodson, is teaching us about how to address envelopes. Looking back, I realize that she could have taught this lesson almost anywhere in the school year, but she decided to teach it around Valentine's Day. Here is what she did. First, she divided us into rows. Then she asked us to name our rows using the words, *road, street,* and *boulevard.* Next she taught us how to properly address an envelope. Then over the next week, she had us write a valentine for each member of the class. Thus, each of us addressed about 25 envelopes. At the same time, we also had the opportunity to make actual cardboard mailboxes, which we got to decorate. When Valentine's Day rolled around, each of us delivered our 25 valentines to the appropriate mailboxes.

What made the activities fun and memorable was not the addressing of the envelopes but the decorating of the mailboxes; the changing of our seat assignments into streets and boulevards; the thought behind who would get which valentine; the wondering about what kind of valentines we would get from whom; and even the actual delivering of the mail, which allowed us to get out of our seats and move around in the room.

Bruce's experience is one that fostered "heightened vitality," in which he was engaged in "active and alert commerce" with those in his classroom and, ultimately, the larger community. Dewey might have pointed out that this is due to the activity's interdisciplinary nature; its practicality; its social elements; and, of course, its educational value. Perhaps most important, he would have liked the fact that it is a fully engaging educational experience. But what does that really mean? Isn't *engagement* just another educational buzzword? Let's follow Dewey's thinking.

Dewey's understanding of how we come to know and learn may be illustrated with a simple drawing and described as follows. First, a person (represented by the handsome stick figure) has some interaction with the world. The interaction, signified by the large spiral, illustrates an exchange between person and environment (shown as mountains). From Dewey's point of view, we are always situated in an environment. In terms of an educational environment, if a teacher wants her students to learn how to address an envelope, she could model the writing on the blackboard and have students repeat it. Although the learning target might be met—that students learn how to address an envelope—little else is accomplished.

To refer to the drawing, the large spiral is the experience of copying down an address onto an envelope. But notice the small spiral hovering over the larger one. For Dewey, hovering over any ordinary experience is the possibility of an aesthetic one—"complete interpenetration of self and the world of objects and events." Such "wow" experiences are fostered when the teacher orchestrates a rich environment such as the valentine project. Subsequently, everything depends

on the quality of the interaction between the student and the learning material. According to Dewey, if the interaction is satisfying to the student, he or she will want to continue to learn and grow. If the interaction is unsatisfying, the student may want to stop learning. But if the experience is powerfully engaging, the student may remember the actual activity for a lifetime, as well as its associated joy and meaning.

Such engagement can happen in a shortened time span, for example, while watching a flock of geese fly overhead on a beautiful blue day or while enjoying a play at the theatre. Such wow experiences in which we feel fully present in the moment, when we lose a sense of time, when our mind does not wander, when our senses are alive, can, from Dewey's point of view, happen in all walks of life. The arts offer quintessential moments of an aesthetic experience, but such experiences can happen anywhere and everywhere. Hovering above any experience is the possibility of an aesthetic ("active and alert commerce") experience. And if this is true, then hovering above any teaching and learning experience is the possibility of an aesthetically engaging learning experience. Such experiences can spur students into alertness, into active commerce with the content and the world.

Our own work has been dedicated to understanding how to provide the possibilities for such experiences to happen to students in schools and classrooms (Moroye & Uhrmacher, 2009, 2010; Uhrmacher, 2009); but in this essay, we focus on what Dewey has helped us all to see. An aesthetic experience does not necessarily take one away from the world to be mired in one's imagination and lost in the pleasure of the senses. On the contrary, an aesthetic experience means that one is alive, active, and alert; one is engaged to the fullest extent possible. It is this kind of engagement—an aesthetic engagement—that we should wish for students to have regularly in schools and classrooms.

References

Christensen, C. M., Horn, M. B., & Johnson, C. W. (2008). *Disrupting class: How disruptive innovation will change the way the world learns.* New York, NY: McGraw Hill.

Dewey, J. (1987). Art as experience. In J. A. Boydston (Ed.), *John Dewey: The later works, 1925–1953: Vol. 10. 1934* (pp. 1–352). Carbondale: Southern Illinois University Press. (Original work published 1934)

Moroye, C. M., & Uhrmacher, P. B. (2009). Aesthetic themes of education. *Curriculum and Teaching Dialogue, 11*(1&2), 85–101.

Moroye, C. M., & Uhrmacher, P. B. (2010). Aesthetic themes as conduits to creativity. In C. J. Craig & L. F. Deretchin (Eds.), *Cultivating curious and creative minds: The role of teachers and teacher educators* (Teacher education yearbook XVIII, pp. 99–114). Lanham, MD: Rowman & Littlefield.

Uhrmacher, P. B. (2009). Toward a theory of aesthetic learning experiences. *Curriculum Inquiry, 39,* 613–636.

16

LISTENING FOR THE GENTLE WHISPER

Rick Breault

> *Will the proposed activity give that sort of expression to these impulses that will carry the child on to a higher plane of consciousness and action, instead of merely exciting him and then leaving him just where he was before, plus a certain amount of nervous exhaustion and appetite for more excitement in the future?*
> —*The School and Society*, Middle Works 1: 84

The prophet Elijah stood at the entrance to the cave where he was spending the night while fleeing his enemies. God had told him to wait there and he would soon experience the presence of the Lord. As he waited, he first experienced a powerful wind that "shattered rocks." Next came an earthquake, then a fire. Each time, Elijah expected the presence of God to be in overwhelming expressions of natural power. Each time, he was wrong. After the fire came "a gentle whisper," and it was in that whisper that the prophet heard the voice of God and was strengthened to return and confront his enemies (1 Kings 19: 8–13, New International Version). Elijah expected to be awed by the physical presence of God. He was waiting for the excitement. The excitement, however, left him where he had been before—unfulfilled and still waiting. Only when he learned to be still and listen for a gentle whisper did that enlightenment come.

This is one of the first stories that came to mind the first time I read the quotation from *The School and Society* (Dewey, 1899/1976). Much in a child's world comes across like a sensory jackhammer—fast, loud, and repetitive. Nearly 20 years ago, Neil Postman (1985) observed that the average length of a shot on network television was only 3.5 seconds. That was before the influence of MTV and the quick-cut, shaky, handheld video used in so many current television shows and advertisements. In the same book, Postman described the Lincoln–Douglas debates in which each candidate spoke for 2 to 3 hours and hardly lost an audience member. Compare that with modern political debates in which candidates have no more than a few minutes to make or rebut a statement and to summarize their positions.

Toward a "Higher Plane of Consciousness"

With rare exceptions, the entertainment industry seems to tell us that everything we need to know about any given issue, product, or scene can and should be taken in several seconds. Any more than that is time that could be spent putting yet another issue, product, or scene in front of you. Besides, if you get too close a look, you just might see that nothing was worth looking at in the first place. There seems to be little chance that the child will be able to hear, or even to know to listen for, the gentle whisper that might carry him or her to what Dewey calls a "higher plane of consciousness and action."

An article I read reported a problem that occurred during an Oscar telecast: The high-definition image was unforgiving of the various natural physical "flaws" such as an actress's less-than-perfect complexion or an actor's signs of old age. I believe that "high definition" is exactly the kind of curriculum that Dewey would like us to implement. This type of curriculum and teaching would lead to deeper and more insightful learning. It would be a curriculum that required students to listen for the gentle whisper of intellectual reflection and engage in the intense gaze of scientific inquiry. That sort of curriculum is unlikely to excite the student in the way he or she typically expects to be excited. And Dewey would have said that's a good thing.

The excitement children experience in their entertainment leaves them addicted to only more excitement or, more accurately, agitation or stimulation. Children used to that kind of excitement become adults who require a 30-second shot clock so they do not have to wait too long for another basket. They need computers that are ever faster and meals that are fast and easy to "fit their busy lifestyle." Dewey's words, therefore, present a challenge and a bit of a quandary for me in my role as a teacher and now as a teacher educator. Amid those rushing images, do we need to adjust today's curriculum and teaching to a new generation of children who were raised on video games and 100-plus cable channels?

A Conducive Learning Environment

Years before I first read the quotation I chose here, I taught fifth grade. On days when achievement tests were being given and the kids were under stress (though nothing compared with the stress kids feel now that none of them are being left behind), I would begin the morning with a brief session of progressive relaxation—a technique in which one focuses on certain muscle groups, tensing and relaxing them one group at a time. I remember being disturbed by how many students simply could not be still.

More recently, the parents of a fourth-grade boy shared with me what happened during a visit to a medical specialist to get advice regarding their son's nervous tics. The specialist told them not to worry too much because "it's pretty common among kids nowadays because of all their activities and schoolwork." As appalling as was the physician's response, I found the cultural situation that led to his observation to be just as frightening. Is today's learning environment one that Dewey would have believed to be conducive to carrying a child "on to a higher plane of consciousness"?

References

Dewey, J. (1976). The school and society. In J. A. Boydston (Ed.), *John Dewey: The middle works, 1899–1924: Vol. 1. 1899–1901* (pp. 5–112). Carbondale: Southern Illinois University Press. (Original work published 1899)

Postman, N. (1985). *Amusing ourselves to death: Public discourse in the age of show business.* New York, NY: Penguin.

17

WORK IN SCHOOL

Donna Adair Breault

> *There is very little place in the traditional schoolroom for the child to work.*
> —*The School and Society*, Middle Works 1: 22

As an assistant principal, I had the pleasure of bus duty each day. This was one of my favorite administrative tasks because it enabled me to watch the children as they began and ended their days at school. One thing I always noticed was the amazing amount of energy the students had at the end of the day. I often had to help them "contain" that energy as they hurried to their buses. In contrast, I would enter the school building at the end of bus duty and see some of the teachers dragging themselves to their mailboxes, utterly exhausted. It was quite clear from my observations that these teachers had done all the work, not their students. This fact was supported by my visits to these teachers' rooms where I would see them spend hours pulling together information to give to their students and then additional hours reading the worksheets the students completed to demonstrate that they had received the information.

Who Is Doing the Work?

I believe Dewey (1899/1976) addresses the situation best in *School and Society,* when he describes the trouble he had finding desks for his laboratory school. He notes that after looking in shop after shop, one salesperson finally commented that he wanted tables where children could work, but the shop only had desks where children could listen. Similarly, in *Democracy and Education* (1916/1980), he laments,

> Why is it, in spite of the fact that teaching by pouring in, learning by passive absorption, are universally condemned, that they are still so entrenched in practice? That teaching is not an affair of "telling" and being told, but an active and constructive process is a principle almost as generally violated in practice as conceded in theory. (p. 44)

Wong and Wong (1991) concurred. In their book *The First Days of School,* they reminded their audience of new and practicing teachers that the person who is doing the work in the classroom is the person who is learning.

Why do teachers seem to have the tendency to do all the work in their classrooms? I can speak only from personal experience. When I first started teaching, I felt a tremendous responsibility for the academic and emotional well-being of my second graders. Although I did not fall into the workbook and worksheet routine, I nevertheless recall spending countless hours making manipulatives and creating learning centers all evolving around weekly themes: outer space, the sea, insects, and so forth.

Meanwhile, I was coming to my class intellectually unprepared. I knew very little about the subjects I "taught"—dinosaurs, planets, plants, and animals. I had plenty of cute activities, but I did not have the grounding through which I could ask the truly meaningful questions. Without that grounding, I was forced into the role of entertainer instead of being a facilitator for higher levels of learning. As such, I created a vicious cycle for myself. Staying busy with the cute activities and manipulatives prevented me from spending time learning and modeling learning. Without deeper knowledge of the subject matter, I had little choice but to continue entertaining.

Intellectually Engaging Activities

Over time I learned from my many mistakes. I realized *entertaining* activities and *intellectually engaging* activities were not synonymous. I began to reassess my priorities and use of time to make sure the experiences I provided for my students were first and foremost educative—whether or not they resulted in something that would make a great display outside my classroom door. Most important, I realized the critical prerequisites for the kind of active learning Dewey describes throughout his work: thoughtful planning, solid understanding of the subject matter, a willingness to experience ambiguity in the learning context, and a relationship of mutual trust between the teacher and the students. Seems like a tall order, doesn't it?

I recall a beautiful example of this type of active learning from a 1st-year teacher I once observed. This teacher was using a math word problem as the focus of her lesson that day. The fifth-grade students were given a piece of paper with an outline of a shopping mall and stores of various shapes and sizes. The only information provided for the students was the monthly rent for one of the stores. No store dimensions were provided. They had to determine an appropriate monthly rent for all the other stores in the mall diagram.

The students, already divided into teams, immediately began working on the problem. They knew where the necessary materials—the rulers, calculators, and so on—were located in the room, and they knew they could use them when needed as long as they returned them to their appropriate places. The teacher walked around the room, commenting on each group's progress, posing challenging questions, and responding to students' questions with additional questions to deepen the level of thinking on the project. There was no need for the teacher to remind students to stay on task or to provide any sort of extrinsic motivation for good behavior. They were very interested in the problem, and they hardly noticed others around them as they worked. Like many elementary classrooms, this lesson was interrupted by their lunchtime and their physical education period, but after each interruption the students eagerly picked up where they had left off.

The groups of students took very different routes to solving their math problem. They used multiple forms of computation, including multiplication and division and working with fractions. Some groups recalled formulas to determine the area of spaces, while others found common units of measurement from various objects in the room. The teacher, well-grounded in math, was able to facilitate each of the routes the groups took. Ultimately, students provided thoughtful suggestions for rent along with justifications for those prices. In addition, each group assessed its effectiveness in problem solving on the basis of a critical thinking rubric provided by the teacher.

What made this lesson an exemplar of active learning in a Deweyan sense? The students were intellectually engaged with a meaningful purpose. They were able to use their experiences and their collective understanding of math to solve a problem. Further, they were able to see themselves as problem solvers and recognize the significance of their capacity to think. This 1st-year teacher had achieved something that took me years. She had created a dynamic classroom environment where active learning through meaningful engagement—not activity generated through entertainment—was the force and focus of her instruction.

References

Dewey, J. (1976). The school and society. In J. A. Boydston (Ed.), *John Dewey: The middle works, 1899–1924: Vol. 1. 1899–1901* (pp. 5–112). Carbondale: Southern Illinois University Press. (Original work published 1899)

Dewey, J. (1980). Democracy and education. In J. A. Boydston (Ed.), *John Dewey: The middle works, 1899–1924: Vol. 9. 1916* (pp. 1–370). Carbondale: Southern Illinois University Press. (Original work published 1916)

Wong, H. K., & Wong, R. T. (1991). *The first days of school.* Sunnyvale, CA: Harry K. Wong Publications.

18

ACTIVE LEARNING AS REFLECTIVE EXPERIENCE

William H. Schubert

> *Mere activity does not constitute experience.*
> —*Democracy and Education*, Middle Works 9: 146

When someone calls my office and reaches my answering machine, they hear some variation on "You have reached the Schubertian Center for Curricular Speculation where we ponder what is worth knowing and experiencing. Please leave a message after the beep and have a good day and life." Note that the Schubertian Center is fictional and unfunded, which gives it great latitude in speculation that ranges from the subatomic to the everyday to the cosmic and does not diminish its realness in a postmodern and Deweyan pragmatic sense.

Although this message is partially offered with tongue-in-cheek humor, it also embodies a deep seriousness with which I have pursued education since my years as an elementary school teacher in the late 1960s and early 1970s. The message remains central today to doctoral students of curriculum studies, practicing teachers and school administrators who engage with me through courses or consultancies, and colleagues in the curriculum field.

Though my experience as an elementary school teacher occurred more than 30 years ago, I remember it vividly, and it still informs my current endeavors as a professor. Working with elementary students is always *active,* but it is not *experience* in the Deweyan sense if the activity does not embody reflection. Dewey

(1916/1980) says that mere activity is "dispersive, centrifugal, dissipating" (p. 146). But serious reflection on activity can transform activity into growth experience.

My List of Activities

When I completed the elementary school teaching episode of my life, knowing that my next episode would be one of teaching teachers, I sat down to make a list of what I had learned. I brainstormed about 150 activities that I considered successful; most of them started with student interests and concerns (Dewey's *psychological*) and led them to integrate funds of knowledge from experienced persons or disciplines of knowledge (Dewey's *logical*) with their own project of growing their life in a sociocultural context. Nevertheless, the list was one of mere activities—for example, invent a language, create a game to teach younger children, make a family genealogy, use catalogs to find $1,000 worth of gifts to help someone in need, observe planet Earth as if you were extraterrestrial explorers, bring in broken things to repair, interview others about important matters, and on and on.

I remembered that these teaching strategies did not usually derive from completion of lesson plan forms or from writing behavioral objectives. Instead, they emerged as I experienced literature, art, and philosophy. I created spaces for myself to do this. Sometimes I found friends or colleagues who could ponder with me. This pondering stimulated my imagination and challenged the assumptions on which I based my life.

This calling to self-educate was my professional development. From the context it provided, I could invent possibilities with children—activities that started from a sense of direction and evolved through places that surprised us, stimulating wonder, which lies at the heart of reflection. Reflection spurred by wonder, then, is a seed that transforms mere activity into experience. An "experience," as Dewey (1934/1987) points out in *Art as Experience,* is making meaning of any dimension of one's life so that it connects who we are and have been with who we are striving to become.

Sources of Inspiration

As I pondered my list, I thought of the wonder inspired by art, literature, and philosophy that stimulated development of these activities. Then a shadow crept over my pondering as I thought of teacher in-service days. Usually, these days were one of two extremes: make-it-take-it or theory-research-sprinkled-with-jokes. The former showed how to make a specific project or lesson to use in the classroom. I recall a colorful, painted sun on burlap. All the suns looked about the same when displayed throughout the classroom. However, the project had no generativity. It was an activity only. The other extreme was the theorist or researcher who gave a talk splotched with humor, after which teachers chuckled a bit while finding no direct relevance to their classroom.

I recall a case in which I thought such a research-oriented in-service was just plain wrong. The researcher said that students in the intermediate grades could not understand metaphorical thinking. He said that it was fruitless to try it with them. The researcher illustrated his point with the adage, "A rolling stone gathers no moss." He said that students would, at best, give a literal interpretation of such a statement. However, I had engaged in discussions with students that told me otherwise. So I followed with a study of my own. I returned to my sixth-grade students who were busy working on individualized projects and called them one by one to my desk, quietly whispering the illustrative adage to each and asking for an interpretation. Some could not relate; others gave literal interpretations of a stone on a mossy hill; a couple related it to the Rolling Stones; and several provided philosophic advice about the value of stopping to enjoy life. One immediately retorted with an adage of his own, which is still etched in my memory: "Well I guess it means that if you are a nail and don't get into hot water, then you won't get rusty." *This* was clearly more than mere activity!

Invention Strategies

So, as I pondered my list of 150 activities, I decided that I wanted to do teacher education that would speak to teachers' needs more fully than the make-it-take-it or dissemination of theory-research orientations. I wondered what enabled me to think of these activities. Was it the literature, art, and philosophy directly, or was there a more intermediate source of imagination? I expressed what I searched for—this intermediate point between make-it-take-it and research-theory—as *invention strategies.* Invention strategies, as I now consider them, were partially unconscious themes from the literature, art, and philosophy that helped me tailor activities from sources of meaning, concern, and interest in students' lives. I made a list of 20-some invention strategies, and for 30 years I have offered them to teachers who sought to enliven their teaching. Among these were limiting, traveling, playing, classifying, rating, interviewing, acting, doing, dialoging, conversing, dreaming, daydreaming, producing, gaming, and feeling (carried away with gerunds). If a teacher can't think of an interesting lesson, I encourage focus on one of the invention strategies. For example, with *traveling:* travel back to a specific time period or to a literary scene and act out how it might feel to be there, or travel in a molecule through the circulatory system, or plan a trip through the continent of Africa (noting language phrases, monetary units, historical places to see, cultural ways, places to stay, customs, climate, sites to see, foods, and traditions). With *playing,* try to reinvigorate the desire to play—noting that when students enter school, pompous adults tell them that play (their mode of learning that taught them more in the first 5 years of life than they will learn in the rest) is over, and work (too often drudgery) has begun. Play, like travel, can transform education from activity to experience because inherent in it is a continuous recreating of oneself in a sociocultural context. Space here does not permit elaboration on all of the invention strategies. (I am contemplating a book to do this.)

The point behind invention strategies is that these strategies are processes born of reflection on central sources of wonder in human life. Robert Ulich (1955) characterized them vividly as "the great mysteries and events of life: birth, death, love, tradition, society and the crowd, success and failure, salvation, and anxiety"

(p. 255). If activities embody such concerns, and invention strategies often do, they constitute experience. They integrate remembrance of one's past and anticipation of one's future in the search for present meaning.

What to Reflect on

For 15 years after I developed the invention strategies, I admonished teachers and school leaders to reflect. Then a well-known educational scholar who visited our university conducted a colloquium in which he raised an issue that astounded me because I thought everyone already knew the answer. He said something to this effect: "Everyone tells teachers to reflect, but no one says what it is that they should reflect on." Then, I thought that perhaps I had too little empathy for teachers who work amid a swirl of activity without enough time to reflectively experience it. So I made another list, which I have used as a basis for discussion in classes and workshops. I share it here, knowing full well that elaboration would be better if space permitted. (I think I might include this in the book, too, or create yet another book.)

1. Reflect on education as a calling that enables personal and social growth.
2. Reflect on what you have to share (your strengths).
3. Reflect on what is worth knowing and experiencing.
4. Reflect on who decides (and should decide) this.
5. Reflect on who benefits (and who does not) from such decisions.
6. Reflect on yourself as a curriculum for others.
7. Reflect on others as a curriculum for you.
8. Reflect on the most important things you have learned (e.g., knowledge, skills, values, appreciations, interests, dispositions).
9. Reflect on how, where, and under what circumstance you learned these important things.
10. Reflect on the hidden curriculum of your educational setting, that is, what is taught and learned by the context, rules, and expectations.
11. Reflect on what is learned by the out-of-school experiences (outside curriculum) of your students (e.g., from homes, families, mass media, work, hobbies, nonschool organizations, peer relationships).
12. Reflect on how to identify and build on students' strengths.
13. Reflect on what it means to broaden and deepen students' perspectives and abilities.
14. Reflect on how to speak the multiple languages of students.
15. Reflect on how to feel the hurt and joy inside students.
16. Reflect on the balance between realities and ideals in education.
17. Reflect on the central, driving ideas that you embody, that is, that are part of who you are as a person and as a teacher.
18. Reflect on what you want to contribute to others as an educator through knowledge, skills, values, social reform, personal growth, and spiritual connectedness.

19. Reflect on what you have learned each day.
20. Reflect on why reflection helps and what else to reflect on.

This last call for reflection epitomizes the essence of Dewey's distinction between activity and experience. To engage in Deweyan experience requires continuous revisiting of such reflections, never considering them fully answered, and making them one with the process of living. So, this is what I mean by my encouragement to ponder in my message on the telephone answering machine at the Schubertian Center!

References

Dewey, J. (1980). Democracy and education. In J. A. Boydston (Ed.), *John Dewey: The middle works, 1899–1924: Vol. 9. 1916* (pp. 1–370). Carbondale: Southern Illinois University Press. (Original work published 1916)

Dewey, J. (1987). Art as experience. In J. A. Boydston (Ed.), *John Dewey: The later works, 1925–1953: Vol. 10. 1934* (pp. 1-352). Carbondale: Southern Illinois University Press. (Original work published 1934)

Ulich, R. (1955). Comments on Ralph Harper's essay. In N. B. Henry (Ed.), *Modern philosophies of education, The fifty-fourth yearbook of the National Society for the Study of Education, Part I* (pp. 254–257). Chicago, IL: University of Chicago Press.

19

PROVIDING ENVIRONMENTS CONDUCIVE TO PROPER DIGESTION

Lisa Goeken-Galliart

It is as if the child were forever tasting and never eating; always having his palate tickled upon the emotional side, but never getting the organic satisfaction that comes only with the digestion of food and the transformation of it into working power.
—*The Child and the Curriculum,* Middle Works 2: 281

John Dewey's quotation from *The Child and the Curriculum* (1902/1976) is just as timely today as it was more than 100 years ago—or is it even more so? With the frenzied way in which we travel through our 2-inch textbooks, our curriculum guides, our lessons, and our days, it is difficult to imagine that Dewey would be impressed. He probably would be saddened and disappointed that adults have evolved into such hurried creatures, but he most likely would be devastated by the way we are modeling and pouring it into our children's lives as well.

Making Connections Takes Time

Our world is so compulsive, immediate, and reactive that we just seem to ramble on without much thought. Our children are doing the same thing as they mirror their parents' lives. Children are not making connections, and that is because that process takes *time.* We are so convinced that there is not enough time, and we are so scheduled, that we miss the newness, the inspiration, and the wonder of it all! That is precisely what Dewey is cognizant of in 1902 and what he means by "forever tasting and never eating."

In the classroom, teachers have to make decisions about how best to spend every minute of the day; time is a precious commodity and it must be spent wisely. That is not at all an overexaggeration or oversimplification. Every minute matters, and each one needs to be viewed as a learning opportunity. How a teacher chooses to use those minutes is an individual decision that is based on experience, attitude, knowledge, and philosophy. Dewey teaches us that a chance to "strike while the iron is hot" should not be neglected but seen as a once-in-a-lifetime opportunity that realistically may not come again. He knows that it is the teacher who is ultimately responsible for providing the environmental conditions necessary to guide a thought or an action—a process that involves the senses, movement, and missteps taken during the journey, and many times a sense of not knowing.

A Taste Is Not Enough

When practitioners skim the surface of a unit or topic of study, Dewey would say that we are giving the child only a "taste." Per his quote, he argues that this is simply not enough. By going into depth, one can "digest." Further, the "transformation into working power" is the empowerment students gain from being able and prepared to apply what was learned previously to new situations.

When we allow students to struggle with a problem and include the extra "space" needed in the day to do so, we help to provide the type of learning environment and appropriate stimuli needed to aid digestion. When we fail to resist the urge to rush in and provide comfort, when we control a given situation too tightly, or when we tell an answer too quickly, we clog up the system.

Practitioners need to trust in collaboration and risk taking so that students can see the benefits of their newfound discoveries. This process allows transformation to take place.

Learning is active; it is moving and flurried; and, many times, it is loud. Many classrooms and schools need to adapt to allow this "movement" versus the mindless, orderly, and passive style that Dewey calls "pouring in." He knows that this is unacceptable back in the early 1900s, and he would not find it palatable to discover it still being practiced in some classrooms today.

Processing the Big Ideas

He would applaud those who take the big ideas and process through them so thoroughly and thoughtfully, enabling students to explore, make the best use of carefully selected stimuli, and draw inferences on new topics. Dewey would say that by going "deep" and not "long," teachers are emphasizing the process and realizing the interdependence of it with the outcome. Students are then better able to let ideas emulsify, to note relevance, to apply new principles to other experiences, to inquire about different situations, and to persevere through the whole process with a sense of true and earned accomplishment.

Dewey's thoughts on this topic are arguably even more relevant today because of the time schedules chosen and placed on the inhabitants of this new century. As the curriculum continues to become more and more multitudinous, teachers will need to challenge themselves even more so to find "space" within their own classroom schedules for some real "digestion" and "transformation." This "freeing up" may be a 100-year-old notion, but if implemented promptly, it may save a generation from a serious case of indigestion!

Reference

Dewey, J. (1976). The child and the curriculum. In J. A. Boydston (Ed.), *John Dewey: The middle works, 1899–1924: Vol. 2. 1902–1903* (pp. 271–292). Carbondale: Southern Illinois University Press. (Original work published 1902)

20

BECOMING A STUDENT OF TEACHING

Robert V. Bullough, Jr.

> *The teacher who leaves the professional schools with power in managing a class of children may appear to superior advantage the first day, the first week, the first month, or even the first year, as compared with some other teacher who has a much more vital command of psychology, logic, and ethics of development. But later "progress" may with such consist only in perfecting and refining skill already possessed. Such persons seem to know how to teach, but they are not students of teaching. . . . Unless a teacher is such a student, he may continue to improve in the mechanics of school management, but he can not grow as a teacher.*
> —*The Relation of Theory to Practice in Education*, Middle Works 3: 256

When educators speak about their teacher preparation, they commonly use the word *training* to describe the process. We tell others that we attended a teacher-training program at a university or college. We graduated trained and certified to teach. It is easy to dismiss use of this term by saying, "Oh, it's just a word." But words name worlds and form realities; and the use of this particular word brings with it much mischief, as Dewey implies.

Dogs are trained by their masters to walk on their hind legs and beg for a biscuit. Elephants are trained to sit on a barrel, raise their trunks to the sky, and trumpet for adoring crowds. On the human side, soldiers, among others, also are trained. On the darkest of nights, infantry soldiers can disassemble and reassemble M-16 rifles with staggering speed. Soldiers are trained to react, and to react swiftly and seemingly without thought to signs of danger. Through drill and practice, responses are wired in. When facing danger, procedures that have been learned click in and direct action. In each of these examples, four-legged and two-legged, ends are known in advance. There is no room for deviation or for individual initiative. So it is in teaching, as Dewey suggests, that an emphasis on training over education leaves little room for teacher growth.

Recognizing Potential in the Unexpected

In teaching, outcomes are rarely, if ever, predictable. No matter how hard we try to manage teaching and to make our actions produce the results intended by us or desired by others, they never do—not quite. When teaching, something inevitably happens that disrupts the flow of the day and forces the setting aside of even the most carefully crafted plan. Something more important for learning suddenly presents itself to us, or something grimly insistent comes along and demands precious classroom time and moral space: A child gets hurt and tears flow; a dirty joke is told, a gasp heard, and muffled and disruptive conversation ensues; a child realizes an amazing and unexpected achievement, and spontaneously the class erupts into clapping and loud cheering; Snowball, the beloved class rabbit, gets sick and dies; and, looking outside the school walls, a space shuttle explodes or two airplanes slam into the World Trade Center.

To manage uncertainty, teachers need procedural knowledge, knowledge of routines, and the ability to implement them. But given the nature of our work and of the work context, teaching routines often stretch and snap, and our teacher habits fail. Then what? At that moment, teachers face a choice: Exercising power, they can bring punishments and rewards to bear in the attempt to reestablish a failed routine by altering the context to better fit that routine; they can switch to another routine (assuming another is known); or they can reconsider the entire situation and reorganize it to achieve another and different end. The last response is only possible when the teacher understands self, teaching, and the context of teaching deeply and richly—when the teacher is educated, not merely trained, to teach and is a student of teaching, just as Dewey suggests. Otherwise, routines define the day and, in defining the day, bind the teacher and limit learning. Maintaining routines becomes the end of education rather than a means for its achievement.

Realizing Personal Potential

Dewey's statement requires consideration here of an additional word and distinction: the word is *professional*. Over the past few decades, designating someone a professional has lost much of its meaning and nearly all of its cachet. It is a word that has been co-opted by barbers; plumbers; and, if we can believe the movies, hired killers. But the distinctive feature and defining characteristic of a professional compared with a nonprofessional is that the professional learns from experience: The professional is a student of his or her own practice and development and, in studying that practice and development, is one who constantly grows in understanding and in ability.

In the hands of professionals, a practice becomes increasingly personal, nuanced, and subtle; problems—when something does not unfold as anticipated or falls outside of preferred practice—are taken as invitations to reconsider personal and professional beliefs, knowledge, including subject matter, and skills and not as reasons for dismay or disillusionment. Problems are invitations to get deeper into ourselves, those we teach, our subject matter, and our situations. Ever learning, the professional teacher knows himself or herself well, and seeks to uncover blind spots, prejudices, and weaknesses as well as to discover strengths upon which to build. He or she is forward looking, imagining and then seeking better and more interesting ways of being with and for young people. Self-critical, the professional can attribute causes, but does so in humility and without placing blame. Instead, he or she accepts responsibility for his or her actions and their educational consequences.

Like trained teachers, newcomers to teaching often look outside of themselves when something goes awry. They tend to blame others, their own teachers, cooperating teachers, and their teacher-education programs, as well as their students and their backgrounds, for failure. Having long been the recipients of teacher classroom offerings, they tend to assume that teaching is a simple matter: One dispenses what one knows and disciplines recalcitrants. Not being privy to the professional's inner logic, its evolution, or to the origins of that logic, they inevitably underappreciate the difficulty and complexity of effective teaching. Assuming that one learns to teach by teaching—one just does it—they sometimes succumb to the temptation to reduce especially artful performance to a matter of time and training, of learning, and then practicing the application of a few rules that folk wisdom and occasionally researchers promise will lead to skilled practice. But the promise inevitably proves to be only somewhat or sometimes true. This is one of the sources of what, among beginners, is called "reality shock"—the discovery that teaching is not quite as easy as it looked from the student side of the teacher's desk and that learning to teach is much more difficult than ever imagined. Practice, they discover, does not make perfect, especially when practice is made routine and inflexible. Nor does mimicry equal mastery.

Making Opportunities Out of Chaos

Teachers are surrounded by events that call forth wonder and surprise, and it is precisely these emotions that make teaching such a potentially interesting and satisfying relationship and a fascinating and fulfilling form of human expression. Only teachers who are students of teaching, who are knowledgeable and engaged professionals, who are morally centered, and who can flexibly and purposefully respond to the shifting emotional and intellectual terrain of the classroom are capable of realizing this potential or even of recognizing it. Students of teaching know that chaos is forever residing just around the corner and that teachers face it mostly alone. They feel vulnerable and exposed but not fearful, for they also know that opportunity stands just around that corner, and they are prepared and willing to embrace it. If, as teachers, we are merely trained and generally are fearful of failure and desirous to contain the unexpected, we are going to miss the opportunities for growth that teaching provides—perhaps not today, but most assuredly tomorrow. Clearly, teaching is not for the faint of heart but is a calling for the adventurous of mind and spirit.

Reference

Dewey, J. (1977). The relation of theory to practice in education. In J. A. Boydston (Ed.), *John Dewey: The middle works, 1899–1924: Vol. 3. 1903–1906* (pp. 249–272). Carbondale: Southern Illinois University Press. (Original work published 1904)

21

EFFORT

The Outgrowth of Individual Interest

Robert C. Morris

> *If the subject-matter of the lessons be such as to have an appropriate place within the expanding consciousness of the child, if it grows out of his own past doings, thinkings, and sufferings, and grows into application in further achievements and receptivities, then no device or trick of method has to be resorted to in order to enlist "interest." The psychologized is of interest—that is, it is placed in the whole of conscious life so that it shares the worth of that life.*
> —The Child and the Curriculum, Middle Works 2: 288

As a young educator beginning my career in 1970, I quickly came to realize that finding and developing the interests of my students was paramount if I wanted to be successful. Identifying the appropriate teaching experiences that would begin the process for student involvement and interest is where many of my early struggles were focused. Like many aspiring teachers, I saw my task as clearly that of directing my students toward a given end, such as getting the correct answer or scoring high on a test. But therein likely would be found my greatest early weakness. Instead of "directing," I should have been only "facilitating" my students toward their own given ends. Student interest, as I have come to see it, is not teacher interest or parent interest; it truly must be student interest.

Know Your Students

By identifying and focusing on each individual student and his or her own driving interests and desires, teachers and even parents have a much better chance not only of reaching students but also of understanding them. Knowing your own students has to be the beginning point. Recognizing things about each student that make up his or her world and understandings is an essential ingredient. This is not to say that one is restricted, as Dewey (1902/1976) notes, "to the chains we wear" (p. 288) but only to understanding the chains each student brings and maybe how these chains affect each student. For students, these chains could be socioeconomic, geographic, or any number of other restrictive elements.

Knowing where a student is "coming from" is an important first criterion for developing interest. Naturally, to find out about your students, you have to investigate and search. Asking questions is a beginning. Inquiry also must be a continuous activity, especially as your students grow and develop. As a teacher, I'm always pleased to see the interests of my students increase and expand over a period of time. Seeing former students and finding out where their interests took them over a lifetime always has been intriguing to me.

Identify Pertinent Subject Matter

A second criterion for developing student interest has to do with clearly identifying pertinent subject matter. Looking for appealing and appropriate curricular and instructional activities is essential. I have come to believe that keeping students on task and focused is not that difficult as long as I've done my homework. When I have found appealing subject matter that fits nicely with the learning experiences I'm creating, students usually are on task.

Consider the Environment

I'm not exactly sure when something that is appealing turns into something "interesting," but the concept of making things agreeable rather than disagreeable is, no doubt, a motivational factor. Like the subject matter, the environment also should be agreeable. The environment or setting is a third criterion for developing student interest. From both a psychological and sociological standpoint, the school's environment can be monumental in its effect on a child. Imagine a classroom where students are not challenged or stimulated, where instructors are mechanical in nature or, worse yet, on a video or being telecast with no possible interaction. Though a lot rides on teacher-directed activity, a school's overall environment and the individual atmosphere of each classroom are factors to consider when developing student interest.

Of course, for Dewey, the end result of student interest is "action" on the part of the student. I tend to favor his later use of the term *effort* as the outgrowth of individual interest. Effort put forth by students truly interested in the idea or activity they are investigating has always been my realization of the Dewey quote cited. Effort seems to represent the final and end result of individual interest, and effort best asserts Dewey's concept of the complete experience for the child.

Reference

Dewey, J. (1976). The child and the curriculum. In J. A. Boydston (Ed.), *John Dewey: The middle works, 1899–1924: Vol. 2. 1902–1903* (pp. 271–292). Carbondale: Southern Illinois University Press. (Original work published 1902)

PART III
Critical Thinking

THE "VARIED AND UNUSUAL" ABUSES OF CRITICAL THINKING

Donna Adair Breault

As a 2nd-year teacher, I sat in the media center ready for an afternoon staff development seminar. An outside consultant was coming in to teach us "Talents," a critical thinking curriculum. From what I can recall 15 years later, there were five "talents" that we were to teach our students. Although I cannot remember them exactly, I know that one dealt with planning, another with brainstorming, and one involved predicting problems; the two remaining were similar in fashion regarding the depth of thought involved. What I do remember quite clearly, however, was the "teacher talk" that the consultant drilled into our heads that day.

"Teachers, can you think of the many *varied* and *unusual* uses for this button?" the consultant asked as she held up a simple black button. The manner in which she drew out the terms *varied* and *unusual* immediately indicated their importance within the program. Teachers spent the next few minutes brainstorming uses for the button with varying degrees of engagement. Following a definition and discussion of brainstorming, the consultant proceeded to share pictures students had made demonstrating the varied and unusual uses of the button; then she reinforced the need to use the "teacher talk" we would be given as part of the program. "There needs to be consistency from grade level to grade level," the consultant contended, "so you always need to ask for 'varied and unusual uses' of objects when conducting a brainstorming activity."

Prescribed Lessons

As I looked around the room, I was surprised that I did not see physical signs from any of the teachers that they too recognized the irony in our experience that day. Finally, annoyed by the whole experience, I spoke up. "Isn't it a bit ironic that you are giving us a prescribed script to teach children to think critically?" My question was met with harsh glances from my administrators and countless protests from the consultant. The seminar continued without question. As dutiful teachers, we took our "Talents" curriculum to our classrooms and immediately began to implement it. Before long, you could see bulletin board displays up and down the hall: "Varied and Unusual Uses for a Button," "Varied and Unusual Uses for a Spoon," "Varied and Unusual Uses for a Tire," and the list went on and on.

Throughout my 9 years of teaching, I saw a number of critical thinking curricula come and go, and unfortunately most were not much better than my first exposure to "Talents." Most were skill-based with prescribed lessons, and throughout them all, I marveled at the irony that surrounded my life as a teacher: "How can you expect me to teach critical thinking when you don't allow me to think critically as a professional?"

Nurturing Thinking

Once I became an administrator, I was in a position to build professional development that would promote critical thinking. To plan the professional development, I had to stop and seriously think about some important questions: "What is critical thinking? Is it something that can be taught? If so, how do we teach teachers to teach it?" Faced with these and other questions, I turned to two valuable resources—a trusted colleague and Dewey.

Based on my readings of Dewey, I believe that critical thinking is an inherent capacity to be nurtured and developed. The "skills" that seem to be the focus of so much of the critical thinking curricula I had known may be instrumentalities to aid in critical thinking, but in and of themselves are not critical thinking. To delineate them as such is like confusing the bow and arrow for the goal of shooting a target. Dewey (1916/1980) makes this analogy:

> But we must remember that the object is only a mark or sign by which the mind specifies the activity one desires to carry out. Strictly speaking, not the target but hitting the target is the end in view. . . . The different objects which are thought of are means of directing activity. (p. 112)

With this in mind, I also considered other things I had read from Dewey regarding the nature of critical thinking to determine what was needed in the professional development experience: a sense of mental unrest (1910/1978), real opportunities to engage the learner to solve relevant problems (1929/1984), encouragement for playful consideration of possibilities (1899/1976; 1902/1976), challenges to suspend judgment (1910/1978), and hopes for even the "audacity of imagination" (1929/1984, p. 247).

Conversations with Teachers

Using these images, my trusted colleague and I planned and implemented the critical thinking professional development. The half-day sessions looked very different from what I had experienced as a teacher. Instead of prescribed materials, we had conversations with teachers. We also offered relevant, though fun, situations in which the teachers themselves had to think critically to solve problems. We offered images from the past, such as the life and work of Leonardo da Vinci; and we explored images from film that captured moments of incredible problem solving, such as the scene from *Apollo 13* when the scientists were trying to find a way to create breathing apparatuses for the astronauts from the materials they knew were on the capsule.

From there, we discussed ways teachers could alter what they were doing in their classrooms to foster higher levels of critical thinking, and we continued the conversations after I or the teachers attempted the various lessons in the classrooms. Ultimately, my colleague and I were trying to help teachers see their work differently—to begin to think critically about their work as teachers so they could, in turn, help students think more critically about their work.

Although I cannot claim to have achieved a pinnacle in professional development in my work with teachers that year, I do believe it was a fairly significant step in the right direction and certainly a more meaningful experience than the afternoon staff development I had endured as a teacher years earlier. I hope that when you read the contributions in this section regarding critical thinking, you too will develop significant images of its potential in your work. Although your definition may not be identical to the one I have outlined here, the fact that you are developing that image is in itself a significant act of critical thinking and a wonderful opportunity for your own professional development.

References

Dewey, J. (1976). The school and society. In J. A. Boydston (Ed.), *John Dewey: The middle works, 1899–1924: Vol. 1. 1899–1901* (pp. 5–112). Carbondale: Southern Illinois University Press. (Original work published 1899)

Dewey, J. (1976). The child and the curriculum. In J. A. Boydston (Ed.), *John Dewey: The middle works, 1899–1924: Vol. 2. 1902–1903* (pp. 271–292). Carbondale: Southern Illinois University Press. (Original work published 1902)

Dewey, J. (1978). How we think. In J. A. Boydston (Ed.). *John Dewey: The middle works, 1899–1924: Vol. 6. 1910–1911* (pp. 177–356). Carbondale: Southern Illinois University Press. (Original work published 1910)

Dewey, J. (1980). Democracy and education. In J. A. Boydston (Ed.), *John Dewey: The middle works, 1899–1924: Vol. 9. 1916* (pp. 1–370). Carbondale: Southern Illinois University Press. (Original work published 1916)

Dewey, J. (1984). The quest for certainty. In J. A. Boydston (Ed.), *John Dewey: The later works, 1925–1953: Vol. 4. 1929* (pp. 1–250). Carbondale: Southern Illinois University Press. (Original work published 1929)

22

THE DANGERS OF IMAGINATION

Robert Boostrom

> *Knowledge falters when imagination clips its wings or fears to use [hypotheses]. Every great advance in science has issued from a new audacity of imagination.*
> —*The Quest for Certainty*, Later Works 4: 247

The surprising thing about these lines from Dewey's *The Quest for Certainty* (1929/1984) is that they seem so obvious. Certainly "knowledge falters" without imagination. Certainly "every great advance in science" requires imagination. Who would doubt such assertions? Why does Dewey feel the need to make them?

The answer, I think, is that John Dewey is afraid of imagination. He feels the need to reassure himself (and us) that imagination really is part of the method of intelligence. He fears that imagination devolves too easily into "mere fooling" (1910/1978, p. 350), into "romantic castles in the air" (1916/1980, p. 305), so that we find that our action is pointless and our experience meaningless.

Now, my claim may seem to be rebutted by the dozens of times that Dewey refers to the positive power of imagination in *The Quest for Certainty* (1929/1984), *Democracy and Education* (1916/1980), *School and Society* (1899/1976), *Art as Experience* (1934/1987), and *How We Think* (1910/1978). But constantly lurking behind his acknowledgment of the playful power of imagination to drive thinking forward is the fear "of escape from the vicissitudes of existence by means of measures which do not demand an active coping with conditions" (Dewey, 1929/1984, p. 14), of "the tendency . . . for the imagination to run loose" (Dewey, 1916/1980, p. 358), of the possibility "we permit our imagination to entertain fancies at pleasure" (Dewey, 1910/1978, p. 189), of the "arbitrary fancifulness" that encourages us "in building up an imaginary world alongside the world of actual things" (Dewey, 1910/1978, p. 308).

Rather than allowing imagination to run loose, Dewey wants it to be rooted in everyday fact. He wants us never to forget the "distinction between hypotheses generated in that seclusion from observable fact which renders them fantasies, and hypotheses that are projections of the possibilities of facts already in existence and capable of report" (Dewey, 1929/1984, p. 63). He also wants our imagination to be rooted in work, not in play. He wants us to fear with him the dangers of the freedom released by the "playful attitude" if we ever forget that it "should gradually pass into a work attitude" (Dewey, 1910/1978, p. 308).

Yet, Dewey knows that these distinctions between good imagination (rooted in the work of fact-based hypotheses) and dangerous imagination (too playful, too fantastic) cannot be maintained. Imagination *is* play. The effort to chain imagination to "hypotheses that are projections of the possibilities of facts already in existence and capable of report" so that "reason" can do its work is doomed at the start." 'Reason' at its height cannot attain complete grasp and a self-contained assurance. It must fall back upon imagination—upon the embodiment of ideas in emotionally charged sense" (Dewey, 1934/1987, p. 40).

Dewey may wish to dismiss imagination as something we "fall back upon," but he knows we cannot reason without it, nor can we escape the risks of "arbitrary fancifulness." Without imagination, we lose too much of ourselves.

> Unless culture be a superficial polish, a veneering of mahogany over common wood, it surely is this—the growth of the imagination in flexibility, in scope, and in sympathy, till the life which the individual lives is informed with the life of nature and of society. (Dewey, 1899/1976, p. 38)

It is not simply that we need imagination to get from "what is" to "what if?"; without imagination, we cannot even know "what is." Our world, our culture, our selves, depend on playful, fanciful, arbitrary, dangerous imagination.

References

Dewey, J. (1976). The school and society. In J. A. Boydston (Ed.), *John Dewey: The middle works, 1899–1924: Vol. 1. 1899–1901* (pp. 5–112). Carbondale: Southern Illinois University Press. (Original work published 1899)

Dewey, J. (1978). How we think. In J. A. Boydston (Ed.), *John Dewey: The middle works, 1899–1924: Vol. 6. 1910–1911* (pp. 177–356). Carbondale: Southern Illinois University Press. (Original work published 1910)

Dewey, J. (1980). Democracy and education. In J. A. Boydston (Ed.), *John Dewey: The middle works, 1899–1924: Vol. 9. 1916* (pp. 1–370). Carbondale: Southern Illinois University Press. (Original work published 1916)

Dewey, J. (1984). The quest for certainty. In J. A. Boydston (Ed.), *John Dewey: The later works, 1925–1953: Vol. 4. 1929* (pp. 1–250). Carbondale: Southern Illinois University Press. (Original work published 1929)

Dewey, J. (1987). Art as experience. In J. A. Boydston (Ed.), *John Dewey: The later works, 1925–1953: Vol. 10. 1934* (pp. 1–352). Carbondale: Southern Illinois University Press. (Original work published 1934)

23

THE IMPORTANCE OF FREEDOM OF THOUGHT

Matthew Keeler

> *Let us admit the case of the conservative; if we once start thinking, no one can guarantee where we shall come out, except that many objects, ends and institutions are surely doomed. Every thinker puts some portion of an apparently stable world in peril and no one can wholly predict what will emerge in its place.*
>
> —*Experience and Nature,* Later Works 1: 172

Children are educated in large part so that they may become independent members of society. But there are generally two sorts of ways to characterize what is meant by the notion of independence and, in turn, two sorts of approaches to the purpose of education.

In one approach, the purpose of education is to train students in the existing socioeconomic mores, along with providing a necessary set of skills for succeeding in accordance with prevailing social structures and institutions. Education is only instrumentally important and is, at bottom, little more than the inculcation of certain values that primarily benefit existing concentrations of power. It is a process that, as Dewey (1897/1972) writes, "results in subordinating the freedom of the individual to a preconceived social and political status" (p. 82). This approach rarely (if ever) makes its purpose explicit, but that matters little—as long as education is *functionally* carried out in this way, the result comes out the same. The independent members of society that it produces are independent only in the trivial sense of being an adult, not in the sense of being able to think, evaluate, and make choices freely.

An alarmingly high number of schools and classrooms take this first approach to education, at least implicitly. Children are indoctrinated from their first years in grade school to be obedient, to retain certain bodies of facts that can be recalled at test time and then forgotten later, and to do little to no critical thinking. Teachers are viewed as authority figures not to be questioned, rather than as guides through unexplored territory. By the time students reach the university level, they are people who are utterly bored by the entire process (though they're quite good at remaining quiet and still in class), who either hold no views or else cannot give them coherent expression, and who consider their college career as analogous to a temporary jail sentence to be endured. This approach to education is ultimately in the business of making a product: the docile worker and uninformed consumer.

The second approach, by contrast, takes the purpose of education to be the cultivation of thoughtful, socially engaged individuals through inquiry, critical thinking, experimentation, and creative self-expression. It begins with an eye toward the individual's natural capacities and curiosities, but is also an inherently social process. Dewey (1897/1972) writes that "the school is simply that form of community life in which all those agencies are concentrated that will be the most effective in bringing the child to share in the inherited resources of the race, and to use his own powers for social ends" (pp. 86–87). This approach considers the student not to be merely a future worker or consumer, but a developing peer with unique burgeoning endowments that he or she will use to participate in society as an equal. Independence is understood to be a function of the individual's capacity for freedom of thought and judgment, which in turn allows for a genuine freedom of action and social engagement.

Few schools or classrooms take this second approach to education, and it's clear why. In the first place, it requires more effort on the part of educators than the simple delivering of instrumentally important facts and skills. An intimate relationship between student, teacher, and world is needed, and this will typically require of the teacher a thorough reevaluation of his or her role qua educator. In the second place, there is in general no real push from society itself for the sort of progressive education that Dewey champions. Progressive education leads to social progress, and social progress upends existing power structures that benefit from the status quo. Dewey is exactly right here: Once we set people on the path of thinking for themselves, we run the risk of overturning entire systems of values and the very institutions that they underpin. This liberating aspect of education— the possibility that understanding and self-determination can be put in the hands of each individual—has always been the reason for its simultaneous promise to some and danger to others.

We as educators must constantly keep in mind that our responsibility to our students is likewise a responsibility to our community. We are at once Socratic midwives to our students' understanding and shapers of a freer and more equal society. Or, at least, that's what we should be. The need for freedom of thought is no less urgent in a democratic society than it is in a totalitarian one. It's only that the mechanisms of control are different: Totalitarianism controls through force, whereas democracies tend to control through the much more insidious notion of the engineering of consent—persuading people to hold views that are not in their own interests. Without the freedom to think in a democracy, we don't have freedom at all.

Cultivating critical, socially engaged thinkers is the responsibility of educators at all levels, and it is a process that should begin from early childhood. Young children have an inherently inquisitive and philosophical demeanor, but they are also particularly susceptible to accepting beliefs on authority alone. Conformity begins early. We have to guard against it by instilling in them from the beginning the importance of both scrutinizing the merits of *any* purported truth or power before accepting it as legitimate and always being open to the revision of their beliefs and values in the face of new evidence.

Kant (1784/1991, p. 54) famously wrote that the motto of the Enlightenment is "*Sapere aude!* Have the courage to use your *own* understanding!" This is the motto that we should inscribe above the doors to all our classrooms.

References

Dewey, J. (1972). My pedagogic creed. In J. A. Boydston (Ed.), *John Dewey: The early works, 1882–1898: Vol. 5. 1895–1898* (pp. 81–95). Carbondale: Southern Illinois University Press. (Original work published 1897)

Dewey, J. (1981). Experience and nature. In J. A. Boydston (Ed.), *John Dewey: The later works, 1925–1953: Vol. 1. 1925* (pp. 1–326). Carbondale: Southern Illinois University Press. (Original work published 1925)

Kant, I. (1991). An answer to the question: "What is enlightenment?" In H. Reiss (Ed.) & H. B. Nisbet (Trans.), *Kant: Political writings* (pp. 54–60). Cambridge, England: Cambridge University Press. (Original work published 1784)

24

TRANSCENDING FALSE DICHOTOMIES

Confronting One of Life's Consistently Compelling Challenges

Thomas E. Kelly

> *Taken merely as doubt, an idea would paralyze inquiry. Taken merely as certainty, it would arrest inquiry. Taken as a doubtful possibility, it affords a standpoint, a platform, a method of inquiry.*
>
> —*How We Think*, Middle Works 6: 265

Dewey's quote poses this stiff challenge: How can teachers help their students steer a steady course between the Scylla of impulsive doubt and the Charybdis of absolute certainty? Put differently, in the context of a democratic society, there are at least two perspectives that can undermine the ideal of thoughtful, fair-minded consideration of ideas, whether the ideas are familiar or novel, commonsensical or improbable. On the one hand, habitual doubt about the merits of any idea may embody a relativistic view toward truth or goodness, a view (not necessarily held consciously) that entails the twin notions that all ideas are as good or bad as any other and that there is no valid way of determining whether one idea is true or better than proposed alternatives. Because nothing definitive can be proven by rational thought or argumentation, deliberation is essentially arbitrary, fruitless, mere bluster.

The second problematic perspective presumes that ideas that deviate from what individuals believe to be absolutely true or good deserve to be summarily dismissed as essentially false or evil. Inquiry is unnecessary, misguiding, subversive. Rather, devoted intolerance toward competing perspectives is dutiful for those passionate, courageous, and wise enough to embrace the Truth.

Fortunately, Dewey also hints at a path toward minimizing these twin threats to sustaining civil discourse. Drawing on Dewey and others (Elbow, 1986; Kelly, 2004, 2010, Palmer, 1998), several promising perspectives can be outlined. The first centers on the idea of "doubtful possibility ... [as] a method of inquiry." With supportive insistence, teachers can facilitate their students taking on alternating stances of methodological doubting and methodological believing. Methodological doubting or skepticism, in one version, is widely embraced in school rhetoric and practice. As a brand of critical thinking, it is aimed at engaging students' minds in logical analysis with an eye toward recognizing formal flaws in reasoning (inconsistencies, contradictions, faulty assumptions).

Perhaps less popular in school practice but nonetheless significant in purpose is social–political critique, which encourages students to examine texts (e.g., commercial advertising, political campaign literature, subject matter textbooks) to uncover their biased manipulations and propaganda. The presumption is that dominant power seeks to perpetuate its own interest and will use all available media to do so, with truth and justice, fairness and inclusiveness continually put at risk in the process. Thus, vigilant, disciplined doubting of received "truths" represents a vital force to safeguard the very integrity of democracy.

But as Dewey suggests, helping students perceptively question logical claims and social arrangements that might be marred, manipulated, or marginalizing is only half of what's needed to advance thoughtful, fair-minded inquiry. To counterbalance the standpoint of discriminating doubt, students need to develop the complementary capacity for methodological believing. Methodological believing can be likened to a game where the explicit purpose is to approach an idea provisionally from a generous, assenting, empathic viewpoint. Students are encouraged not only to temporarily suspend their disbelief but more affirmatively and imaginatively to embrace the strong possibility that the idea is intriguing, helpful, and worthy of their efforts to deeply understand its meaning and favorable implications.

Where confusion exists, an embrace of this provisional standpoint disciplines students to assume that the problem likely lies in their own insufficient understanding, not in the inadequacy of the idea. Hence, further inquiry, not dismissal, is activated along the following lines, directed to the author of the idea or to those appearing to understand it well: "Help me see what I might be overlooking or blocking. Help me experience the force of this perspective as you experience it."

Because of the alarm bells that misunderstanding of methodological believing can generate, it is essential to emphasize that the intent of methodological believing is not to have students become obsequious, self-deprecating, indiscriminate adherents to any and all ideas that come down the pike. Just the opposite. It is to have students develop a deeper understanding and appreciation of the potential merits of all viewpoints as part of the process of deliberate, disciplined inquiry, which, when coupled with methodological doubting, is designed to lead to more informed, fair-minded judgments of the overall worth of any idea.

Because methodological believing corrects for the half-empty and dismantling platform of methodological doubting while the latter moderates the acts of incorporating and appreciating characteristic of the former, we experience Dewey's tendency to integrate apparent opposites in the process of exposing false either–or dichotomies. Witness how in the chapter quote, he frames doubt and certainty not as oppositional forces, as they are characteristically understood, but as dynamics that possess common propensities within the interpretative context of inquiry. A significant implication for teachers follows from understanding Dewey's sustained critique of accepting false dichotomies. For Dewey, false dichotomies in general and the excesses of doubt and certainty highlighted in the quote in particular often function to choke curiosity, invalidate inquiry, incriminate interaction, intensify ignorance and solidify stereotypes. They promote and perpetuate a preemptive polarization that tends to preclude complexity and overlook opportunities that can authentically create connection and community.

To help students examine the dynamics of either–or and both–and perspective taking, teachers might well focus on three sets of ideas: ambivalence, paradox and contradiction, and provocative declaratives. Exploring ambivalence can provide students with a felicitously familiar context for understanding how contrary emotions and directives—for example, love and hate, holding on and letting go—are often experienced simultaneously yet make utter psychological sense. In fact, with insightful exploration, they emerge as intimately interdependent; that is, as precious paradoxes, not as contradictions at all. If apparent opposites can exist sensibly within us, maybe they can so exist between us as well. Thus, distinguishing between contradictions and paradoxes in particular contexts seems to be a fruitful line of intellectual and social inquiry. Consider these samples:

- Being deliberate in judgment precludes being decisive.
- As a term, *democracy* has been so corrupted that it risks becoming an empty slogan or, worse, a serious impediment to understanding political discourse.
- To be female and critical is invariably to be or be seen as a bitch.
- The language of victimization on which rights-oriented advocacy depends actually functions to corrode a sense of empowerment.
- Conviction inevitably leads to close-mindedness.
- On principle, teachers should avoid disclosing their own point of view when addressing controversial issues in the classroom.

Facilitated well (Kelly, 2004), one can imagine a number of exemplary benefits occurring from students confronting these provocative declaratives: greater attentiveness to both the precision and malleability of language and the prevalence and preciousness of paradox, an appreciation for uncommon commonalities, fresh insight into taken-for-granted socialized "truths," and a keener affirmation of this enterprise called *inquiry*.

References

Dewey, J. (1978). How we think. In J. A. Boydston (Ed.), *John Dewey: The middle works: 1899–1924: Vol. 6. 1910–1911* (pp. 177–356). Carbondale: Southern Illinois University Press. (Original work published 1910)

Elbow, P. (1986). *Embracing contraries: Explorations in learning and teaching.* New York, NY: Oxford University Press.

Kelly, T. (2004). A teacher educator's story. In J. G. Henderson & K. R. Keeson (Eds.), *Curriculum wisdom: Educational decisions in democratic societies* (pp. 144–158). Upper Saddle River, NJ: Pearson.

Kelly, T. (2010). Engaging dissensus: Selected principles and reflections. In J. G. Henderson & J. L. Schneider (Eds.), *The path less taken: Immanent critique in curriculum and pedagogy* (pp. 91–96). Troy, NY: Educator's International Press.

Palmer, P. J. (1998). *The courage to teach: Exploring the inner landscape of a teacher's life.* San Francisco, CA: Jossey-Bass.

25

EDUCATORS' PROFESSIONAL FREEDOM FOR STUDENTS' DEMOCRATIC LIBERATION

James G. Henderson

> *Genuine freedom, in short, is intellectual; it rests in the trained power of thought, in ability to "turn things over," to look at matters deliberately, to judge whether the amount and kind of evidence requisite for decision is at hand, and if not, to tell where and how to seek such evidence. If a man's actions are not guided by thoughtful conclusions, then they are guided by inconsiderate impulse, unbalanced appetite, caprice, or the circumstances of the moment. To cultivate unhindered, unreflective external activity is to foster enslavement, for it leaves the person at the mercy of appetite, sense, and circumstance.*
>
> —*How We Think*, Middle Works 6: 232

I have a deep faith in educators' intellectual abilities. I think they are capable of engaging in sophisticated pedagogical judgments inspired by a democratic love of wisdom. Such judgments require the practice of evidence-based reflective inquiries informed by open-minded conversations and eclectic deliberations. In short, John Dewey's "genuine freedom" involves the integration of informed experience, conversation, and deliberation. Samuel Fleischacker (1999) linked this professional judgment to student liberation:

> It may sound unexciting to announce that one wants to make the world free for good judgment, but this quiet doctrine turns out to be the most sensible, most decent, and at the same time richest concept of liberty we can possibly find. . . . A world where everyone can develop and use their own judgment as much as possible is closer to what we really want out of freedom. (p. 243)

I agree with Fleischacker that a worthy aim of education is to "make the world free for good judgment." Consider the implications of this curriculum aim for educational practices. Teachers would exercise their best professional judgments concerning their students' educational experiences so that their students could practice good judgments about the subjects they are learning and the life they are living. This is a generous, transactional way of working. It is a wonderful democratic vision of liberated teachers liberating students under their care. But can teachers work in this way? I firmly believe that the vast majority of teachers, if provided with the proper study-based collegial support, can elevate their pedagogical judgments in this way. They can practice professional freedom for democratic liberation.

Freedom as Good Judgment

Teachers, who are "freeing" themselves through "freeing" their students, must deeply consider the *hows* and the *whys* of teaching. They can't function as narrow technicians. They must cultivate the skills of their craft while thinking deeply about what they are doing. Their pedagogical practices must necessarily be informed by disciplined inquiries, reflections, deliberations, and conversations centered on the vital relationship between educational experience and human liberation. They must embrace a love of wisdom. Human *wisdom* is defined in the *Oxford English Dictionary* (1989) as "the capacity of judging rightly in matters relating to life and conduct; soundness of judgment in the choice of means and ends." Educators, who practice a love of wisdom, humbly consider the long-term goodness of their decisions. They attempt to solve immediate problems while cultivating enduring values. Their judgments are situated in both present reality and visionary future.

John Dewey serves as a model for this professional commitment. In a concise and insightful narrative on Dewey's philosophical work, Philip Jackson made two key points. First, near the end of his life, Dewey considers replacing *experience* with *culture* as his key organizing term. Jackson (2002) wrote,

> Dewey's choice of the word *culture* to replace *experience* rested on what he had come to understand. . . . What Dewey found to be attractive about the notion of experience in the first place was its breadth of coverage. . . . [He was] openly committed to the goal of social betterment through the continued criticism of ongoing social practices and cultural traditions. (pp. 52–54)

Even after a long and productive scholarly career, Dewey is still studying and rethinking the relationship between educational experience and the "good" life. Second, there is no discernible method underlying Dewey's philosophical efforts. His inquiries are best understood as a way of living. Jackson (2002) (author's emphasis) explained: "For Dewey . . . there was only the struggle *within experience* to . . . make life better for oneself and for others through an artful blend of thought, feeling, and action." (p. 101)

Reflective Inquiries Informed by Deliberative Conversations

I believe that teachers can cultivate this "artful blend" through a study-based approach to curriculum development. They begin by examining the vital inter-connections between three forms of reflective inquiry: three ways of practicing continuous reflections in the context of circuits of inquiry (Ryan, 2011). The first reflective inquiry is a recursive, back-and-forth movement between educational aims, curriculum designs, and teacher–student transactions for the purpose of fostering democratic educational experiences. Such experiences foster a deepening understanding of a particular *Subject* with a deepening *Self* and *Social* understanding of democratic liberation—in short, a deepening *3S* understanding. The second reflective inquiry involves recursive cycles of inspired awakening, mindful attending, and critical self-examining by teachers for the purpose of embodying and modeling 3S understanding for their students. The third reflective inquiry involves recursive cycles of peer inviting, peer transacting, and public reviewing for the purpose of establishing adult learning communities that support classroom learning communities. These three reflective inquiries are informed by four deliberative conversations on (a) negotiating wisdom judgments in standardized management contexts, (b) advancing democratic humanism, (c) advocating for social justice, and (d) embracing transactional poetics. This seven-topic study agenda is an open set, meaning that educators can incorporate additional reflective inquiries and/or deliberative conversations as they deem necessary.

Conclusion

Over the past 3 years, I have observed the excitement of experienced teachers working as lead learners for this study agenda. I conclude with three insights based on these observations. First, the study and the practices that flow from this study can be enacted in the small decision-making openings that exist in most teachers' workdays. Though the current educational policy environment is dominated by standards-based management with its command-and-control logic tied to high-stakes testing, there is generally some wiggle room to exercise professional judgments. Second, not all teachers are ready to build their capacities for good judgment, so this laboratory effort must begin with voluntary educators who, in turn, function as collegial lead learners. Third, the enormous structural barriers to practicing good judgment in education must be honestly acknowledged and addressed. Experienced teachers must work as determined study activists. This book is a collection of concise reflections on John Dewey's writings. Dewey has a deep faith in educators, as articulated in "My Pedagogic Creed" (1897/1972). I celebrate and share Dewey's faith as I contemplate educators' freedom for students' liberation.

References

Dewey, J. (1972). My pedagogic creed. In J. A. Boydston (Ed.), *John Dewey: The early works, 1882–1898: Vol. 5. 1895–1898* (pp. 81–95). Carbondale: Southern Illinois University Press. (Original work published 1897)

Dewey, J. (1978). How we think. In J. A. Boydston (Ed.), *John Dewey: The middle works, 1899–1924: Vol. 6. 1910–1911* (pp. 177–356). Carbondale: Southern Illinois University Press. (Original work published 1910)

Fleischacker, S. (1999). *A third concept of liberty: Judgment and freedom in Kant and Adam Smith.* Princeton, NJ: Princeton University Press.

Jackson, P. W. (2002). *John Dewey and the philosopher's task.* New York, NY: Teachers College Press.

Oxford English Dictionary. (1989). "Wisdom" definition 1a. *Oxford English Dictionary* (2nd ed.). Oxford: Oxford University Press.

Ryan, F. X. (2011). *Seeing together: Mind, matter, and the experimental outlook of John Dewey and Arthur F. Bentley.* Great Barrington, MA: American Institute for Economic Research.

26

AMERICAN STUDENTS AND THE EXPLORER'S MIND

Laura Dawes

> *The undisciplined mind is averse to suspense and intellectual hesitation; it is prone to assertion. It likes things undisturbed, settled, and treats them without due warrant.*
> —*Democracy and Education*, Middle Works 9: 196

When I was younger, like many children, I had a fear of ghosts and monsters living in my room. Every shadow at night looked like some unknown creature about to attack. Instead of checking for the ghosts and monsters or reassuring me there were no such things, my mother simply said, "We can't afford to have monsters or ghosts." That was it; this concept made perfect sense to me, I never questioned her, and I was no longer afraid of something attacking me while I was trying to sleep. Instead of arguing with my irrational thought, my mother played into it, giving me a perfectly justifiable reason to not be afraid in my own house.

History is riddled with irrational ideas that we now look back on and openly mock. No longer do we fear boats sailing off the edge of the world or believe that the earth is the center of the universe. Now ask yourself: Why do you not believe those things? Is it because you sailed around the world and lived to tell about it or that you personally studied and marked the layout of our solar system? Chances are you have done neither of those things; you know the world to be round and the sun to be the center of our universe because someone told you that was the nature of the world, that person supported the position logically (perhaps with pictures or a textbook), and you believed it as being the truth. You may be thinking, "Yes I was told those things, but that does not make them any less true." But how can you be certain if you have never explored the topics yourself?

Traditional education involves governments, administrators, and teachers deciding what should be taught to students and the materials that will be used to do so. The students sit perched in their perfectly aligned rows and try to absorb everything that the teachers and their textbooks tell them while never getting the opportunity to question what they are taught. Many who have gone through this educational style would argue that it is a good system. They went on to be successful, and our society is functioning fine, so why fix a system that is not broken? The reasons are many, but the primary objection to the traditional classroom system is that it has led to an overreliance on standardized test scores to prove that the educational system is achieving its goals. This testing forces the curriculum the children are taught to be narrower and narrower, limiting their futures.

As Dewey's quote shows us, it is human nature to be curious, but it is also human nature to stop looking for the answer to a question once one has been given. We want certainty in our lives, and when someone we trust (e.g., a parent or teacher) provides an answer, we take that to be a truth and no longer wonder. Just like when I was little and my mom gave me the answer I needed to stop being afraid, today's students are being told the information they need for the state mandated tests, which they are taking to mean that is all they need to know. They stop wondering, and as they get older they start to expect the answer to always be given to them because history has shown them if they wait long enough, someone will eventually answer the question for them.

In today's school system, children believe that the tests are the entire reason they are learning the information. Moreover, the way they are learning the information is through standard rote memorization. This pattern leads them to request the simple "truth" so they can take the test and move on. They are graduating without having gained the skills or having had the opportunities to discover the answers to questions they have on their own, and that means schools are producing mindless drones that are trained to believe whatever authorities tell them. Think about the implications this can have not only for our children but also our society.

We are producing citizens who will believe anything that seems to be a valid explanation, and they will not be able to check proffered theories because they will not be prepared to think outside of what they have been told. Is this what we want for our children? To be followers who believe whatever they are told? If not, then we need to reform our educational system so that it allows students the opportunity to discover information and ideas on their own in a structured environment. The teachers in this new system would then help students discover the tools they need to find the answer to their questions, present their solutions, and apply them. If we do not make these changes, then we will produce more and more citizens who will reproduce only things they were taught and who are not only unable but also unwilling to problem solve or explore new uncharted areas. It is in these uncharted areas that we most desperately need bold and creative thinkers who will prove that we are not sailing off the edge of the world.

Reference

Dewey, J. (1980). Democracy and education. In J. A. Boydston (Ed.), *John Dewey: The middle works, 1899–1924: Vol. 9. 1916* (pp. 1–370). Carbondale: Southern Illinois University Press. (Original work published 1916)

27

DEWEY'S FREEDOM OF INTELLIGENCE

Linda O'Neill

The only freedom that is of enduring importance is freedom of intelligence, that is to say, freedom of observation and of judgment exercised in behalf of purposes that are intrinsically worthwhile.

—Experience and Education, Later Works 13: 39

Teaching philosophy of education over the past 2 decades, I have returned to Dewey again and again, always finding something new. Dewey provides rich justification for a vision of education that was only a vague intuition during my earlier career in training and development. As professor of teacher education Robert V. Bullough Jr. (2005) explained, the emphasis in training is often to "contain the unexpected," whereas education, at its best, invites "wonder and surprise" as teachers depart from safe routines to find "better and more interesting ways of being with and for young people" (pp. 22–23). Leadership consultant Robert Farson (1997) also identified important distinctions between training and education: "Training makes people more alike, because everyone learns the same skills. Education, because it involves an examination of one's personal experience in the light of an encounter with great ideas, tends to make people different from each other" (p. 155). Dewey's *Experience and Education* (1938/1988) offers just such an encounter with great ideas.

Dewey wrote *Experience and Education* at the request of the International Honor Society in Education, Kappa Delta Pi (KDP). In 1938, KDP asked Dewey, then approaching age 80, to comment on the national debate between traditional and progressive education. Although the particulars of the debate have shifted over the past seven decades, we continue to wrestle with some of the same threats to freedom of intelligence Dewey identifies. These threats include the lure of simplistic choices, the temptations of our blind desires, and the tyranny of external purposes.

The Lure of Simplistic Choices

Observing that we tend to reduce even our most complex dilemmas to either/or questions, Dewey identifies simplistic choices between "sides" in educational debates as threats to freedom of intelligence. In *Experience and Education,* Dewey explains that we need *not* choose between rigid specifications and unfocused activity, abject obedience and unruly behavior, enforced silence and noisy confusion, or past traditions and present interests. In Dewey's philosophy, these are false dichotomies. Instead, we can experience continuity between the richness of the past and the concerns of the present as we live each day in a dynamic interaction of internal impulses and external conditions. To cultivate freedom of intelligence, we must resist the temptation to oversimplify our choices; we must recognize that truth and falsehood, pain and pleasure, failure and success, freedom and control can coexist. Dewey reminds us to avoid the trap of simplistic either/or choices.

The Temptations of Blind Desires

Dewey (1938/1988) argues that students may gain the "illusion of freedom" (p. 42) when they are granted permission to move about the classroom. But if they are reacting impulsively to the circumstances of the moment, they remain slaves to their own "blind desires" (p. 43), driven by forces over which they have no "control" (p. 41). In Dewey's view, to become masters of our own desires, we must take time to reflect, combining memories of past actions and their consequences with careful observations of the situations before us. For Dewey, this "union of observation and memory" (p. 41) is vital to a reconstruction of experience enriched by judgment and significance. With freedom of intelligence comes the power to combine observation and memory, judgment, and significance in the formulation and execution of thoughtful plans.

Although we would love to believe that our technological advances bring us greater and greater opportunity to exercise freedom of intelligence, we can easily be overwhelmed by the barrage of information and conditioning stimuli we experience daily. With wireless communication comes "perpetual connectivity" as we submit to systems that often defy our attempts to control them (Castells, 2010, p. *xxx*). As residents of global networks, we are constantly multitasking, racing to follow whatever captures our attention. In fact, we may be more *under* than *in* control of our technologies—and in ways we have yet to fully understand. In our buzzing, beeping, chiming, flashing virtual worlds, we need to safeguard time for "the union of observation and memory" at the "heart of reflection" (Dewey, 1938/1988, p. 41). Dewey reminds us that unexamined impulses, conditioned responses, and blind desires can all threaten freedom of intelligence.

The Tyranny of External Purposes

Dewey (1938/1988) asserts that to exercise freedom of intelligence, students must have both time for reflection and space for the "individuality" that comes with freedom of movement. Freedom of movement can allow students to reflect on activities that make use of the body as well as the brain. It can channel students' natural vitality instead of allowing destructive energies to build. It can foster students' physical and mental health. But freedom of movement is not enough by itself to cultivate freedom of intelligence. If students are to develop freedom of intelligence, they must go beyond movement and naïve reflections on their activities. As they mature, they must be taught to recognize cause-and-effect relationships with increasing skill, developing confidence and the capacity for self-direction. In cultivating freedom of intelligence, students ultimately become capable of pursuing freely chosen and personally fulfilling goals.

Building on Plato's definition of the slave as one who is directed by another's purposes, Dewey does *not* suggest that students, teachers, or administrators automatically reject policies or plans established by others. Effective policymakers and planners can help balance purposes, trade-offs, and consequences, strategically anticipating what might come next from multiple perspectives. But despite their potential strengths, externally imposed policies and plans may miss significant insights educators possess about their own communities, schools, and classrooms. Dewey reminds us to gather our courage in order to pursue those purposes we find most worthwhile, honoring the freedom of intelligence grounded in our own experience.

Some of Dewey's critics have claimed that his philosophy of education promotes activity for its own sake. In *Experience and Education,* Dewey clearly dispels this notion. Freedom of intelligence includes freedom of movement as a "means, not an end" (Dewey, 1938/1988, p. 39). Freedom of intelligence requires that we avoid simplistic choices when faced with the complexities of our current dilemmas. It requires that we draw on the past while carefully analyzing conditions of the present, forming judgments rather than relying on habitual responses or blind desires. It requires that we honor insights from our own experiences and pursue purposes that are personally meaningful, even when external pressures seem overwhelming. Dewey's writings encourage us to reimagine what "freedom of intelligence" might mean for education in our own time.

References

Bullough, R. V., Jr. (2005). Becoming a student of teaching. In D. A. Breault & R. Breault (Eds.), *Experiencing Dewey: Insights for today's classroom* (pp. 20–23). Indianapolis, IN: Kappa Delta Pi.

Castells, M. (2010). *The rise of the network society: The information age economy, society, and culture* (2nd ed., Vol. I). Malden, MA: Wiley-Blackwell.

Dewey, J. (1988). Experience and education. In J. A. Boydston (Ed.), *John Dewey: The later works, 1925–1953: Vol. 13. 1938–1939* (pp. 1–62). Carbondale: Southern Illinois University Press. (Original work published 1938)

Farson, R. (1997). *Management of the absurd: Paradoxes in leadership.* New York, NY: Simon & Schuster.

28

UNEXAMINED PRESUMPTIONS

George W. Noblit

> *Prejudice is the acme of the a priori. Of the a priori in this sense we may say what is always to be said of habits and institutions: They are good servants, but harsh and futile masters.*
>
> —*Experience and Objective Idealism,* Middle Works 3: 136

Our view of people and things different from us has little to do with them per se. It springs not from our direct experience with others but from beliefs that exist beneath our consciousness—presumptions that we have not examined and that are not always evident to us. From these unexamined presumptions emerge prejudgments of experiences. These exist before experience and stop us from learning fully from our experience.

The bind of a priori beliefs is strong, and many people never see beyond them, accepting them as natural and therefore correct. As Dewey notes, the a priori beliefs left to their own master us, making us pawns of our culture and society. However, the a priori belief examined is the tool, the servant, of learning from our experiences—for seeing the opposite gender, people of other races, the poor, and so on, anew from our experiences, not from our biases. Such experiences are truly educative, and I believe understanding them is necessary to be able to teach well.

Commitment to Equity

As an educator, I long ago decided to devote my work and life to equity. I came of age in the 1960s when it seemed we were clearer about the inequities in our society and more committed to broad-based social action to reduce, even eliminate inequity. I did not come to a commitment to equity easily. I grew up in a small industrial mountain community full of the prejudices of class, ethnic heritage (against Southern and Eastern Europeans), gender, and race. I inherited these as natural facts of life. I also perpetuated these in many ways because I defined myself superior based on my maleness and Whiteness.

Probably through the lens of class and ethnicity, I first saw the unfairness of prejudices. To be honest, however, I was more attuned to the unfairness of class hierarchies because they directly affected me. Because I was working class, I was unable to date some girls and hang out with some boys. I was unable to see much further than myself at that time. In retrospect, I had little consciousness of my role in creating inequities, nor did I have a language to enable me to talk about inequity beyond my own self-absorption.

Consciousness Raising

Later in my life, my consciousness was "raised," to use the language of the 1960s. In a world rocked by civil disobedience, all my prejudices were assaulted. The civil rights movement, women's movement, antiwar movement, and the youth movement gave way to race riots, marches, and political and personal confrontations. I recall being both scared and exhilarated. I was seeing the world and myself anew, and I was learning from my experiences in ways no book could teach.

Learning from these experiences changed my perspective on the world and thus confirmed for me Dewey's observation that prejudice emerges from the a priori. However, the immediacy of my experiences and the severity of the challenges to the boy I had been meant that the changes I focused on were internal.

Later, as a professor, I came to embrace the a priori in a new way. Up to that point, I was recounting my changes and my new beliefs as testimony to what others could, and should, believe. This, however, was not much of a pedagogy. As I struggled to find a way to teach against racism and sexism, I rediscovered the a priori not as an enemy but, as Dewey notes, as a servant of learning. My goal then became to be less a proselytizer of my way of understanding and more a teacher. I began to structure lessons ("gigs" I have come to call them for their performative, improvisational nature) that would reveal a priori beliefs and demonstrate how these beliefs were not only unfair to others but also reduced the possibilities that could be conceived of by the person with the a priori beliefs.

One of my favorite types of gigs requires students to face the hidden curriculum of a writing assignment. I ask them to analyze how my assigning them a paper that I will grade is reproductive of the social order and how one might create from the assignment an emancipating experience. The important element of this gig is that the paper has no assigned content—just that they are to write a paper and I will grade it. My students tell me that they alternatively love and hate the assignment, and me, as they work through it. The assignment comes at a point where we have read and discussed a set of ideas about structure and agency, how societies reproduce themselves, and how knowledge and reality are social constructions.

The result is almost always that students discover they have a language for expressing their ideas—one that I did not have in my youth or young adult years. Moreover, if one of us does not find the language, then we all go back and work through the material again. For me, seeing the a priori and struggling with it must be a collective accomplishment. If it is not, then the a priori is left a "harsh and futile master" for some, and students are left to believe that learning from experience is limited to personal awareness—but not a tool for educative development of our society.

As a teacher, I know that I still have much to learn. Yet this quotation from Dewey largely encapsulates what I have learned so far and also what I see as the most important substance I can teach.

Reference

Dewey, J. (1977). Experience and objective idealism. In J. A. Boydston (Ed.), *John Dewey: The middle works, 1899–1924: Vol. 3. 1903–1906* (pp. 128–144). Carbondale: Southern Illinois University Press. (Original work published 1906)

PART IV

Democratic Citizenship

PREPARING CHILDREN FOR DEMOCRATIC CITIZENSHIP

Rick Breault

Little in the typical teacher-preparation program encourages teachers to think about what it means to prepare children for democratic citizenship. You can search the various teacher standards, regardless of their acronyms (NCATE, INTASC, NBPTS, PDS), and you will not find any emphasis on preparing young people for a life in democratic society. You might find references in the social studies content area standards or in the general standards to nurturing qualities that are implicit in good democratic citizens, but nothing that mentions democratic citizenship as such. Once you get into the school environment itself, things are even worse. Any deliberate discussion of schooling for democracy has been nearly completely drowned out by the rallying cry, "Get a score and get a job!" Dewey would not be pleased.

This set of reflections is intended to leave you with a challenge. If you read only the other parts of this volume, there is the possibility that you will walk away with a better, but incomplete, understanding of Dewey's purpose. The intellectual development of individual students was certainly a concern for Dewey. However, he reminds us in *Democracy and Education* (1916/1980),

> A being connected with other beings cannot perform his own activities without taking the activities of others into account. For they are indispensable conditions of the realization of his tendencies. When he moves he stirs them and reciprocally. (p. 16)

And later in that same book, Dewey (1916/1980) tells us,

> The essential point is that isolation makes for rigidity and formal institutionalizing of life, for static and selfish ideals within the group. (p. 92)

Educating for Democratic Citizenship

Dewey is seldom more clear or definitive on a point than he is when explaining that we cannot help but live in society, and society is most effective when it is lived as a democracy. Dewey's vision of educating for democratic citizenship, however, bears little resemblance to the simplistic version we currently see in most schools, or what I call the "3 Ps"—be productive (get a job), be patriotic (say the Pledge of Allegiance), and participate (vote).

Even in some of the better curricula, democratic citizenship is something that you learn *about* so you can participate later in life. It is an established body of knowledge or set of behaviors you learn so that you can be a better citizen. If democracy is practiced at all in the classroom, it is usually in the form of voting on choices determined by the teacher or maybe developing classroom rules together. Although the latter is not a bad idea, it focuses on society's role in controlling its citizens rather than on releasing their potential.

What you will read in the following selections should both trouble and excite you. Dewey pulls no punches in describing the school's responsibility in nurturing democratic citizenship, and it is not an easy task. Consider these words from *The School and Society* (1899/1976):

> We must conceive of them [school work] in their social significance, as types of the processes by which society keeps itself going, as agencies for bringing home to the child some of the primal necessities of community life . . . in short, as instrumentalities through which the school itself shall be made a genuine form of active community life, instead of a place set apart to learn lessons. (p. 10)

A Dynamic Process

Where Dewey differs from what we currently call education for democracy is in his emphasis on democracy and democratic education, not as established content but as a dynamic process. The community and the school always must be asking, "What kind of society do we want and what kind of school will help bring about that society?" This idea permeates Dewey's (1916/1980) writing (all emphases have been added):

> The conception of education as *a social process* and function has no definite meaning until we define the kind of society we have in mind. Democracy is the faith that the *process of experience is more important* than any special results attained, so that special results achieved are of ultimate value *only as they are used to enrich and order the ongoing process.* (p. 103)

Dewey would not oppose the idea of preparing young people for the world of work. In fact, he would encourage it. However, there is an important difference between a curriculum that helps children become integrated into the working life of the community and one that is narrowly focused on careerism and stresses simply getting a job, especially if that emphasis leads to the perpetuation of a privileged class and a more limited curriculum "conceived for the masses" (Dewey, 1916/1980, p. 200). He might also have a problem with the understanding of democracy and economics that is currently dominant in our schools, and culture in general, which emphasizes individualistic consumerism as an expression of freedom.

Where we currently have "token economies" in which young children are "paid" or rewarded with trinkets from the school store for doing their schoolwork, Dewey would have us provide meaningful and productive activities that students would want to do for their intrinsic reward. Where the present trend in field trips is to visit toy and sporting good stores—paid for by those stores— Dewey might have suggested visiting local craftspeople and small factories to see the importance and contribution of work and cooperation in the life of the community. The emphasis would be better placed on the ingenuity of the creative process and what the individual contributes to communal life than on helping to create early brand loyalty to a megacorporation that might well have rent the fabric of the local community by driving small business owners into bankruptcy or sending local factory jobs overseas.

Preparing Students for Democratic Living

Yes, you will find that this part of the book presents quite a challenge. To prepare your students for democratic living, you must allow them to live democratically. That means you will need to implement a curriculum that takes into consideration everything you have read to this point. Classrooms that model thoughtful, participatory democratic living are characterized by experiences that focus on active learning, meaningful inquiry, and critical thinking. If all this sounds overwhelming, and it probably does, keep in mind that Dewey also describes democracy and education as a process in which we move gradually toward the kind of society— or classroom—we seek. To conclude with Dewey's (1937/1987) own words:

> The foundation of democracy is faith in the capacities of human nature; faith in human intelligence and in the power of pooled and co-operative experience. It is not belief that these things are complete but that, if given a show, they will grow and be able to generate progressively the knowledge and wisdom needed to guide collective action. (p. 219)

References

Dewey, J. (1976). The school and society. In J. A. Boydston (Ed.), *John Dewey: The middle works, 1899–1924: Vol. 1. 1899–1901* (pp. 5–112). Carbondale: Southern Illinois University Press. (Original work published 1899)

Dewey, J. (1980). Democracy and education. In J. A. Boydston (Ed.), *John Dewey: The middle works, 1899–1924: Vol. 9. 1916* (pp. 1–370). Carbondale: Southern Illinois University Press. (Original work published 1916)

Dewey, J. (1987). Democracy and educational administration. In J. A. Boydston (Ed.), *John Dewey: The later works, 1925–1953: Vol. 11. 1935–1937* (pp. 217–225). Carbondale: Southern Illinois University Press. (Original work published 1937)

29

TEACHING DEMOCRACY FOR LIFE

John M. Novak

> *Democracy is a way of life controlled by a working faith in the possibilities of human nature.*
> —*Creative Democracy: The Task Before Us*, Later Works 14: 226

Teaching in and for a democracy is a daunting and creative challenge. It is much more than emphasizing the importance of voting or being informed about the governmental process. Both of these are important, but democracy goes much deeper than that. Teaching in and for a democracy is about learning to live a shared life and finding ways to grow through meaningful participation in important social issues.

Democracy as a way of life emphasizes that people grow as they learn to bring their individuality and intelligence to the many communities they inhabit. Human growth and development do not come merely from the inside or the outside. That is, human beings do not have a specific inborn human potential that emerges regardless of what happens in their environment. Neither are they blank slates that are mechanically stamped out by their surroundings. Individuals and their communities grow as a result of the unique contributions people bring to group tasks and challenges. Through this give-and-take process, individuals learn to understand the perspectives of other people and develop one another's ability to be heard and taken seriously.

Participative Living

Teaching for a democratic way of life means being able to model this way of participative living. Teachers realize that students attend not only to what they say but, more importantly, to what they do. A democratic way of living requires that teachers and students engage in a "doing with" relationship. The lived experience of this "doing with" relationship communicates the message that "we are all in this together."

Looked at metaphorically, this way of teaching should be more like participating in a jazz band than marching in a drum and bugle corps. In the latter, people are interchangeable parts that follow a set of specific instructions to arrive at a predetermined goal. Though there may be energetic engagement, the process is closed—participants are merely following orders. The job of the teacher is to make sure that everyone stays in line and is in the right place at the right time.

In a jazz band, individuals participate in a developing theme that is enhanced by their anticipated creative extensions. Participants are expected to want to be competent, committed, and creative. The job of the teacher is to make this metaphorical possibility a creative reality. The role involves, on the one hand, knowing who your students are and where their interests and talents lie. On the other hand, the role means having a solid grasp of what you are teaching and the creative possibilities that exist in connecting subject matter with individual student interests and abilities. This role develops by having a feel for your students and your subject matter and possessing the artistic desire and competence to bring them together in vitally enhancing ways.

Positive Possibilities

There is no guarantee that this jazz-like effect will occur in its most artistic form every time a teacher encounters a class. This is not an all-or-nothing affair, but it has a better chance of developing if it is a part of a melioristic faith in human possibility. Seasoned meliorism for democratic teachers needs to be distinguished from naïve optimism and cynical pessimism. The former implies that good things will result regardless of what we do as teachers. The latter perspective is resigned to the belief that teaching cannot make any real difference in people's lives. The mistake of both of these positions is that they imply that good or bad things are guaranteed regardless of a teacher's actions. A seasoned meliorism necessary for democratic living is based on the idea that jazz-like encounters are more apt to develop if teachers approach teaching and learning situations with an energetic openness to positive possibilities and reflectively learn from previous and present experiences.

A working faith in human nature is a stance from which a teacher operates. In baseball, a batter digs in and takes his or her stance. Stances can differ, but their aim is to enable the batter to make a solid connection with the ball. Good hitters modify their stance according to previous experience and current conditions. Similarly, a democratic teacher digs in with a stance that is built on a working faith in human possibilities. This working faith says that all people are valuable, able, and responsible and can behave accordingly in cooperative and collaborative activities. Enacting this stance is not easy and does not negate the fact that people may at times be apathetic, self-centered, or narrow-minded in their actions. At the very least, a working faith in human possibilities assumes that human nature is not fundamentally evil, that social life can be filled with meaningful encounters, that intelligence can handle more complex problems, and that teachers can learn from successful and unsuccessful endeavors. This working faith in human nature points a teacher in the right direction and enables self-correcting strategies to develop.

Modeling Democratic Living

Teachers need to model this democratic stance outside as well as inside the classroom. In the governance of their school, teachers should be active leaders for democratic living. Their voices need to be heard and artfully combined as they participate in a creative endeavor to make their school a model for creative democratic processes. Connecting the school to the larger outside world, this working faith in human nature means that teachers also attend to the societal resources, strategies, and commitments that make this way of life available to all.

A commitment to a democratic way of life is not easy and is never finished. But what is the alternative for creative and committed teachers in a democratic society? The democratic teachers I have encountered have found ways to grow personally and professionally in bringing this ideal to life and in bringing life to this ideal.

Reference

Dewey, J. (1988). Creative democracy: The task before us. In J. A. Boydston (Ed.), *John Dewey: The later works, 1925–1953: Vol. 14. 1939–1941* (pp. 224–230). Carbondale: Southern Illinois University Press. (Original work published 1939)

30

EDUCATION FOR A CHANGING WORLD

William Ayers

> *The individual is to be the bearer of civilization; but this involves a remaking of the civilization that he bears.*
> —*The Significance of the Problem of Knowledge*, Early Works 5: 20

The individual and society are not separate worlds, discreet planets orbiting past one another in infinite space, untouched and unaffecting. No. Individuals are brought forth in a shared space, forever created and shaped in a social surround; every society is constructed, deconstructed, reconstructed at often dizzying speed by actual persons. This is a dynamic, never-ending wheel, spinning and whirring without end. We change the world; the world changes us.

Reaching the Full Measure of Humanity

John Dewey's ideas are as alive and powerful today as ever because he was brilliant, of course, but more because he employed his brilliance in a particular pursuit. Dewey is a dialectician, and he sees teaching as an enterprise geared toward helping every human being reach the full measure of his or her humanity. Education changes lives; education changes the world—simple to say, and yet in countless ways, excruciatingly difficult to enact.

Education, no matter where it is practiced, enables each of us to become more self-consciously human. It embraces as principle and overarching purpose the aspiration that people become more fully human. It impels us toward enlightenment and liberation. And at the center of the whole adventure, students and teachers in their endless variety—energetic and turbulent, struggling, stretching, reaching—come together in classrooms and community centers, workplaces, houses of worship, parks, museums, or people's homes. They gather in the name of education, assembled in the hope of becoming better, smarter, more capable and powerful and in the hope of creating a better, more human world. In Paulo Freire's cosmology, this precious, humanistic ideal is an expression of every person's true vocation—*the task of humanization*.

But humanization is not possible in isolation. Rather, it is achieved with others. The dialectical push and pull that Dewey sees so clearly is the engine of personal as well as social growth and change.

In the opening pages of José Saramago's *The Stone Raft* (1995), the Iberian Peninsula, without warning or explanation, breaks free of Europe and begins to drift slowly out to sea. The peninsula migrates east, stops, spins suddenly, and heads south, a kind of large stone raft adrift on an unknown expanse of blue. "You can see where the crack originates," says the narrator, "but no one knows where it ends, just like life itself" (Saramago, 1995, p. 16).

Five strangers are thrust together through a strange set of circumstances, and soon they set off on a voyage of their own. "Don't worry about things making sense," one says. "A journey only makes sense if you finish it, and we're still only half way there, or perhaps only at the beginning, who knows, until your journey on earth has ended I cannot tell you its meaning" (Saramago, 1995, p. 133).

Saramago's stone raft is, of course, also the planet Earth, gliding through the fathomless blue, turning and turning around a rather small and insignificant star, charted but not, fated but free, so large that none of us feels like a sailor, so small that we tremble at our insignificance. So many gigantic things lie outside our control, so much seems to just happen to us; it's difficult to take hold of our power and our agency, to make something of it.

Asking Risky and Baffling Questions

We need to learn to ask questions of ourselves and others, risky questions and baffling questions, dynamic questions, and then to live within them—within the contingent answers and the tentative conclusions and the deeper, more disturbing questions that emerge. Even when we think of ourselves as open-minded, we are in some large part prisoners of constrained definitions of society, narrow conceptions of human capability. We accept too much.

Perhaps the hardest lesson for all of us to learn is that human identity is not settled but rather in motion; that reality is not fixed and solid but dynamic. History is not finished, and we are not living at the point of arrival. People act as if the future is going to be a lot like the present, only more so; but the future is unknown, of course, and also unknowable. Think of any decade in the past century; no one could have predicted the changes just ahead and the impact of those changes on so many aspects of life. Hip-hop. Reality TV. AIDS. email. The atomic bomb. Starbucks. DVDs. Genocide in Rwanda and Bosnia. Knowing this, it is obviously foolish to imagine the future as the present plus, now in spades, and yet our imaginations fail.

"So often we need a whole lifetime in order to change our life," Saramago (1995) wrote.

We think a great deal, weigh things up and vacillate, then we go back to the beginning, we think and think, we displace ourselves on the tracks of time with a circular movement, like those clouds of dust, dead leaves, debris, that have no strength for anything more, better by far that we should live in a land of hurricanes. (Saramago, 1995, p. 70)

For better or for worse, we do indeed live in a land of hurricanes, and we ride the crest of a zephyr. Paradoxically, and a little sadly, it is also a land disguised as calm, and we too often experience ourselves as little more than dead leaves and debris.

Living in History

We might cultivate as an article of faith the belief that every human being can exceed where he or she is now—is capable of surpassing himself or herself, of going beyond. One of our challenges, then, is to live and work in the belief that we can do what's never been done, and we might. This requires embracing a most hopeful if scary proposition: We are each, and civilization itself is, a work in progress. We are living in history. What we do (or don't do) will make a difference. The outcome is unknown. We act, we doubt, we learn, and we act again.

References

Dewey, J. (1972). The significance of the problem of knowledge. In J. A. Boydston (Ed.), *John Dewey: The early works, 1882–1898: Vol. 5. 1882–1898* (pp. 3–24). Carbondale: Southern Illinois University Press. (Original work published 1897)

Saramago, J. (1995). *The stone raft* (G. Pontiero, Trans.). New York, NY: Harcourt Brace.

31

JOHN DEWEY AND THE AMERICAN CREED

Daniel Tanner

> *It should be a commonplace, but unfortunately it is not, that no education—or anything else for that matter—is progressive unless it is making progress.*
> —Introduction to *The Use of Resources in Education,* ix

So writes John Dewey in his last piece of published writing before his death on June 1, 1952. In his last work, Dewey reviews some of the successes of progressive education but also notes the lack of progress in many quarters and the difficult road ahead for the democratic transformation of school and society. He points to the difficulties of recent years in which "organized attacks on the achievements of progressive education have become more extensive and virulent than ever before" (Dewey, 1952, p. viii).

Fallacies and Failures of Dualistic Thinking

For Dewey, the progressive education movement, as part of a wider democratic social movement, never can rest as long as it is committed to the improvement of the human condition. Throughout his life, he exposes the contradictions and conflicts of dualistic thinking in impeding the method of intelligence and preventing problem resolution and solution. He prophetically exposes the Soviet fallacy in holding that democratic ends would emerge from undemocratic means. He exposes the erroneous belief that restrictions on civil liberties are necessary to protect American democracy and that gains in social welfare are made at the expense of individuality. In the present-day wake of international terrorism, the American public is led by its leaders to believe that security can be protected only through sacrifices in civil freedoms. But Dewey makes it clear that democracy is the best guarantor of freedom and security.

Dewey advances the needed interdependence of knowledge and exposes the hazards of knowledge dualism—such as the divorce between the sciences and humanities—decades before C. P. Snow (1959) addressed the issue and exposed its inevitable losses to humanity when the branches of knowledge are isolated or set against one another. Dewey forewarns researchers in the behavioral sciences against setting a divide between the qualitative and quantitative research in educational investigation. Early in the 20th century, he holds that all research must be grounded in an intellectually coherent and inclusive system of ideas and quality and must employ appropriate techniques if the results are to attain generalized significance.

Nature of the Learner

Dewey orchestrates a theory of democracy and education on a global scale. Yet some of his deepest and most far-reaching insights and realizations on human nature and behavior grow out of his observations of children in his laboratory school. Just imagine a curriculum built on what Dewey identifies as the four impulses of children—the social, the investigative, the constructive, and the expressive/artistic—or what may be termed the *fourfold functions of developmental learning.*

Dewey anticipates Piaget by decades—and he goes further, for he systematically interrelates the design and function of the school curriculum to child and adolescent development. He anticipates and contributes to the emergence of modern cognitive/developmental psychology in answer to the warring sects in psychology that impeded progress in understanding the nature of the learner in a free society.

Transformation of the Curriculum into the Working Powers of Intelligence

Dewey systematically conceives of and demonstrates the means for constructing the school curriculum to advance the learners' growth. He explains the processes of reflective thinking and the method of intelligence for social and personal problem solving necessary for productive citizenship in a democracy. He conceives of education as the process through which experience is reconstructed for growth—both in the meaning of experience and in advancing the ability to direct the course of subsequent experience. He holds that the process of education must empower the learner in the control of his or her destiny by transforming the curriculum into the working power of intelligence. Dewey provides educators with a paradigm revealing how the success or failure of educational reform hinges on the extent to which the curriculum is in harmony with the nature and needs of the learner and the democratic prospect.

Many authorities on Dewey have failed or refused to recognize that what they regard as his greatest single work, *Democracy and Education* (1916/1980), systematically integrates educational theory and democracy through the very structure and function of the school curriculum. Indeed, Dewey defines philosophy as the general theory of education. Through education and its agency of curriculum, the rising generation develops its fundamental intellectual, emotional, and instrumental dispositions toward life in all of its manifestations.

Education and the American Creed

More than any other figure of the past century, Dewey promotes and strengthens the belief in education as the principal conclusion of the American creed (Myrdal, 1962). Among the multitude of cultures that have found conflict in American and global society, Dewey envisions an overarching intercultural education to build a sense of unity through diversity.

He conceives of community not as a group set against other groups by special interests but as a cosmopolitan association of people who draw their strength through finding common cause in their diverse talents. He never doubts the democratic prospect and is an activist for virtually every democratic social movement—educational opportunity, human rights, child welfare, academic freedom, and social justice. He advises his fellow philosophers that they should study the problems of humanity rather than the problems of philosophy.

Throughout his life and over the course of the half-century since his passing, Dewey has been vilified, honored, betrayed, vindicated, attacked, and defended. But when all is said and done, he gave America and the world the most provocative, comprehensive, and powerful vision for human progress through democracy and education for the 21st century. He was a man for his times and a man for all times. He knew full well that progress is never made. By its very nature, progress is in the making.

References

Dewey, J. (1952). Introduction. In E. R. Clapp, *The use of resources in education* (pp. vii–xi). New York, NY: Harper & Row.

Dewey, J. (1980). Democracy and education. In J. A. Boydston (Ed.), *John Dewey: The middle works, 1899–1924: Vol. 9. 1916* (pp. 1–370). Carbondale: Southern Illinois University Press. (Original work published 1916)

Myrdal, G. (1962). *An American dilemma* (20th anniversary ed.). New York, NY: Harper & Row.

Snow, C. P. (1959). *The two cultures and the scientific revolution.* New York, NY: Cambridge University Press.

32

JOHN DEWEY AND THE IMPORT OF A CURRICULUM DEVOTED TO STUDENT EXPERIENCE

Chara Haeussler Bohan

> *When nature and society can live in the schoolroom, when the forms and tools of learning are subordinated to the substance of experience, then shall there be the opportunity for this identification, and culture shall be the democratic password.*
> —*The School and Society,* Middle Works 1: 38

In 1899, when John Dewey gave the three lectures that make up the material for *The School and Society* (Dewey, 1899/1976), lecture and recitation remained a primary method of education (Trenholme, 1909). At that time, Dewey is not satisfied with such passive learning, and he seeks to describe a means of educating students in which they actively participate in their learning through lived experience. He believes that the classroom should be an environment where nature and society happily coexist rather than a place in which students passively prepare for their future role in the world of work.

Because students engage in life through the use of imagination and develop deeper understandings through lived experiences, Dewey seeks to cultivate students' imagination and experiences in the classroom. For students, the Deweyan classroom opens up a world of possibilities.

Considering Students' Interests

Dewey's recommendation to make the methods of learning subordinate to experience has several lessons for teachers in classrooms today. The first is to consider the interests of children and to invest in the learning process by developing activities that can further students' experiences (Tanner, 1997). For example, in an elementary classroom where students are to learn basic economic principles, rather than lecturing students and having them only read text, teachers might engage students in an economics fair (Bohan, 2003). Students can make a product; earn wages for their labor; and advertise, buy, and sell their products.

In a secondary economics course, students can participate in a classroom activity where they play a game of buying and selling stock on the New York Stock Exchange and then follow their investments. By considering students' interests and developing a curriculum with experiences to match those interests, teachers necessarily enhance the learning experience. Dewey's attention to experience highlights the difference between learning a foreign language by reading a textbook and learning a foreign language by living in the country where the language is spoken. The latter is a more authentic and effective means of learning.

Arranging the Environment

A second lesson to consider is practical in nature. A teacher must reflect on how the classroom space fosters students' experiences. When Dewey (1899/1976) seeks desks and chairs for his laboratory school, he has difficulty finding the proper equipment. He wants to create an environment in which students could work rather than simply listen. Similarly, a teacher today must consider the classroom space. The simple task of taking rows of desks and rearranging them in a circle can change the dynamics of student and teacher interaction. As a teacher, standing in the front of the room at a podium lends itself to the lecture format, whereas sitting among the students at a table or in a circle fosters discussion. Some lessons require lecture to convey understanding, particularly to large groups, but at other times, actively engaging students to foster dialogue is more prudent.

A teacher ought to be purposeful and careful about how the classroom space is arranged and the type of learning promoted by the physical environment. A welcoming and inviting classroom is a place where learning is easily facilitated. Would a student prefer to read a book in the Magic Tree House series or a classic such as *All Quiet on the Western Front* while sitting on a hard desk chair or in the comfort of a plush and pillowed couch? Students typically spend 7 hours of their day in the school environment. Do teachers want students to spend the majority of their day sitting in one position? When the environment presents obstacles rather than offers an invitation, learning is more difficult to accomplish.

Fostering Democratic Character

A third and final component of Dewey's elevation of experience in the learning process is the democratic nature of an education that actively engages students in the world. To foster democratic character in students, Dewey believes, the school has to be organized as a cooperative community (Westbrook, 1991). Traditional lecture and recitation demand a more autocratic methodology, but the world of experience requires students to participate in a more democratic form of learning.

Students learn from one another, the world around them, and the projects in which they engage, in addition to seeking assistance from the teacher. When students understand that they are participants in their learning rather than simply receivers of knowledge, they develop a greater commitment to their education.

For students, learning in a democratic environment might mean selecting a topic to research rather than being assigned a research paper.

Dewey's attention to a curriculum based on experience is important to today's teachers and students alike. In an educational world filled with standardized curricula, tests, textbooks, and worksheets, Dewey's philosophy is a gentle reminder about possibilities and ideals in schools where students are the heart of learning. Cultivating students' experiences is a means to promote a lifelong love of learning. Dewey understands the value of a curriculum devoted to student experience.

References

Bohan, C. (2003). A fair to remember: Elementary economics. *Social Studies and the Young Learner, 15*(4), 6–8.

Dewey, J. (1976). The school and society. In J. A. Boydston (Ed.), *John Dewey: The middle works, 1899–1924: Vol. 1. 1899–1901* (pp. 5–112). Carbondale: Southern Illinois University Press. (Original work published 1899)

Tanner, L. N. (1997). *Dewey's laboratory school: Lessons for today.* New York, NY: Teachers College Press.

Trenholme, N. M. (1909). The organization of the recitation. *History Teacher's Magazine, 1*(4), 74–76.

Westbrook, R. B. (1991). *John Dewey and American democracy.* Ithaca, NY: Cornell University Press.

33

THE BEST AND WISEST PARENT

David J. Flinders

> *What the best and wisest parent wants for his own child, that must the community want for all of its children. Any other ideal for our schools is narrow and unlovely; acted upon, it destroys our democracy.*
>
> —*The School and Society,* Middle Works 1: 5

How do we decide who are the "best and wisest" parents? What makes them best, and what do these parents want for their children? Though Dewey does not take the meaning of "best" parent for granted, at least generally speaking, we might assume that the best and wisest parents watch out for their children's interests and well-being. Such parents want to provide for their children, comfort them, and protect them from harm. But more than this, they want their children to have opportunities to succeed. We might even say that the best parents are those who want the best for their children—including the best health care, the best teachers, and the best education.

Available Resources

Though this initial line of thinking might seem straightforward, we quickly run into some hard economic facts. We live in a society of rich and poor, and the disparity between these groups has grown increasingly wide. Some parents have more resources and more wealth—much more wealth—than others. Their resources allow them to provide more for their children. However, we would not on this basis conclude that all poor parents automatically must be excluded from the "best and wisest" category. By the same token, we would not want to equate "best" simply with being rich. Either way of defining "best" would constitute what Dewey refers to as a "narrow and unlovely" view of parenting.

Individual Needs

Dewey also would caution us on another point: He would argue that any definition is inadequate that attempts to set out the criteria for good parenting without regard for the differences among individual children. Even children who seem alike, such as siblings raised under the same roof, often possess quite different interests, abilities, and aptitudes. Thus, what is best for one child may not be best for others.

The differences among individual children are important in education for the same reason. They raise issues of equity by suggesting that we cannot provide the same course of study for all students without privileging those students whose interests and abilities happen to match the curriculum. Conversely, a one-size-fits-all education would disadvantage those students whose interests and abilities fall outside its scope. Put another way, the best and wisest parents would want each of their children to receive an education matched to his or her individual needs.

Social Criteria

Though Dewey is known for arguing that the needs and interests of children should play a critical role in their education, he does not argue that those needs and interests were the *only* criteria we should consider. Social criteria, for example, are suggested directly in Dewey's references to the vital connections between education and democracy. Dewey's best and wisest parents not only want each of their children to be happy, but they also want them to be acceptable members of the society in which they live. Our culture often pits social and individual concerns against one another, but Dewey sees these concerns as complementary rather than oppositional. It would be difficult, in his view, to raise a self-actualized child who also was entirely unacceptable to a democratic society, or vice versa.

Nowhere is this close integration of social and individual interests more evident than in teaching. In the classroom, as in families, the sacrifice of either interest seriously flaws the entire process. On one side of the issue, we might imagine parents who say, "We love our own children and work hard to provide for them, so why should we be concerned about anyone else's kids?" Or, "Yes, we know many children go hungry and are homeless, but those children are not our problem as long as our own kids are safe and well cared for." We might be sympathetic with what such parents want for their children and even admire their hard work to provide it. Yet, we should take time to consider their "my child first and only" attitude. This narrow perspective seems uncaring and shortsighted. In what this attitude models or conveys by example, it may fail even the particular children it is meant to serve.

Broad Interest in the World

The care that teachers provide for particular students in their charge involves more than sentimental affection for individual children. It also involves more than helping each child feel special. Rather, caring is reflective work that includes taking a broad interest in the world of which children are a part. Child-centered teachers need not take up social causes directly, but any claim to child-centeredness logically commits them to acknowledging that their own work is something of a social cause.

On the topic of social causes, we might imagine parents fully devoted to various political and philanthropic activities. Perhaps these activist parents are so devoted—as they rush from Habitat for Humanity sites to voter registration tables, to canvassing for Greenpeace, to their volunteer jobs at the local humane society—that they have no time left for their own children. Would children be comforted in knowing that such family sacrifice is for noble and worthy causes? If the parents' neglect is genuine, we should be concerned regardless of their otherwise admirable commitments to social betterment.

In the context of teaching, Dewey views the needs of the child and the needs of a democracy as serving complementary ends. Schools do not serve democracy, for example, by requiring students to engage in "service learning" against their will. Rather, genuine and lasting social reform involves the nurturing of positive attitudes, abilities, and dispositions. Democratic reform, in short, is more than simply good works. It must also educate people if it is to make a difference. On this count, teachers who say they are reform minded implicitly are committing themselves to child-centered schools.

Reference

Dewey, J. (1976). The school and society. In J. A. Boydston (Ed.), *John Dewey: The middle works, 1899–1924: Vol. 1. 1899–1901* (pp. 5–112). Carbondale: Southern Illinois University Press. (Original work published 1899)

This photo of Dewey in academic gown at the
University of Chicago was taken around 1902.
Special Collections Research Center, Morris Library,
Southern Illinois University Carbondale. Used with
Permission. Photo by Eva Watson Schutze.

John Dewey portrait, inscribed "To my friend [?] Wang,
with best regards, John Dewey, Peking, July 5, 1921."
Special Collections Research Center, Morris Library,
Southern Illinois University Carbondale. Used with
Permission.

John Dewey portrait.
Special Collections Research Center, Morris Library,
Southern Illinois University Carbondale. Used with
Permission. Photo by Blackstone Studios.

Included among formal portraits of department heads at
the University of Michigan was this one of Dewey, taken
in 1893 right before he left there.
Special Collections Research Center, Morris Library, Southern
Illinois University Carbondale. Used with Permission.

John Dewey poses with Matthias Alexander.
Special Collections Research Center, Morris Library, Southern Illinois
University Carbondale. Used with Permission.

Dewey (standing, center) is photographed with the Quadrangle Club at the University of Chicago around 1896. Special Collections Research Center, Morris Library, Southern Illinois University Carbondale. Used with Permission.

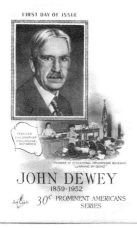

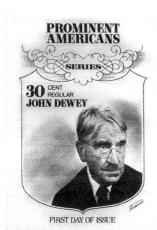

U.S. Government issued postcards.
Courtesy of Craig Kridel.

34

BUILDING A COMMUNITY OF INQUIRERS

Sam F. Stack, Jr.

> *We must conceive of them (school work) in their social significance, as types of the processes by which society keeps itself going, as agencies for bringing home to the child some of the primal necessities of community life of man; in short, as instrumentalities through which the school itself shall be made a genuine form of active community life, instead of a place set apart to learn lessons.*
>
> —*School and Society,* Middle Works 1: 10

Written in 1899 as part of a lecture to the parents of the Dewey lab school at the University of Chicago, this quote emphasizes some of the primary concerns Dewey has about the changing nature of society and the need for education to change accordingly. Dewey describes the changes in society in the late 19th century as a "revolution" (Dewey, 1899/1976, p. 6) the schools could not ignore. Dewey believes this revolution, born through technology, industrialization, and urbanization, had led to the dissolution of community life, a life he believes was better understood in earlier rural–agrarian communities. This was not an intellectual retreat to the "good ole days" but was an attempt to bring to the modern era a sense of connection, identity, and place, nurturing an understanding of shared interest and how people can better understand living in the modern world. Dewey senses the modern era had created an imbalance between individualism and one's responsibility to the society or social order. This imbalance was exacerbated by capitalism and its distorted stress on freedom and materialism. Capitalism had turned work into something one does for material gain rather than giving the individual a sense of contribution, such as work well done.

Occupation and Activity

Dewey discusses work in the larger conception of what he called *occupation.* Dewey does not define occupation until a later chapter in *School and Society* entitled "The

Psychology of Occupations" (Dewey, 1899/1976, p. 92). "By occupation," he writes, "I mean a mode of activity on the part of the child which reproduces, or runs parallel to some form of work carried as in social life" (p. 92). There is more here in Dewey's definition of occupation than personal satisfaction; in an aesthetic sense, a type of creativity is associated with the definition, along with the notion "I can see where in the greater scheme of things I am making a contribution." Simply put, through the study of occupations, one can see the "entire industrial process" being revealed. For Dewey, it is through this experience or process that one builds character, and helps one gain "habits of order and industry and obligation to self and others" (Dewey, 1899/1976, p. 7).

Occupation and Democracy

Undergirding Dewey's use of occupations and an understanding of work are his thoughts on participatory democracy. Dewey (1899/1976) writes, "A society is a number of people held together because they are working along common lines, in a common spirit, and with reference to common aims" (p. 10). It is through occupations that he wished to emphasize our connection and potential role in democratic society. Our conception of occupation as something one does to make a living is only partially what Dewey wishes to convey. He believes that occupations should be at the center of school life.

An occupation goes beyond mere work and is something we do to contribute to society at large, a type of social spirit rather than the concept of it as an individualistic pursuit, or what Dewey termed, in the ideal, a harmonizing of power "along certain lines" (Dewey, 1899/1976, p. 95). Dewey understands that the school in his day is out of touch in many ways and uses manual training as training for trades rather than helping children become intelligent problem solvers. He grasps the tension or dualism between manual and intellectual labor and tries to attack it through the study of occupations. He understands that studying occupations alone captures the interest of children, but this is only a starting point to gain knowledge, the key being knowing how to interact in society. The school is a place and perhaps the best place for students to learn about the things people do (occupation) and how they create the world they live in.

Dewey envisions the study of textiles as a means (or instrumentality) to teach subject matter through activity and problem solving; however, the key to learning how to weave or separate the boll from the cotton is not as important as engaging in a process by which we as human beings interact or experience nature, using our knowledge to the benefit of humankind or the common good. Information is not something we merely acquire but something we gain from our inquiry— what Dewey terms in the chapter quote as the "growing insight and ingenuity of man." The school should be a place that is alive with energy and where there is "a spirit of free communication, of interchange of ideas, suggestions, results" (Dewey, 1899/1976, p. 11). The school is the place to build a community of inquirers.

21st-Century Learning

The problem of modern education, or what is often termed *21st-century learning*, is that it perceives occupation in a narrow and individualistic sense. Education has become less an activity of intellectual enrichment and inquiry as Dewey envisions it and more training for a job so one can make a living wage, contributing to the global economy at large. Current educational reform tends to sacrifice inquiry for acquiring, clearly a danger Dewey sees as a threat to democratic society.

For Dewey, true 21st-century learning must be fully transformative and refuse to maintain the status quo, and, as he advocates, "saturating him (the student) with the spirit of service, and providing him the instruments of self-direction, we shall have the deepest and best guarantee of a larger society which is worthy, lovely, and harmonious" (Dewey, 1899/1976, p. 20).

Reference

Dewey, J. (1976). The school and society. In J. A. Boydston (Ed.), *John Dewey: The middle works, 1899–1924: Vol. 1. 1899–1901* (pp. 5–112). Carbondale: Southern Illinois University Press. (Original work published 1899)

35

A BEING CONNECTED WITH OTHER BEINGS

Audrey M. Dentith

A being connected with other beings cannot perform his own activities without taking the activities of others into account. For they are the indispensable conditions of the realization of his tendencies. When he moves he stirs them and reciprocally.
    —*Democracy and Education,* Middle Works 9: 16

Each semester in my curriculum theory class, I ask my graduate students to research their own communities to find examples of reciprocity of learning and living in everyday life. Using ethnographic methods, I ask them to find examples of human exchange that include the sharing of knowledge, skills, or other resources in a face-to-face human format. These exchanges must be largely nonmonetized and not reliant on or wholly dependent on consumerism. These should leave little or no ecological footprint and they should be activities that are in harmony with the local context. They can be activities that highlight local cultural or ethnic origins, but not necessarily so. Ideally, these practices involve an intergenerational exchange through the sharing of knowledge and show evidence of positive relationships that foster democratic processes and civil liberties. Over the course of the semester, these graduate students, who are practicing teachers, community educators, and school administrators, enthusiastically set out to find these practices in their local communities.

By the end of the semester, they submit the fruits of their labor. Typically, they have garnered rich examples of community life, including many examples of the creative arts and crafts knowledge in their communities; the growth and production of food and its cultivation; diverse forms of bartering; cultural dances and other forms of artistic expression; oral history and forms of intergenerational narratives; healing and medicinal practices; and the many ceremonies, games, and heritage languages that are a part of every single community in myriad ways. Their iMovies, YouTube videos, Wiki pages, PowerPoint presentations, and other forms of mediated representation depict the "cultural commons" (Bowers, 2012) they have uncovered through their ethnographic efforts. They are always surprised to find that these practices are strongly evident in every community and that they are a fundamental part of their own lives, too. They never considered these practices, which are often taken for granted, as pedagogical, emancipatory, democratic, or ecological in nature.

To frame their thinking, I use Bowers's (2012) concept of the cultural commons as the guide for this ethnographic work. Bowers asserted that people are waking up to the reality that has been hidden behind a facade of limitless consumerism and rampant individualism. He urged us to recognize the nature of sustainable wealth through the cultural commons or the nonmonetized forms of wealth that have sustained people in their communities for thousands of years. This wealth is a fundamental source of empowerment and is apparent in the daily practices, everyday actions, patterns of reciprocity, and ways of thinking that are shared through conversations; mentoring; observation; and the sharing of knowledge, skills, and mutually beneficial practices.

Over the years, I've reviewed the artifacts gathered by my graduate students. They have included local articulations of the slow food movement, farmers' markets, and the resurgence of food contests at county fairs. The events at community charity centers including food and clothing exchanges have been increasing in number and scope. Free youth league sports, walking clubs, and yoga events have also proliferated. In addition, they have researched and captured ways of childbirth and the raising of children through organized movements including narrative birthing and La Leche League activities. They've witnessed new ways that young people are reclaiming spaces for nonconsumer activities, including swing dance mobs, youth-built skating parks, and large community gardens. Often the exploration of these students results in uncovering some local and revitalized ethnic traditions such as Folklorico or Irish dance that have become popular again among youth. Sometimes they report on the work of organizations that serve communities through the arts, such as Say Sí, a San Antonio community art center where young people learn the arts through the mentorship of craftspersons without incurring any fees. Or, they uncover a local restaurant that serves only locally grown, organic foods and hosts many free community events. The examples seem to multiply each year.

In animated exchange, we share our experiences and we reflect collectively on the ways that every action within a community has a particular and certain reaction. Reciprocity is evident in the practice of exchanging knowledge, skills, and practices with others for mutual benefit. The exchange of these cultural commons leads not only to the new knowledge but also to stronger communities, less reliance on consumerism, and a sounder ecological mindfulness.

Anthropologist Gregory Bateson (1972) acknowledged this understanding as a central basis unit of information that circulates through the micro and macro levels of the life cycle. He called this unit, "the difference that makes a difference" (p. 459).

No other event in my curriculum theory class has been more powerful or has found more resonance among students than this one simple activity. This activity does more to connect students to the power of community knowledge, the reciprocity of community relations, and the ecology of life than any other project I've assigned in my classes.

Dewey understands this simple yet profound principle—all actions are connected, and each one constitutes a difference that stirs others and impacts the lives of others in the web of life. As educators, we are obligated to understand this fundamental concept, particularly in this time of great ecological peril and amid the proliferation of techno-scientific forces that thwart community, foster fear, and threaten the collective knowledge and sound practices that can ultimately sustain us all.

References

Bateson, G. (1972). *Steps to an ecology of mind*. San Francisco, CA: Chandler.

Bowers, C. A. (2012). *The way forward: Educational reforms that focus on the cultural commons and the linguistic roots of the ecological/cultural crisis*. Eugene, OR: Eco-Justice Press.

Dewey, J. (1980). Democracy and education. In J. A. Boydston (Ed.), *John Dewey: The middle works, 1899–1924: Vol. 9. 1916* (pp. 1–370). Carbondale: Southern Illinois University Press. (Original work published 1916)

36

THE VALUE OF COMMUNICATION IN A CLASSROOM COMMUNITY

Barbara J. Thayer-Bacon

> *Not only is social life identical with communication, but all communication (and hence all social life) is educative. To be a recipient of a communication is to have an enlarged and changed experience. One shares in what another has thought and felt and in so far, meagerly and amply, has his own attitude modified.*
>
> —*Democracy and Education*, Middle Works 9: 8

I am sure that when we, as teachers, look at our classrooms full of students, we are able to see that social life exists. Where at least two people are together, there is social life. People who are together in a particular setting at a particular time will communicate with one another in some manner. If they are unable to speak the same language, they will resort to using body language, such as facial expressions and physical posturing, and succeed in establishing some kind of social interaction.

In the classroom, where communication is taking place, there is social life. Even if only two people are in a classroom and they both decide to go to opposite corners of the room and sleep during their time together, they still have communicated something to each other and established a social life. Granted, it is not a very interesting or exciting social life, but all we need is some kind of interaction between at least two people to declare a classroom a place where social life exists.

The Classroom as a Community

When we look again at our classrooms full of students, I wonder whether we can see a community. I believe that a classroom is not only an example of social life but also is an example of a community—a group of people who have confirmed that they have something in common.

Our students come from diverse contexts, even if our larger school community is ethnically homogeneous. We probably have boys and girls; only children;

twins; adopted children; and children from single-parent homes, widowed-parent homes, and extended-parent homes as well as students from homes of varying shapes and sizes, with parents of various educational levels or criminal records, just to name a few diverse examples. Given that most towns in the United States today are not ethnically homogeneous, our students probably don't all share the same religious and political beliefs, economic or historical backgrounds, or even the same language.

Still, given all that diversity, they share the fact that they attend our class, are exposed to the same curriculum, have you or me as their teacher, and are together as students. I suggest that our classrooms are communities and that there are enough commonalities among individuals to establish some kind of shared experience and shared interest that connect us.

Communicating Shared Experiences and Interests

How does the group of people within our classroom confirm that individuals have shared experiences and interests in common? We do this through communication. If we do not share the same language, then we have to work together to try to learn or create a common language so that we can try to understand one another. If we are lucky enough to share the same language, we don't have to work as hard at finding common terms and establishing common meanings so that we can communicate. However, in spite of sharing the same language, all the diverse backgrounds and experiences we bring to the shared classroom space create many opportunities for us to misunderstand one another. Even in our own homes, miscommunications happen all the time. So why might we think that they wouldn't occur in our classrooms? Of course, they do!

Let's look closer at the challenges of communicating within a diverse classroom community to help us appreciate the educative value of allowing and encouraging communication in our classrooms. When we try to communicate with others, we cannot do so by remaining within our own perspectives. We have to use our imaginations to help us try to think from others' perspectives, to find ways to reach out to them and have our meaning received. We cannot communicate with others by staying within ourselves. We have to get out of our own worldview and try to see the world from others' worldviews.

That effort to reach out allows us to enlarge our thinking. The reaching out we do to communicate is what opens us up to being changed by our communicative efforts. Even if our exchange with others goes smoothly and there are no misunderstandings, we are changed by the effort we made to reach out to others. And if our communication does not go smoothly, that creates opportunities for more growth and learning as we try to figure out what went wrong and why. No matter what, we cannot lose; all communication with others leads to growth, and growth leads to education. All communication opens the possibility for us to further our own education as well as the education of others.

Encouraging Communication

The logical conclusion we can draw is that if communication leads to personal growth and education, then we should encourage lots of communication in our classrooms. We should not judge students talking to one another or to us as being "off task" or "wasting time." Instead, we must try to see these communications for what they are—valuable experiences that enlarge our thinking and change us.

I know that teachers are judged in U.S. schools, indeed all over the world, for how quiet their classrooms are. A quiet classroom is a common criterion used for measuring whether we are good teachers. Quiet seems to be associated with control, authority, and efficiency, hence more knowledge gained. However, I suggest that our classroom communities need to have many opportunities for communication among members so that we, as teachers, can enhance our students' growth and further their education as well as our own.

Like Dewey, I encourage you to allow your students more opportunities, not fewer, to communicate with one another and with you in class. Next time you look at your classroom full of students, I hope you will see a place where there is the chance for much growth to take place. Don't be afraid to open up the classroom space to more conversation and discussion. Much learning will take place as a result.

Reference

Dewey, J. (1980). Democracy and education. In J. A. Boydston (Ed.), *John Dewey: The middle works, 1899–1924: Vol. 9. 1916* (pp. 1–370). Carbondale: Southern Illinois University Press. (Original work published 1916)

37

REALIZING A COMMON GOOD

Randy Hewitt

> *The desired transformation is not difficult to define in a formal way. It signifies a society in which every person shall be occupied in something which makes the lives of others better worth living, and which accordingly makes the ties which bind persons together more perceptible—which breaks down the barriers of distance between them.*
> —*Democracy and Education,* Middle Works 9: 326

As Dewey professes, life means growth, development, and change over time. However, simply to say that life means growth tells us nothing about the extent, intensity, and content of this growth as it takes concrete form.

To ask what life *is* at any one moment in time, to inquire into growth as it takes shape and develops qualitative characteristics, is to ask an empirical question. To ask what concrete form life *should* take, to ask in what direction and how growth *should* proceed, is to ask a philosophical question. To be concerned with the philosophical question is to be concerned with what kind of individual and community *should* be in the making. It is to take a conscious interest in what ends *should* guide individuals' growth in shared experience. Furthermore, it is to be concerned with the capacities, skills, affections, and dispositions necessary to realize these ends.

Desirable Ends

If philosophy serves as the means by which we imagine a better state of human affairs from the one that now exists, then education serves as the means by which we deliberately bring this better state of affairs into being. Philosophy, then, identifies the desirable ends within individual and social growth, and thus defines the aims and purposes of education.

What does it mean to say that the aim of education should be to bring about "a society in which every person shall be occupied in something which makes the lives of others better worth living, and which accordingly makes the ties which bind persons together more perceptible—which breaks down the barriers of distance between them"? Furthermore, why should this be the aim of education? To answer these two questions, it is necessary to sketch out the philosophical foundation that gives warrant to this aim of education.

Shared Activities

Human beings unavoidably share in concrete activities that yield concrete results. That is, an individual's environment always includes other human beings already engaged in activities ("occupations," as Dewey sometimes calls them) aimed at common ends. Therefore, any individual's particular tendencies of action are inextricably social and thus are socially cultivated and learned activities.

Simply put, shared activities provide human beings with the fundamental means of living and learning. They supply specific ends, aims, and purposes for human conduct through which individuals first develop interest, desire, judgment, and motive. Shared activities stimulate, organize, and direct individuals' senses, attention, and motion. Shared activities provoke thought and incite emotion necessary for personal—and social—growth. They are the essential substances through which individuals acquire and refine their special affections, dexterities, and aptitudes. In short, shared activities are organs of intelligence. They form the central nerves whereby the individual not only develops specific tendencies to act but also more or less realizes his or her inherent connection to others as an indispensable condition for nourishing personal growth.

Shared activities, furthermore, help form the moral fiber or character of the individual. They serve as the medium through which the individual filters the demands of others on himself or herself and refines personal abilities in light of their claims. Because the individual must continue enlisting the support of others for growth, he or she must develop some degree of interest in their modes of response and their expectations of the consequences as a result of these responses. If he or she is to acquire the skills necessary to become a part of the group, he or she must assimilate not only its likes, dislikes, desires, purposes, and plans but also its demands that these plans be carried out in particular ways.

Others command the individual to consider the significance of his or her actions more carefully. They demand that an individual develop his or her interests and act in a way that is considerate of others as they attempt to develop their own interests. As claims of right, their expectations sharpen judgment about the direction and control over specific desires and inspire and enlarge the individual's idea of the good to be served. In a general, more formal way, shared activities provide the individual with an intrinsic ideal for conduct that serves as both a good and standard.

As the good or aim of conduct, the ideal refers to the individual's conscious tendency to develop his or her particular capacities and interests *in harmony* with the demands and needs of others as they develop their own powers. From the point of view of the self, the goal of any activity or occupation is to act in a way that will improve one's interests, skills, desires, attitudes, habits, and judgment. From the social point of view, the goal is to act in a way that will improve the specific shared conditions (the arrangements, opportunities, and materials) that nourish the activities and growth of others.

As a standard of judgment, the ideal refers to the degree to which the individual actually brings about this harmony by acting on his or her conception of good. In their attempts to realize a common good through their various activities, individuals come to share lives and communicate with one another in more intimate and varied ways. As a result, they come to learn from one another. They come to identify new interests and capacities for further growth as well as responsibilities intrinsic to these new potentials. Thus, the ideal of self-growth inherent to shared activities entails two principles whose just relation makes up the democratic ideal: individual liberty and social equality.

Social Experience

An enriched democratic experience, however, cannot be secured merely by virtue of collective acceptance and general appeal to its abstract principles. The work of democracy can be made concrete, secured, refined, and extended only through the day-in and day-out activities that human beings share. Democracy as a moral ideal challenges each individual to be actively engaged with the particular problems that arise within his or her shared occupations and that limit free and full contact with others. Only through active concern for the community can problems be immediately felt, understood, and appreciated with sympathy. Only through constant communication, persistent questioning, and critical reflection about shared ends and purposes, and the special needs and capacities of all involved, can existing efforts to satisfy social needs be measured, deficiencies be identified, and further work be suggested.

A flourishing democratic experience requires free flowing and broad communication about the consequences of shared activities. Mutual reference and exchange of ideas is vital to making "the ties which bind persons together more perceptible," for multiplying perceptions of possible human resources, sharpening consciousness of shared ends, and stoking the desire to excel beyond existing conceptions of good. Constant vigilance over existing efforts to meet social demands helps detect conditions that set up unequal relations of power and stifle human interaction and freedom of individual growth. An education most fitting to democracy is one that consciously aims to cultivate what Dewey (1916/1980) calls "robust trustees of its own resources and ideals" (p. 15).

Education, in the most general sense, is the means by which a democratic society consciously modifies itself to enhance the depth and range of shared meaning and bring about a more unified social experience. In light of the philosophical foundation stated here, education should entail the cultivation of democratically minded individuals charged with the responsibility of bringing about a more intimate, harmonious experience. Therefore, the aim of instruction is to develop democratic characters who are socially and politically engaged according to their own specific interests.

Good teaching, then, aims to provide the experiences necessary to direct individuals, on their own, to sense, test, measure, reflect on, and develop an idea of their experiences. Put differently, good teaching cultivates the emotional and intellectual powers of attention, perception, memory, imagination, conception, and judgment in individuals such that they widen and enrich the significance of their own interests by reference to the interests and needs of others. Fundamentally, the aim of instruction is to develop in students the affections, sympathies, and conceptual habits necessary for critical analysis of ideas and assumptions that work to preclude or enhance a more intimate experience with others.

Reference

Dewey, J. (1980). Democracy and education. In J. A. Boydston (Ed.), *John Dewey: The middle works, 1899–1924: Vol. 9. 1916* (pp. 1–370). Carbondale: Southern Illinois University Press. (Original work published 1916)

38

TEACHER AS SHAPER OF SOCIAL PROCESS

Louise M. Berman

> *The conception of education as a social process and function has no definite meaning until we define the kind of society we have in mind.*
> —*Democracy and Education*, Middle Works 9: 103

Business cannot be as usual! Changes in society for good and for bad have suddenly brought the realization that we live in a relatively small global village. And, in this village, we see

- increasing gaps between the haves and the have–nots,
- insecurity about the variety of ways life can be diminished or extinguished through terrorist attacks,
- inadequate access by many to both medicine and medical services,
- school systems with little teaching of our democratic heritage or possibilities,
- lack of will on the part of many persons to become politically active in causes beyond those that have an immediate impact on themselves,
- the tendency of people to fill their lives with endless activity without giving adequate attention to what really matters, and
- lack of reflection because of a surfeit of information and choice.

People today are faced with multilayered problems as well as possibilities; therefore, they may give inadequate attention to the spirit and vision that have inspired persons for generations. Dewey probably would ask us to consider the kind of society we have in mind, just as he continues to raise that question into the 1940s.

One way of dealing with societal vision and purpose might be the constant refinement of the meaning of *social process*. The term lends itself to considering a variety of topics that might be included in a society's statement of purpose. How a society views the social processes it seeks to teach, or neglects to teach, its young partially determines the direction of that society.

Creating a Societal Vision

That Dewey is concerned about constant change and reform suggests that no one statement of the ends of society will be complete. Within Dewey's philosophy, such a statement constantly will be shaped and reshaped. Allow me then to raise a few questions about education that teachers, students, parents, and concerned citizens might ponder and act on as they think about the kind of society they wish for themselves and others.

What thoughts, ideas, and values energize teachers and others interested in thinking about the process of finding some common perspectives? A dynamic society is not a ho–hum entity. Teachers and others bring to their settings themselves as persons. Each individual, therefore, must reflect on that which makes him or her a fully functioning human being so that the excitement, newness, and considered values of each person are inviting to human contact, communication, and connection. The teacher who is vibrant and sharing of a considered self is attractive to other human beings. Teaching and learning are then fostered through both indirect and direct means.

How do we establish contexts, including schools and classrooms, so that mini communities are formed? In such communities, social processes are taught. These processes might include, but are not limited to, sharing power, showing compassion to others like and unlike one's self, using minds actively, searching for just and moral means of dealing with human problems, uncovering goodness in people's actions, and teaching civility as a way of honoring and respecting the opinions of others.

How will persons learn to make a difference in the various communities in which they are involved? Possibilities for such action will vary depending on the ages of the students, the nature of the context, and the yearnings of the people within the community to help bring about needed societal changes. The key is to provide settings in which persons can identify problems and dilemmas and work on them in concert. Questions might be addressed, such as the following: How can persons learn to exercise political power by communicating with different kinds of persons; asking piercing questions; mediating conflicting ideas and ideologies; and showing civility, compassion, and concern in difficult situations? What does it take to stay with a tough project until some resolution is achieved? For example, volunteerism is sometimes part of school programs. Such activities help individual students develop certain ways of showing interest in others and fine-tuning intellectual and emotional skills. But when fundamental societal change is a major purpose, students must learn political skills of negotiation, conflict resolution, and consensus building. How can additional skills be built into an existing program?

How will teachers and leaders help students and their communities to develop the will to think about fresh priorities in society and schools? For example, what can be deleted from the curriculum to make time and space for the enhancement of knowledge, skills, and feelings necessary to our living together harmoniously? How do we use these skills to encourage better schools for all children or more adequate health services for poor neighborhoods or countries?

How can schools and communities interact so that the quality of life for all is enhanced? For example, in neighborhoods with students from diverse political, socioeconomic, and ethnic backgrounds, conversations between school personnel and neighbors invite parties to hear the backgrounds and purposes of one another. Schools may help through their attempts to look for commonalities and differences in neighborhood diversity. We seem to have done well in acknowledging diversity, but perhaps we have to search for fresh ways to talk about our common humanity.

How do the academic disciplines contribute to students' building of projects based on life in their mini communities? Geography, history, philosophy, literature, mathematics, the arts, physical education, and the sciences all provide insights and ways of thinking that are important to Dewey's focus on mind as capable of continuous growth, integration, and change. Although Dewey's thinking about organized subjects is sometimes misunderstood, he strongly emphasizes the use of the disciplines in learning how to live well, solve problems, and live ethically with others. The disciplines provide incentives for imagining the lives of others, making extraordinary observations, engaging in creative renderings of thought, and judging with exquisite sensitivity.

How do we as teachers help persons learn to live with the uncertain, the ambiguous, and conflicting perspectives as students search for answers to perplexing questions? Perhaps one of the most important and compelling aspects of teaching is helping persons live imaginatively and wisely in a world full of contradictions and unanswerable questions. Providing settings where students look for alternative possibilities and connections among contending points of view may enhance their ability to live with joy and satisfaction in a world of perplexities and paradoxes.

Paying Attention to What Needs Fixing

Education is not business as usual. I started this reflection with a number of societal changes that need attention. Clearly, I could list numerous things that are good in our world and immediate society. Ignoring the problems, though, is dangerous. When the brakes or transmission in a car begin to give out, the persons in it are in trouble. Unless we pay attention to what needs fixing, all of us may suffer.

Teachers and communities need to work out the meanings of social process for the settings of which they are part. Such action involves looking and relooking, creating and re-creating answers to society's toughest problems. Such action involves the joy and suffering that frequently accompany newness of ideas and activity. Such action involves naming those attitudes, predispositions, and learnings to live amicably with self and others. Such actions mean persons reaching beyond themselves to apply learnings from their immediate context to the world community with its problems begging for solutions.

So let's get started in the context within which each of us works.

Reference

Dewey, J. (1980). Democracy and education. In J. A. Boydston (Ed.), *John Dewey: The middle works, 1899–1924: Vol. 9. 1916* (pp. 1–370). Carbondale: Southern Illinois University Press. (Original work published 1916)

39

THE SOCIETAL PURPOSE OF EDUCATION

Jesse Goodman

> *The problem of education in its relation to the direction of social change is all one with the problem of finding out what democracy means in its total range of concrete applications: economic, domestic, international, religious, cultural, and political. . . . The trouble . . . is that we have taken democracy for granted; we have thought and acted as if our forefathers had founded it once and for all. We have forgotten that it has to be enacted anew in every generation, in every year and day, in the living relations of person to person, in all social forms and institutions. Forgetting this . . . we have been negligent in creating a school that should be the constant nurse of democracy.*
> —*Education and Social Change*, Later Works 11: 416

Why do we have public schools? Why should Johnny or Mary or Susie spend hours upon hours in buildings that look like factories but are called schools? On the surface, the question seems innocent—a simple question with an equally simple answer. The question is so rudimentary that most individuals currently concerned about our schools seem not to have noticed it; or perhaps they feel that the answer is so obvious that discussing it would be a waste of time. As most individuals can quickly discern, the design of recent educational reforms has been to help young people get jobs when they grow up. Some people also might add that the function of schools and the recent wave of reforms are meant to ensure our competitive edge over other countries in the global marketplace.

I suggest that our society might benefit from considering Dewey's thoughts on the matter. Specifically, we would achieve much by reopening the debate about the societal purpose of public schooling. Throughout Dewey's life and works, he emphasizes two fundamental and closely related purposes for public education. The first might be characterized as a quest for helping individuals create meaning in their lives. The second, as indicated by the quote at the beginning of this essay, is to foster the development of an educated citizenry for the purpose of continually deepening and broadening our democratic society.

The Notion of Public School

Instead of advocating for this or that particular reform, I suggest that what is really needed during these complex times is for us, as a nation, to recast the context within which we debate what should happen in our schools. Rather than situate this discourse within a purely marketplace context, as has been the case for the past decade or so, I propose that we look at public education, as Dewey suggests, within a democratic framework. Let me begin by taking us back to the turn of the century—a time when, as Dewey notes in many of his works, the notion of the public school took on new dimensions.

Though public schools in the United States gradually increased in numbers throughout the 19th century, they subsequently exploded across our country— particularly in our cities—as a result of the massive wave of immigrants that came to live in this land. Thousands of people came to toil in our factories and in the coal mines that produced the energy needed to run a newly electrified society. With these immigrants came their children, and therein was the dilemma. For several years, the prevailing thought was to put these "little beggars" to work alongside their parents; eventually, the cruelty of that existence led to legal prohibitions against that practice. Schools became the solution to the question of what to do with these children, more of whom were coming onto our shores and being born each day.

Teaching Children to Be Good Workers

As schools were built rapidly to keep up with the population explosion taking place in our cities, a debate about the function of these schools began to emerge. Until recently, the debate continued and, at times, thrived in our society. On one side of the issue were those who argued that schools should teach children what they would need to know to be good workers (Bobbitt, 1918; Charters, 1909; Cubberley, 1916). After all, the reason we let these children into our country was because we needed the labor of their parents. It only seemed reasonable that schools should educate these children enough so that they could be even more productive workers than their parents.

Many schools were built with the expectation that the taxpayers' investment would yield a positive return—that is, a more productive workforce. Accordingly, many believed that it was important to teach these children how to speak English;

to read, write, and compute math problems; and to follow directions. In addition, there was a call to inform these "dullards," as they were sometimes called (Thorndike, 1940), what it means to be an American. Often called *civics*, this course of study was designed to minimize the value of their traditional ethnic heritages and to teach these children the innate superiority of our (predominantly masculine, Northern Euro-American) cultural traditions, values, and most importantly governmental and economic institutions. The argument was to drill children until this information and these skills were thoroughly internalized. Sound familiar?

Helping Children Live in a Democracy

On the other side of this debate stood those such as John Dewey (1916/1980) and Boyd Bode (1927), who warn of the dangers embedded in this narrow educational vision. These individuals argue that public schools should be established to help the children of immigrants learn what it means to live in a democracy. Because most immigrants came from societies that were more or less totalitarian and these people often were used to living relatively powerless lives (as victims of economic, social, and ethnic oppression), Dewey argues that we needed schools that could teach children how to thoughtfully participate in not just living in but also developing a more democratic society.

As the quote at the beginning of this essay stated, Dewey does not want young people to take the democracy that was currently being practiced in our society for granted. To the contrary, he sees room for significant improvements, and he suggests that a truly democratic society never assumes that its democracy is complete. Dewey argues that our schools should help to create a society based not only on a political democracy but also a social democracy. Democracy should be thought of as a way of life rather than just the participation of a minority of citizens in a ritual of voting every couple of years.

Ideological Surgery on Our Schools

Throughout the past century, the ideas of Dewey and his colleagues often were overshadowed by those who saw schools as sites for vocational training. However, within the past 2 decades, this marketplace rationale has so completely dominated the public discourse that the notion of schooling for democracy has vanished from public consideration. Both Democrats and Republicans seem to disagree only on minor details of educational reform, with the Bush administration taking this utilitarian orientation toward schooling to new heights.

Unfortunately, many of the most talented teachers and those students who are not academically oriented are being pushed out of our schools (physically or intellectually) at ever increasing rates in Bush's quest to leave no child behind (Aleman et al., 2003; Allington et al., 2003; Black, Goertz, Koretz, & Masters, 2003; DeBray, Horn, Kim, & Sunderman, 2003; Seashore, 2003). The fundamental purpose for schools seems to be taken for granted, regardless of one's political and social values. Americans have been willing to stand by, as if in a trance, while those in power conduct ideological surgery on our schools—cutting them away from any consideration of the relationship between democracy and education and graphing them onto corporate and military interests (Berliner & Biddle, 1995).

Perhaps this surgery has occurred because we have heard so much about the difficulties of economic globalism. However, if educational reform continues to move in its current direction, it is our democracy, not our economy, that will be in peril. One does not have to be a sociologist to recognize that our brand of democracy requires little participation or thoughtfulness on the part of the average individual, and yet the level of even this limited participation is dangerously low. Our national leaders get elected to office in much the same way that soap finds its way into our homes—through slick advertising. We live in an age of sound-bite politics. Instead of engaging in discourses about substantive issues, the focus often degenerates into little more than name-calling. Finding out whether someone has slept with someone other than his or her spouse takes on greater significance than that person's visions and ideas for the country and the world in which we live.

The quality of the political discussions among our population is worrisome to anyone who treasures democratic values. Though many people blame the politicians or the press for this sorry state of affairs, we—the people of this country—must take ultimate responsibility. Slick advertising, mudslinging, and sound bites all work because, as a nation of citizens, we allow ourselves to be swayed by these substitutes for substantive dialogue. Censorship, racial fears and hatred, poverty, and homelessness are increasing, while values of opportunity for average citizens, authentic compassion, and tolerance for diversity seem to be fading away in many sectors of our society.

The efforts to reform schools in the context of a marketplace rationale have resulted in many new proposals, such as limiting our notion of education to scores students receive on a single, standardized test; legislating that all students must pass this test to graduate; requiring schools to improve the scores on this test annually; the emphasis on phonics, math, and other technical knowledge over more substantive study in the social sciences and humanities; creating student voucher systems; and, most recently, initiating a national curriculum. At the same time, we continue to see children alienated from their studies and teachers who are burned out by all the paperwork required to ensure that Johnny has memorized his daily lessons. All these proposals come at the same time that funding for our schools is being cut and is even more inequitable than when Kozol (1992) called the lopsided funding of our children's education "savage."

What might school reform proposals comprise if the goal was not tied merely to helping children get jobs or to successfully outcompeting other cultures but rather to making our country a more democratic society in the manner discussed by Dewey? How might schools be funded? What might schools look like if instead of merely trying to raise children's test scores on a single, standardized test that is often given in an atmosphere of anxiety and fear, schools were dedicated to creating educational experiences that would help students become thoughtful, caring, and active participants in the creation of a more democratic culture? What curriculum might be developed if our goal was to help all children discover their talents, forms of intelligences, and powers of imagination in an effort to make their lives more meaningful? Obviously, the answers to these questions would generate far different visions, ideas, and policy proposals than those being touted by our current government officials.

I am not suggesting that schools should not prepare children for the workplace. After all, every culture has an obligation to educate its young people to participate in the economic activity of the times. However, as Dewey believes, if we are successful in preparing children to thoughtfully take part in improving our democracy, then there would be little need to worry about them acquiring the skills necessary to live in our ever-changing economy. Nor am I suggesting that schooling for democracy would take on one particular form. Dewey does not offer a blueprint. Rather, he simply suggests that if we, as a nation, would begin to discuss the type of education needed to live in a dynamic and socially just democracy, then we would find more viable solutions to the problems that our schools and our society face. Who knows? Perhaps we would once again begin to discuss, as the founders of our nation did long ago, what living in a democracy means.

References

Aleman, E., Alexander, C., Fuller, E., Gamoran, A., Hunault, J., Maxcy, B., ... Yang, S. (2003, April). *Accountability and the politics of education reform.* Paper presented at the Annual Meeting of the American Educational Research Association, Chicago, IL.

Allington, R., Chambliss, M., Croninger, R., Graeber, A., Larson, J., Price, J., & Valli, L. (2003, April). *High-stakes accountability and high-quality teaching: Reconcilable or irreconcilable differences?* Paper presented at the Annual Meeting of the American Educational Research Association, Chicago, IL.

Berliner, D. C., & Biddle, B. J. (1995). *The manufactured crisis: Myths, fraud, and the attack on America's public schools.* Reading, MA: Addison-Wesley.

Black, P., Goertz, M., Koretz, D., & Masters, G. (2003, April). *Effects of accountability on learning.* Paper presented at the Annual Meeting of the American Educational Research Association, Chicago, IL.

Bobbitt, F. (1918). *The curriculum.* Boston, MA: Houghton Mifflin.

Bode, B. H. (1927). *Modern educational theories.* New York, NY: Macmillan.

Charters, W. W. (1909). *Methods of teaching: Developed from a functional standpoint.* Chicago, IL: Row, Peterson, & Co.

Cubberley, E. P. (1916). *Public school administration.* Boston, MA: Houghton Mifflin.

DeBray, E., Horn, C., Kim, J., & Sunderman, G. (2003, April). *The No Child Left Behind education act and its effects on poor and minority students: Findings from the first phase of state-level implementation.* Paper presented at the Annual Meeting of the American Educational Research Association, Chicago, IL.

Dewey, J. (1980). Democracy and education. In J. A. Boydston (Ed.), *John Dewey: The middle works, 1899–1924: Vol. 9. 1916* (pp. 1–370). Carbondale: Southern Illinois University Press. (Original work published 1916)

Dewey, J. (1987). Education and social change. In J. A. Boydston (Ed.), *John Dewey: The later works, 1925–1953: Vol. 11. 1935–1937* (pp. 408–418). Carbondale: Southern Illinois University Press. (Original work published 1937)

Kozol, J. (1992). *Savage inequalities: Children in America's schools.* New York, NY: Harper Perennial.

Seashore, K. (2003, April). *Accountability in educational reform: Tensions and dilemmas.* Paper presented at the Annual Meeting of the American Educational Research Association, Chicago, IL.

Thorndike, E. L. (1940). *Human nature and the social order.* New York, NY: Macmillan.

40

FOUNDATIONS OF DEWEYAN DEMOCRACY

Human Nature, Intelligence, and Cooperative Inquiry

Stephen M. Fishman

> *The foundation of democracy is faith in the capacities of human nature; faith in human intelligence and in the power of pooled and cooperative experience.*
> —*Democracy and Educational Administration*, Later Works 11: 219

For reform-minded teachers like myself, no concept of Dewey's is more important than his concept of democracy. I say this because we live in dark times. Increasing globalization; the widening gap between rich and poor; and the escalation of racial, religious, and ethnic hatreds make it difficult to believe that our individual efforts can yield a more humane and equitable future. Loss of hopefulness about the future is especially hard on reform-minded teachers because the vitality of our classroom practice depends on faith that we and our students can preserve and improve on what is best in our culture.

This is why Dewey's vision of democracy—and his conviction that it is a realistic ideal—is so important at the present time. Dewey's democratic vision balances individual rights and collective responsibilities, seeing every person as entitled to maximum personal growth as long as such growth contributes to respectful, cooperative work with others. Dewey's conviction that his ideal is practicable can help reform-minded teachers regain the hope they need to reinvigorate their classroom work.

Human Nature

On what does Dewey base his optimism that his concept of democracy presents a practicable ideal? In the quote from his 1937 article that is the focus of my short essay, Dewey (1937/1987) tells us that "faith in the capacities of human nature" is one of the foundations of his concept of democracy. What does he mean? Dewey believes that the "capacities of human nature" may be developed or expressed in manifold ways. That is, human dispositions do not have static or fixed ways of expressing themselves. This approach allows Dewey to take an optimistic, evolutionary view of human potential, of our powers of imagination and experimentation to develop more caring and equitable forms of association in the future. In other words, we can redesign ourselves.

For example, whether we express our capacity for combativeness by destroying one another or by trying to solve collective problems depends, according to Dewey, on the channels encouraged by our social customs. According to Dewey, these customs can be altered through intelligent, collective action. Viewing our native capacities in this way allows Dewey to counter those social theorists who were pessimistic about the possibilities of extending democracy, who argued that our combative, self-centered disposition inevitably must lead to oppressive and undemocratic human associations.

At the opening of the 21st century, I believe that Dewey's view is vital for teachers who want to rekindle their hopes for social reform. It can help us find the language and conviction to resist the naysayers who argue that there is nothing anyone can do—not even classroom teachers—to more fully democratize our society.

Intelligence

Dewey's belief that his democratic vision could be realized is based not only on his faith in human nature. It is also based, as he tells us in this same 1937 article, on his faith "in human intelligence and in the power of pooled and cooperative experience." This latter confidence rests, in large part, on Dewey's positive view of modern science. As Dewey understands it, the success of the scientific enterprise is the result of shared inquiry and full exchange of information. Modern science exemplifies the social nature of intelligence, the way individual, creative development goes hand-in-hand with participation in shared, collaborative work.

The personal fulfillment and group cooperation that characterize work in the scientific community give Dewey (and us) a glimpse of the type of relations—the "mode of associated living" (Dewey 1916/1980, p. 94)—that he sees at the core of democracy, the type of relations that he believes can be practiced by the U.S. community at large.

Cooperative Inquiry

Standing in the way of the full development of more cooperative and democratic societies, according to Dewey, are two factors. The first is the continued use of force and intimidation to resolve our differences rather than the use of intelligent discussion and mutually shaped activity. Dewey wants us to alter our socially accepted custom of expressing our combativeness by oppressing others and, instead, develop a new custom, one that uses human combativeness for collective good.

The second impediment to a more democratic society is the continued belief that personal happiness lies in the acquisition of material wealth rather than in personal growth generated in cooperation with others. Our belief that our first human need is to compete for material goods conflicts with what Dewey sees as the core value of democracy. For him, the ultimate justification for democracy is the better quality of life that it affords its citizens. For Dewey, democracy provides more opportunities for meaningful experience—more opportunities to be creative and find one's calling—than any other form of associated living.

Vision of Democracy

At first glance, Dewey's democratic vision may seem unrealistically utopian for contemporary classroom teachers because our world has become more focused on competition than cooperation, on material acquisition than creative expression. However, I believe that we can use Dewey's vision—as well as his faith in human nature, intelligence, and cooperative experience—to go against the current, dominant U.S. grain, to go against the idea that democracy is about competing for material goods rather than about developing fulfilling, shared experiences.

In particular, I believe that we can use Dewey's faith to rekindle our hopes as teachers that our classrooms can be effective places to plant and nourish seeds of a less competitive and more cooperative ethos. As we encourage students to find their calling, as we develop pedagogies that enable students to practice shared, reflective inquiry, we build upon Dewey's faith in human nature and intelligence. We also keep alive his vision of democracy by contributing, in significant ways, to America's ongoing discussion of its own best future.

References

Dewey, J. (1980). Democracy and education. In J. A. Boydston (Ed.), *John Dewey: The middle works, 1899–1924: Vol. 9. 1916* (pp. 1–370). Carbondale: Southern Illinois University Press. (Original work published 1916)

Dewey, J. (1987). Democracy and educational administration. In J. A. Boydston (Ed.), *John Dewey: The later works, 1925–1953: Vol. 11. 1935–1937* (pp. 217–225). Carbondale: Southern Illinois University Press. (Original work published 1937)

41

WHY WE FORGET

Liberty, Memories, and Seeking Simple Answers

David M. Callejo-Pérez

> *Is love of liberty anything more than a desire to be liberated from some special restriction? And when it is got rid of does the desire for liberty die down until something else feels intolerable again?*
>
> —*Freedom and Culture*, Later Works 13: 65

It is in the deeds of the past that a record of the future is created (Hobsbawm, 2002). In this sense, historians must assume the responsibility of discerning the "facts" as well as the burden of rereading, reunderstanding, and rewriting history (Woodward, 1993) with an eye toward finding meaning in what we do and have done. However, this task comes with a caveat: There is uneasiness in the process through which knowledge—the past—is transmitted to future generations and influences our conceptions of what matters. For example, after the tragic events of September 11, 2001, in New York City, how have our notions of liberty been redefined to balance with our need for security? Or how have parents reframed their children's notions of freedom of space after the events at Columbine High School or Sandy Hook Elementary School? Or after the sad episode at Virginia Tech, how have college campuses reconceived a student's freedoms?

Embedded in *Freedom and Culture* (1939/1988) is Dewey's concept of liberty—a defense of democracy—which is a unique perspective rooted in the ideals of *American* liberty. In Dewey's concept, American liberty is simply defined during the American Revolution as limits of personal and property rights and romanticized by memories of the freedom and democracy that coexisted in the early 20th-century United States. This notion of liberty was without the context and complexity of the current political and economic marketplaces.

For example, during World War I, a massive British propaganda operation, known as the "Rape of Belgium," portrayed the German army as defiling "innocent Belgians" and helped influence the United States to enter the war on its side (Taylor, 1954). Moreover, the loans by J. P. Morgan of $12 million to Russia, $50 million to France, and $500 million to the Allies, along with Bethlehem Steel's development and trading of steel to England, frustrated the ability of the United States to remain neutral (Dayer, 1976; Horn, 2000). So when British Intelligence discovered a telegram in January 1917 from German Foreign Secretary Arthur Zimmermann to German Ambassador to Mexico Heinrich von Eckardt urging him to try to get Mexico to fight against the United States alongside Germany, the U.S. decision was all but sealed. The resulting anti-German sentiment and financial relationships invigorated Americans with the hope of improving security and the ability to protect our liberty.

Like the historical analysis that complicates our memory of how we entered World War I, these powerful decisions serve to sacrifice liberty and community in the name of security and safety. As Dewey writes in *Freedom and Culture* (1939/1988), do we want freedom because it is "inherent in human nature" or because it is a "product of special circumstances" (p. 65)? Are we victims of our constantly shifting historicity, continually driven to respond to those shifts ahistorically? Was 9/11 really comparable to the Oklahoma City bombing or to Pearl Harbor?

Oppression of freedom is more likely to occur if we cease to find meaning in the past and act solely on the basis of our present. In a sense, Dewey seeks to explain why and how our nation perceives history in what we do and how we do it. Do we react to this history by searching for liberation and yet continuously oppress our freedoms? Dewey (1939/1988) writes,

> We cannot continue the idea that human nature when left to itself, when freed from external arbitrary restrictions, will tend to the production of democratic institutions that work successfully. . . . We have to see that democracy means the belief that humanistic culture should prevail; we should be frank and open in our recognition that the proposition is a moral one—like any idea that concerns what should be. (p. 151)

Dewey (1934/1987) illustrates that "an experience of thinking has its own esthetic quality" (p. 45). As a historian writing about a historical moment—the Civil Rights Movement in Holly Springs, Mississippi (Callejo-Pérez, 2001), I understood how historians fail. Our own history, education, and beliefs create in us an *overdetermination* to provide an explanation acceptable to the field we specialize in rather than to stay true to the *objectivity* in the method of discovery.

Nicholas Onuf (1989) believed that the problem with the disciplines is the assumption that there are not multiple views but one view guided by objectivity—minus those rich moments that drift through hazy pasts and those concurrent with when the historians choose to write. For example, the murder–suicide committed by Jovan Belcher of the Kansas City Chiefs led columnist Jason Whitlock (2012) to write about how numb we are to gun violence and murder. We accept our insanity, he suggested, rather than "reflecting upon the absurdity of the prevailing notion that the second amendment somehow enhances our liberty rather than threatens it." He continued, arguing, "how many lives have to be ruined before we realize the right to bear arms doesn't protect us from a government equipped with stealth bombers, predator drones, tanks and nuclear weapons?"

This complex notion of the Second Amendment of the U.S. Constitution is one of the many arguments that seem so removed from the initial notions of liberty as conceived by the founders of the United States. Likewise distant from the initial notions of liberty are the origins of World War I, recent events that have brought the United States into the fold of world terrorism, and the senseless violence citizens experience daily.

Knowledge (cultural capital, in particular, such as religious practices, economics, and politics) has constituted—always—one of the pillars of the culture in which society evolves. Sometimes interpreted as causes and other times as effects of cultural and economic development, the transmission of knowledge occupies thousands of pages of texts. Educational contexts similarly are a product of such creations—as validated by the numerous studies dedicated to those who transmit and those who receive that cultural capital.

For those of us involved in the arduous educational enterprise, Dewey provides an intrinsic and rich intellectual path that is symbolic because in its inspiration rests an angst that is motivated by both our stunted memory—with a forward-moving optimism—and the omnipotent hegemony of technology to solve all tribulations—and our desire to do so. However, it is in these times we need to be less distant from our history and reremember the past—and more precisely the origins of our ideas, practices, and desires. In this case we remember not only the greatest, but also the worst—both the pain and excitement of the past that has created the path we travel today.

References

Callejo-Pérez, D. M. (2001). *Southern hospitality: Identity, schools, and the civil rights movement in Mississippi, 1964–1972*. New York, NY: Peter Lang.

Dayer, R. A. (1976). Strange bedfellows: J. P. Morgan & Co., Whitehall and the Wilson administration during World War I. *Business History, 18,* 127–151.

Dewey, J. (1987). Art as experience. In J. A. Boydston (Ed.), *John Dewey: The later works, 1925–1953: Vol. 10. 1934* (pp. 1–352). Carbondale: Southern Illinois University Press. (Original work published 1934)

Dewey, J. (1988). Freedom and culture. In J. A. Boydston (Ed.), *John Dewey: The later works, 1925–1953: Vol. 13. 1938–1939* (pp. 63–252). Carbondale: Southern Illinois University Press. (Original work published 1939)

Hobsbawm, E. (2002). *Interesting times: A twentieth-century life.* London, England: Allen Lane.

Horn, M. (2000). A private bank at war: J. P. Morgan & Co. and France, 1914–1918. *Business History Review, 74,* 85–112.

Onuf, N. G. (1989). *World of our making.* Columbia: University of South Carolina Press.

Taylor, A. J. P. (1954). *The struggle for mastery in Europe, 1848–1918.* London, England: Oxford University Press.

Whitlock, J. (2012, December 1). In KC, it's no time for a game. *Fox Sports News.* Retrieved from http://msn.foxsports.com/nfl/story/jovan-belcher-kansas-city-chiefs-murder-suicide-tragedy-girlfriend-self-leave-orphan-daughter-why-still-playing-sunday-120112

Woodward, C. V. (1993). *The burden of Southern history.* Baton Rouge: Louisiana State University Press.

PART V

The Educative Experience

AN EDUCATIVE EXPERIENCE? A LESSON IN HUMILITY FOR A SECOND-GRADE TEACHER

Donna Adair Breault

What am I going to do today? The question in my head kept getting louder as I approached the school building that morning. It was the next to last day of school. All papers and books had gone out the door with students the previous day, along with the plans I originally made for our time. To find something to keep them occupied and me sane for the next 2 days was a looming challenge. As I paused at a stoplight, it hit me! I pulled into a convenience store, picked up a pile of real estate magazines, and continued on my way to school, somewhat relieved.

"Class, we are going to spend the next 2 days building a city," I announced to my second graders. We spent the first part of the morning discussing what constitutes a city—subdivisions, stores, schools, churches, and so on—and then divided into teams to plan how we would proceed. Well before lunch, all the desks were pushed out of the way, and green, white, and gray bulletin board paper was unfurled across the classroom floor.

I won't say that the 2-day activity was carried out in perfect pedagogical form. There were mistakes—largely because of poor planning. Discussions about the location of major roads, noise pollution from retail areas and its effects on nearby houses, and challenges regarding traffic around business areas came a bit too late to change some of the designs already carved out in magic marker. In the end, the city plan would not have won any great awards, but the primary goals—keeping students occupied and the teacher sane—had been achieved. As students said their final goodbyes and left for the summer break, I felt relieved and frankly a bit cocky about the events that had unfolded over those final 2 days.

Culminating Experiences

Years later, as a teacher educator always in search of anecdotes, I would recall the experience as my students read Dewey's *The School and Society* (1899/1976) and

The Child and the Curriculum (1902/1976), and we would discuss "educative experiences." I believed that the activity was educative because students were actively engaged in cooperative learning and the curriculum was integrated, to a degree. I even would go so far as to say that some learning was going on—as much as I would have expected at the time given that it was the last 2 days of school.

And then I saw it! I ran across a book written by Ida DePencier (1967)—a former teacher from Dewey's lab school. As I was browsing through the book, one picture in particular caught my eye. It was a group of young students, possibly kindergarteners or first graders, busy on the floor of their classroom building a city. My first response was, "Look, they are doing the same activity my students did." It didn't take long for me to realize how wrong I was. The caption under the picture noted: "A primary class builds a city. In addition to ideas in social studies, reading and mathematics played a large part of this activity. Ideas about zoning and city growth patterns became obvious" (DePencier, 1967, p. 151). The more I discovered about Dewey's lab school, the more I realized that activities in that setting did far more than merely keep students occupied. They were culminating experiences through which students actively applied what they had learned in meaningful ways.

With this realization, images of what I could have done those last 2 days besieged me. In what ways could we have reviewed elements of geometry—including area, and parallel and perpendicular lines—as we planned our subdivisions? Rather than just letting students have free reign to draw squiggly lines across the page to represent subdivision roads and paste homes wherever they would fit, we could have discussed electrical, water, and sewage line issues and deliberately planned the location of streets and placement of houses. Had I thought to introduce the idea of zoning, I would have offered students a tremendous opportunity to debate the percentage of area within the city they would allot for commercial development. They would have been able to consider the issues surrounding the location of business areas, the number of businesses to allow, and the opportunities for employment.

We also could have explored issues of community, outlined by such social theorists as James Howard Kunstler (1996), who described the loss of connections with one another that people sense as a result of the current design of homes, subdivisions, and suburban sprawl. Although those ideas may seem to be a bit of a stretch for second graders, students easily could explore the implications of homes being built without porches or what it means when neighbors cannot walk to places such as local stores. Any of these possible avenues would have made my 2-day activity a more educative experience.

Toward Growth in Understanding

I continue to share this lesson as an anecdote in my classes, only now I share it for very different reasons. I offer it as an example of why teachers always should consider this important question: "How can I make my lesson *even more educative?*" Although some lessons are, unfortunately, *mis-educative,* it is safe to assume that most of the lessons a thoughtful teacher will generate are at least *mildly,* if not *moderately educative.* Students will learn something. The challenge, however, always should be to strive to make those lessons *even more educative.*

Dewey offers some valuable advice on how to do this. According to Dewey, an educative experience leading to growth is, foremost, based on the students' prior knowledge and experience. As teachers, we need to honor students' experiences without reducing the complexity of those experiences. In addition, we need to use prior knowledge and experience as sources of working power toward growth in understanding. As Dewey (1916/1980) notes, "We have laid it down that the educative process is a continuous process of growth, having as its aim at every stage an added capacity for growth" (p. 60). Further, the movement toward growth in understanding needs to be real—not contrived or driven by external, superficial reasons. "You need to know this for a test," for example, is not a legitimate justification for a truly educative experience. Whenever we separate the content of our lessons from students' experiences, impose routine for the sake of mere drill, or neglect to draw motivation from outside students' lives, we deny the educative potential of learning.

With these and other images in mind, I often ask my graduate students to develop rubrics for educative experiences that delineate *highly educative, moderately educative, minimally educative,* and *mis-educative* qualities of experience. My students often keep these rubrics in the front of their lesson plan books and refer to them frequently as they reflect on their lessons. I would encourage each of you to do the same. After reading the entries related to educative experiences, try to formulate your own rubric as a tool for reflection and professional growth. With such a tool, you can confidently ask yourself, "How can I make my lessons *even more educative?*"

References

DePencier, I. B. (1967). *The history of the laboratory schools: The University of Chicago 1896–1965.* Chicago, IL: Quadrangle Books.

Dewey, J. (1976). The school and society. In J. A. Boydston (Ed.), *John Dewey: The middle works, 1899–1924: Vol. 1. 1899–1901* (pp. 5–112). Carbondale: Southern Illinois University Press. (Original work published 1899)

Dewey, J. (1976). The child and the curriculum. In J. A. Boydston (Ed.), *John Dewey: The middle works, 1899–1924: Vol. 2. 1902–1903* (pp. 271–292). Carbondale: Southern Illinois University Press. (Original work published 1902)

Dewey, J. (1980). Democracy and education. In J. A. Boydston (Ed.), *John Dewey: The middle works, 1899–1924: Vol. 9. 1916* (pp. 1–370). Carbondale: Southern Illinois University Press. (Original work published 1916)

Kunstler, J. H. (1996). *Home from nowhere: Remaking our everyday world for the twenty-first century.* New York, NY: Simon & Schuster.

42

AESTHETICS OF HUMAN UNDERSTANDING

Margaret Macintyre Latta

> *Tangled scenes of life are made more intelligible in esthetic experience; not, however, as reflection and science render things more intelligible by reduction to conceptual form, but by presenting their meanings as the matter of a clarified, coherent, and intensified or "impassioned" experience.*
>
> —*Art as Experience,* Later Works 10: 295

Dewey's *Art as Experience* (1934/1987) is American Pragmatism's seminal text on the aesthetics of human understanding. Transcending art objects, Dewey's aesthetics conceive the significance and integrity of all human experience through creating meaning with others and concomitantly creating enlarged understandings of the self. Negotiating the aesthetic as this fundamental human encounter between self (subject) and other (world) is at the core of all meaning making for Dewey. Thus, aesthetic experience is a search, attending to given relations of all kinds through constant mediation and participation. Dewey turns to the arts to concretely exemplify such experiential terrain, with meanings "embodied in a material which thereby becomes the medium for their expression" (p. 277). It seems fitting, then, to turn to a particular artwork in search of what Dewey sees as the "formed matter of esthetic experience" (p. 277), offering the sustenance that intensifies meaning making across disciplines and interests of all kinds. While engaged in this search, consider the interdependency with the nature of curriculum alongside considering the potential that aesthetic experience holds for its enactment within classrooms (Macintyre Latta, 2013).

Concrete Practice with the Aesthetics of Human Understanding

The Floodwall is a multidimensional website documenting an art project created by Jana Napoli with graphic artist Rondell Crier (see http://www.floodwall. org), revealing the many experiential tales and entanglements formed and generated by Hurricane Katrina in 2005. Napoli relayed her experience of returning to her home in New Orleans, Louisiana, following the devastating floodwaters of the hurricane as an engulfing silence (Napoli, 2013). From a safe distance, the multimedia news reports and imagery had kept the realities at bay. But the devastation's weight and immediacy overwhelmingly surrounded and deeply troubled her return. Napoli waded into the silence as she wandered through the "tangled scenes" of her community, instinctively seeking ways to "render" meanings. Dresser drawers of every sort and description marked her wanderings, and these found drawers became the "matter" shaping the flood-wall installation and associated website. Crier explained that when Napoli told him about collecting these strewn dresser drawers, it resonated, instinctively knowing why this act held such significance. He articulated how the "depth of life" within items themselves "could explain the magnitude and meaning of loss through objects, forcing others to connect on a direct personal level" (Crier, 2013).

The nature and shape of Napoli and Crier's meaning making became the "matter" of the Floodwall Project, a multidimensional artistic installation. Napoli arranged the retrieved dresser drawers as building bricks that some-times form a wall measuring 8 feet tall and 192 feet in length and at other times fall in disarray across the floor or can be configured into a room. Crier devel-oped an associated interactive database, documenting as much information as could be ascertained through numbering, cataloguing, and photographing each drawer. Audio and video components include a growing collection of oral histories from the original drawer owners. So, the Floodwall website brings all interested nearer to the experiences and lived consequences of Hurricane Katrina through revealing what the silence held for Napoli and Crier and what it prompts in others.

As a whole, the Floodwall Project is a work of art brought into existence by Napoli and Crier to clarify, cohere, and make sense of an "intensified" or "impassioned" experience. Attending to the movement of Napoli and Crier's sense-making calls attention to process—the aesthetics of human understanding. The website invites all who are interested to engage likewise. Such engagement is akin to how Dewey (1934/1987) characterizes aesthetic experience, seeing signif-icances for inquiries of all kinds embedded within attention to the movement of the experiential whole, creating meaning and concomitantly creating self. Dewey claims that to gain access to these significances, personal involvement is necessary. Seeking attunement within process insists on bringing one's perspectives to bear. Such a search entails adapting, changing, integrating, synthesizing and internal-izing understandings of situations in relation to self and others. The Floodwall website at http://www.floodwall.org evidences Napoli and Crier's experience as such. Concomitantly, the Floodwall website fosters aesthetic experience in others through its open invitation to enter the website and put oneself in relation to the "tangled scenes," inciting multiple movements of thinking that clarify, cohere, and make sense, revealing varied tales and interpretations.

Gaining Comprehensibility Through Aesthetic Experience

Curricular enactment in classrooms often isolates self-understandings, subject matter, and inquiry from each other. With little room for interaction and deliberation, curricular enactment as a movement of thinking in self and others is thwarted. The multiplicities and potentialities of curricular enactment as aesthetic experience are masked. After all, it is the entanglements of self with subject matter and inquiry that are a catalyst for seeing, feeling, and acting, that furthers the movement of thinking in self and others. This is why Dewey (1934/1987) goes on to emphasize that aesthetic experience is a parts-to-whole movement "that is what it is because of the entire pattern to which it contributes and which it is absorbed" (p. 295). In doing so, Dewey points out that parts cannot be scrutinized away from each other. All parts interrelate and contribute to the moving experiential whole.

Tracing the parts-to-whole creation of the Floodwall Project via the website, the individual and collective discord is firstly expressed and experienced, but individual and collective reflection is also induced again and again. Hurricane Katrina becomes more comprehensible, "more intelligible," as enlarged perspectives are gained and deepened through individual/collective involvement. Dewey (1934/1987) terms such intelligibility "mind and body" (p. 267), reflecting his persistent argument against dualistic thinking of all kinds that separates the mind from the body, the head from the hand, and the emotion from intellect. That is why Dewey turns to the arts as exemplary forms that embrace mind–body. He explains,

> In art as an experience, actuality and possibility . . . the new and the old, objective material and personal response, the individual and the universal, surface and depth, are all transfigured from the significance that belongs to them when isolated in reflection. (p. 301)

Such an argument for reciprocity and connections embeds meaning making within aesthetic experience. Dewey (1934/1987) explains that aesthetic experience turns away from external organization, toward "ordering of a growing experience, one that involves moreover, the whole of the live creature, toward a fulfilling conclusion" (p. 87). It is the entanglements found within a growing experience that punctuate and characterize the moving experience, offering what Dewey terms moments of "consummation" that move into new moments (p. 23). He reveals how "art celebrates with peculiar intensity the moments in which the past reinforces the present and in which the future is a quickening of what now is" (p. 24). This intensity holds the vitality awakened in self and others.

Thus, Dewey envisions a deep kinship worth cultivating between aesthetic experience, curricular enactment, and what it means to be alive, instilling such intensity. A depth of expression is rendered that seems very fitting for the unfolding processes of self-formation, always in relation to others, that an education ought to entail.

References

Crier, R. (2013). *Artist statement.* Retrieved from http://www.floodwall.org/artist_state-ment_crier.html

Dewey, J. (1987). Art as experience. In J. A. Boydston (Ed.), *John Dewey: The later works, 1925–1953: Vol. 10. 1934* (pp. 1–352). Carbondale: Southern Illinois University Press. (Original work published 1934)

Macintyre Latta, M. (2013). *Curricular conversations: Play is the (missing) thing.* New York, NY: Routledge.

Napoli, J. (2013). Artist statement [web content]. Retrieved from www.floodwall.org/artist _statement_napoli.html

43

GROWTH

The Consummate Open-Ended Aspiration

Paul Shaker

> *We have laid it down that the educative process is a continuous process of growth, having as its aim at every stage an added capacity of growth.*
> —*Democracy and Education,* Middle Works 9: 54

Our greatest sages leave us not only with a legacy of clarity and insight, but also with enigma. As their reflections on life reach the limits of expression, we often are left with claims that transcend language and logic. Such ideas may appear mystical, repetitive, or vague. They are attempts to stretch current language and concepts to offer an understanding of the emerging world. Though such writing may attract the ridicule of contemporaries, it carries quite a different meaning to those who come later. These concepts may become the authors' principal legacy and the reason for their lasting recognition. "Every event in the visible world is the effect of an 'image,' " states the *I Ching* (Wilhelm, 1967, p. vii). Those whose writing reaches across time seek to design those images.

From ancient times, Plato's theory of forms can be seen in this light, foreshadowing Gestalt and certain other schools of psychology that have a structural bent. Two millennia after they were spoken, the Beatitudes of the Sermon on the Mount enunciate spiritual values and a way of life that remain beyond the grasp of all but a few Christians. Buddha's Four Noble Truths also fit this description of a life practice few can adopt or explain but that constellates an ideal. In the 19th century, the Romantic poets and Walt Whitman described sublime states and heightened consciousness. In the 20th century, C. G. Jung coined terms such as *archetype* and *synchronicity* in an attempt to bring science to the mysteries of the human mind. At the same time, John Dewey extends the traditions of the Transcendentalists and American Pragmatists by putting forward his concept of "growth."

Growth as a Metaphor

In its many formulations, Dewey's statements about "growth" typically are marked by their circularity. Growth is described as the aim of life and defined as a continuous process. Truly educative experience is that which leads to further education and growing. Education has as its aim an added capacity for growth. Though the concept of growth is pivotal to Dewey, he nonetheless repeatedly portrays it in puzzling ways. Stylistically, this is not the Dewey to which we are accustomed. Typically, he is a paragon of logic and conventional scientific thought, a consummate rationalist. In the treatment of growth, his central metaphor, he steps out of character with statements that resemble Zen koans more than they do syllogisms. Perhaps in this instance, Dewey seeks to touch something that lies beyond the reach of his normal philosopher's tools.

On one level, Dewey alerts us to the significance of change by employing a familiar natural metaphor to redirect thinking on education toward process rather than product. Dewey subverts traditional thinking about education and its emphasis on "acquiring knowledge" by presenting a central aim that is contentless, open-ended, ineffable, and emerging. Today's lesson can be evaluated only in terms of what happens to the student tomorrow, not what the student "knows" today. A course of study, degree, or program has value in terms of whether graduates go forward into life, striving for further development as a result of their education.

And on those tomorrows, when we look back and try to determine through our current achievements whether the education we have received has been of merit, our answer will be determined by yet another tomorrow's achievements. The process has no end, not even death, because our influence can survive us, as has Dewey's. All our evaluation is formative, not summative. Even the best ideas often become obsolete and a burden on future society, because they are valued for their past effects rather than their current impact. The cost of stasis gives emphasis to the need for a constructive attitude toward change and growth.

The old order changeth, yielding place to new,
And God fulfills himself in many ways,
Lest one good custom should corrupt the world.
            —Alfred Tennyson (1863/2007, line 408)

Accommodating Chance

Through his concept of growth, Dewey also equips us with a way to accommodate chance. Though in our Western tradition we construct elaborate plans that are in turn executed by the application of technology and the exercise of will, we are not impervious to the results of chance. An act of nature, an airplane crash, or a virus can appear without warning and topple our well-laid plans. If the world is a fully predictable place, decoded by cause and effect, we have not yet fully found a way to break that code. Jung offered the maligned or ignored concept of synchronicity as an explanation. In the absence of such explanations, much of what we experience still has the air of chance, coincidence, or even chaos. Dewey's formulation of growth does not demystify chance. Instead, it provides a method of coping with phenomena that are beyond our ability to control or predict. Dewey's "growth" gives us a means of responding to the unforeseen. This guiding principle allows us to encounter the great reversals of life and emerge with our psyches, if not our families or fortune, intact. The great stories of survival and triumph against adversity, as depicted in fiction, are applications of Dewey's concept of growth.

> Everything, even life, is eventually taken away from you. You cannot feel, cannot touch its expression. You can only reach its reflection. If you try to grasp happiness itself your fingers only meet a surface of glass, because happiness has no existence of its own. (Sirk, 1959)

Transformation

Dewey's idea of growth is, however, more than a way of rationalizing fate and coping with the unforeseen. Ultimately, by his formulation, he not only opens the possibility of, but also puts an emphasis on, transformation. "Growth" in this sense is the consummate open-ended aspiration. No static state of perfection, bliss, competence, or control is postulated as a goal. Rather, Dewey invites those who would be educated to join in a noncyclic, unending process of living. Implicit in this address to life is perseverance because, by definition, the process is ongoing and ends for the individual only with the end of consciousness.

As I go through life and reflect on this principle of Dewey's with the benefit of greater experience and maturity, I increasingly appreciate its genius. I feel that I cannot truly grasp the idea of life as a continuous unfolding—that I am touching a "surface of glass" when I attempt to do so. Yet, as time goes by, increasingly I have intimations of the truth of this assertion. Each moment of every day, we are challenged to integrate the experiences that come to us. Living is defined in these encounters, and the quality of our lives is so determined. Each day, we rise to meet the challenges and gifts living presents us; as day ends, we can take stock in a transitory way of whether the capacity for growth in us has been preserved and transformed.

References

Dewey, J. (1980). Democracy and education. In J. A. Boydston (Ed.), *John Dewey: The middle works, 1899–1924: Vol. 9. 1916* (pp. 1–370). Carbondale: Southern Illinois University Press. (Original work published 1916)

Sirk, D. (Director). (1959). *Imitation of life* [Motion picture]. United States: Universal International Pictures.

Tennyson, A. (2007). The passing of Arthur. In *Idylls of the king* (pp. 243–254). Radford, VA: Wilder Publications. (Original work published 1863)

Wilhelm, R. (1967). *The I Ching.* Princeton, NJ: Princeton University Press.

44

THE RELATIONS OF ONE GREAT COMMON WORLD

Gary Weilbacher

We do not have a series of stratified earths, one of which is mathematical, another physical, another historical, and so on. We should not be able to live very long in any one taken by itself. We live in a world where all sides are bound together. All studies grow out of relations in one great common world. When the child lives in varied but concrete and active relationships to this common world, his studies are naturally unified.

—*The School and Society*, Middle Works 1: 54

In theory, public schools in a democratic society are places where all sides should be bound together by the common goals of education. An educated population enhances and advances society by creating an informed, active, and caring citizenry. Seemingly, however, current educational structures are more closely aligned with sorting and stratification than with understanding relationships and promoting unity.

Curriculum Organization

The area where stratification may be most obvious is curriculum organization. Ironically, students come to school with little, if any, understanding that knowledge has been conveniently compartmentalized. They use their knowledge in an integrated manner as they try to solve problems related to their world. As students progress through the educational system, they gradually are provided with fewer opportunities to see how "all sides are bound together." Many elementary schools consist of self-contained classrooms, where one teacher, working with students grouped together because of their ages, tells them, "Now it's time to do our math lesson." Math, to the children, soon becomes a "subject" to be addressed at a particular time. To be fair, many elementary teachers teach subject knowledge by using themes related to dinosaurs and butterflies. Most students, however, begin in elementary school to understand the idea of *subjects* being separate from one another.

Even though interdisciplinary teaching is a hallmark of exemplary middle schools, such schools are few and far between. Most young adolescents see separate math, science, social studies, and language arts teachers and must make hurried choices among electives such as foreign languages, music, and art. Some middle school students are placed in algebra classes, sending the message that certain components of the discipline are more valuable than others. The result of such curricular organization is that the lines between and levels within subjects become more distinct.

Tracks

In many large high schools, students choose or are placed into general, college prep, or vocational prep tracks, where disciplines are further separated into honors, general, and remedial categories. These distinctions are further emphasized as students are separated by wings or floors within their schools. In these schools, quite clearly, groups of students are bound together because of their common characteristics, not because they share a common world.

This sorting process often is influenced by the experiential, cultural, familial, and economic backgrounds that students and teachers bring with them. Schools place differing values on these backgrounds; students coming from less valued backgrounds learn that the skills, knowledge, and actions they used successfully in other contexts when negotiating their world are less effective in school. For many of those students, school becomes another world, distinct from the one in which they grew up. It is not overly dramatic to suggest that students who don't adjust to the school world are not "able to live very long in any one taken by itself." The large numbers of dropouts coming from less valued backgrounds provide for rather convincing evidence. On a larger scale, schools filled with students coming from impoverished conditions find themselves on "watch lists," another form of stratification indicating that such schools are not the same as achieving schools. Our educational system appears to create, foster, and value such distinctions.

Counteracting Stratification

Thus far, there seems to be little evidence to support Dewey's claims. However, the power of Dewey's words is in the possibility that any teacher can counteract the stratification imposed by the educational system, especially on a curricular and cultural level. A long, distinguished, but relatively forgotten history offers alternatives to departmentalized curriculum arrangements, including core curriculum, the project method, and arrangements created during the Eight-Year Study. These alternatives suggest that teachers do not need to teach using separate periods for individual disciplines (Aiken, 1942; Hartzler, 2000; Vars, 1993).

Undoubtedly, such work is challenging—mainly because most teachers were not taught to teach using these ideas. Still, teachers can help their students construct "active relationships to this common world" by engaging them in curriculum planning and service learning. Teachers and students can cooperatively build curricular themes by focusing on common questions and concerns about themselves and the world around them (Beane, 1997). Student concerns are steeped in cultural beliefs and reflective of the worlds in which their knowledge began to develop. Learning about these concerns does not discard the disciplines of knowledge. Rather, such learning activities "grow out of [the] relations [that are found] in one great common world." Studying such relations can reconnect the process of education with the rest of the world, especially with the students' world.

References

Aiken, W. M. (1942). *The story of the eight-year study, with conclusions and recommendations.* New York, NY: Harper & Brothers.

Beane, J. A. (1997). *Curriculum integration: Designing the core of democratic education.* New York, NY: Teachers College Press.

Dewey, J. (1976). The school and society. In J. A. Boydston (Ed.), *John Dewey: The middle works, 1899–1924: Vol. 1. 1899–1901* (pp. 5–112). Carbondale: Southern Illinois University Press. (Original work published 1899)

Hartzler, D. S. (2000). *A meta-analysis of studies conducted on integrated curriculum programs and their effects on student achievement.* Unpublished doctoral dissertation, Indiana University, Bloomington.

Vars, G. F. (1993). *Interdisciplinary teaching: Why & how.* Columbus, OH: National Middle School Association.

45

LEARNING IN AND OUT OF SCHOOL

Bridging the Cultural Gap

Ron W. Wilhelm

> *From the standpoint of the child, the great waste in the school comes from his inability to utilize the experiences he gets outside the school in any complete and free way within the school itself, while, on the other hand, he is unable to apply in daily life what he is learning in school.*
> — *The School and Society,* Middle Works 1: 46

Think back to your most memorable learning experience—one that continues to hold special meaning in your life. To reflect on why it was so valuable to you, consider these questions. Who was your teacher? What actions did that person take to help you learn? How did that person interact with you while you were learning? In what way was your new knowledge or skill connected to your daily life? When I have engaged adults in reflecting on these questions, they have shared that most of their truly significant learning experiences did not occur in the classroom, and most of those experiences embodied practical, life applications. How do we understand the fact that after 12 or more years of schooling, many adults point to learning experiences outside of formal education as their most memorable?

Learning involves making connections between the experienced and the possible, between the known and the imagined. Given rapidly changing demographics in U.S. schools, with increasingly culturally and linguistically diverse student populations, educators are challenged now more than ever to help students make connections and bridge cultural knowledge gaps. Much has been written over the past 30 years about the nature of school culture and the ways it can marginalize students unprepared to function in a basically middle class, White, Protestant, female classroom world. Teachers must design and build cultural bridges so that all students may connect their life experiences outside of the classroom with new knowledge, skills, and attitudes presented as part of the official curriculum. How are monocultural, monolingual teachers to take on that role?

Several practices can help educators fill their own cultural knowledge gaps and create a curriculum and learning environment that privileges student learning outside the classroom while promoting the use of new classroom knowledge in students' daily life. Consider the following questions:

- *How might I be more knowledgeable about and sensitive to students' cultural backgrounds, values, and traditions?* Teachers must be willing to confront their own misinformation, biases, and lack of cultural knowledge. The process is lifelong and involves attending to and reflecting on not only your attitudes and areas of cultural ignorance, but also on what examples you use to illustrate your lessons, what images you display on classroom walls, and what curriculum materials you select to overcome the limited or biased sources you are provided by the district.

  Though initially time-consuming, many educators begin the year with visits to their incoming students' homes. They use the visits to meet the students and parents, to answer questions about the school, and to gain insight into the home culture of each child. One important area to explore is the parents' perceptions of their own schooling experiences. Through such interaction, teachers can better understand the nature of parental involvement and support in their child's learning and then use the information to design meaningful learning experiences grounded in the home context.

- *How do I demonstrate respect for different cultures and backgrounds in my interactions with parents and students?* Some schools organize sessions between parents and teachers to promote ongoing dialogue that focuses on educational issues of local significance. Parents can help teachers examine the norms of the local community, families, and languages for socializing children and identify logistical barriers to parental involvement. Parents also can help teachers secure community support for the curriculum. In turn, teachers can help parents learn to engage in an ongoing dialogue with their children about learning.

- *In what ways do I provide a learning environment in which students' cultures are recognized, shared, and respected?* You can build knowledge bridges by inviting students to comment on their lives as part of the learning experience. You can give students choice and voice in the organization of learning experiences. Your challenge is to help young learners see the personal relevance of new concepts and skills. One important strategy, especially for English language learners, is to focus on how they use both their native language and English. Consider the specific ways you support the child's and family's use of their native language and how you facilitate English language development and use.

- *How do I organize opportunities for students to teach me about their cultures?* You can encourage the adventurous nature of many students by enabling them to switch roles and teach from their area of expertise, whether that be computers, sharks, or *quinceañeras* (15th-birthday celebrations). Astute teachers with little expertise in computer technology have engaged their students in joint learning experiences in which the students teach the teachers new computer skills.

By critically reflecting on our practice, engaging in respectful and frequent dialogue with our students and their parents, and validating students' cultural knowledge as part of the official curriculum, educators can ensure the transfer of classroom learning to life beyond the school. By traversing cultural knowledge bridges between home and school, our students will understand that knowledge and skills gained in the classroom can be used to resolve real-world problems.

Reference

Dewey, J. (1976). The school and society. In J. A. Boydston (Ed.), *John Dewey: The middle works, 1899–1924: Vol. 1. 1899–1901* (pp. 5–112). Carbondale: Southern Illinois University Press. (Original work published 1899)

46

THE CHILD AND THE CURRICULUM

Two Limits That Define a Single Process

William A. Reid

Abandon the notion of subject-matter as something fixed and ready-made in itself, outside the child's experience; cease thinking of the child's experience as also something hard and fast; see it as something fluent, embryonic, vital; and we realize that the child and the curriculum are simply two limits that define a single process.
                    —The Child and the Curriculum, Middle Works 2: 278

Educators tend to work with simple, commonsense models of what and whom they teach. This is not to be critical of teachers. Clearly, they approach teaching this way for good reasons—the demands made on them, their working conditions, and the need to retain their students' attention and administrators' support over the long haul. This inclination, however, typically is balanced by a degree of complexity in the teachers' visions of the point and purpose of education. How, then, might we interpret and apply Dewey's remarks on the fluidity of the relationship between child and curriculum?

Fluent and Vital

For most of us, taking Dewey's advice too literally would be a mistake. It is all too easy to enter a classroom enthused with images of students and subject matter that are fluent and vital, only to find oneself in the midst of chaos and confusion and to end up in a state of disillusionment. Teachers in our schools are not in the enviable situation of Rousseau's (1933) tutor to Emile. Typically, they face 30 or so students of differing characters, while their choice of what to teach is restricted by school and district policies and constrained by testing programs.

An essential part of becoming a successful teacher in such circumstances is to develop an instinct for what works not just today, but next week, next month, and next year. This is what matters most where practical matters of teaching are concerned. Yet, not many teachers would be happy to operate solely on such a simplistic basis. Most feel the need for an overarching vision that helps them aspire higher in their everyday work in their classrooms. Dewey's remarks are important, therefore, because they provide such a vision in addition to offering strong links to practicality.

Practical

These links to practicality operate at two levels. First, in the right circumstances—for instance, if we were tutoring Emile—we could imagine guiding our activities so that they stimulated fluent, profoundly educative encounters between mind and subject matter. Ideally, such opportunities will, from time to time, occur in our own teaching experience. When they do, we will recognize them, know how to make use of them, and feel a sense of exhilaration as a result.

Second, Dewey's proposition has practicality outside the classroom. If, as teachers, we want to improve the nature of our practice, then Dewey can provide us with needed arguments when discussing how schooling might be improved. As noted previously, teachers tend to work with simple models of subject matter and students because of the conditions under which they teach. When debates on how these conditions might be changed arise, teachers must be influential in guiding those debates toward policies that lead to improvements in teaching.

To achieve needed change, teachers must have expertise so that they can offer solid arguments for or against particular proposals. Dewey's idea provides us with an excellent foundation for that expertise. It presents a model of learning that carries not only philosophical conviction, but also practical implications for the organization of the curriculum. As teachers, we should be able to lay out these implications with a purpose strengthened by personal experience of moments in our own classrooms when the truth of his observation manifests itself.

References

Dewey, J. (1976). The child and the curriculum. In J. A. Boydston (Ed.), *John Dewey: The middle works, 1899–1924: Vol. 2. 1902–1903* (pp. 271–292). Carbondale: Southern Illinois University Press. (Original work published 1902)

Rousseau, J. J. (1933). *Emile.* New York, NY: Dutton.

47

THE RECONSTRUCTION OF EXPERIENCE

Edmund C. Short

Experiences in order to be educative must lead out into an expanding world of subject-matter. . . . This condition is satisfied only as an educator views teaching and learning as a continuous process of reconstruction of experience. . . . At every level there is an expanding development of experience if experience is educative in effect.
　　　　　　　　　　　—*Experience and Education,* Later Works 13: 60–61

Too often we teach discrete facts or concepts that are easily ignored or soon forgotten by our students. A better approach is to conceive of our teaching as providing educative experiences. An *educative experience* is one that has the potential for being meaningfully connected to students' previous experiences and for leading to fuller, deeper understandings based on what has already been learned. The key issue for teachers creating educative experiences is to grasp what experiences students have had that can be tied into the new understandings, skills, or attitudes that are the focus of immediate curriculum aims and objectives being addressed.

Or, as Dewey (1938/1988) states,

It thus becomes the office of the educator to select those things within the range of existing experience that have the promise and potentiality of presenting new problems which, by stimulating new ways of observing and judgment, will expand the area of further experience. (p. 51)

Dewey (1938/1988) further notes, "Any experience is mis-educative that has the effect of arresting or distorting the growth of further experience" (p. 11).

Exemplifying Principles

The significance of this way of thinking lies in its two exemplifying, sound educational principles. First, we know that when students assume ownership of their learning, it is more valued, meaningful, cognitively clear, and accurate than when mental or dispositional tasks are imposed on them with little or no personal investment. Creating truly educative experiences for and with students enables them to engage such experiences with thought and emotional involvement; quick memorization and fragmented information no longer suffice as indicators of successful learning. Attention is drawn to the meaning, purpose, and interconnection of learning tasks.

Second, we know that doing one's own thinking is essential for true understanding to occur. This requires paying attention to what one has understood previously, how new information or evidence fits with or contradicts this, and how these differing understandings can be reconciled or integrated. Students must do this for themselves. A teacher cannot tell students the results or impose the answers. Each student must consider these things based on his or her own previous knowledge. Teachers can provide only the circumstances and stimulation for this educative experience to occur.

What must the nature and content of these educative experiences be? Dewey (1938/1988) writes of the teacher providing "an expanding world of subject-matter" and of the student engaging in "a continuous process of reconstruction of experience" (p. 59). These components of educative experience would appear, at first glance, to be simple to spell out and enact. Yet Dewey gives few specifics on what is involved. I offer from my own years of teaching experience what I think is involved and invite other teachers to create appropriate educative experiences for students in concrete teaching/learning situations and to share with all who are interested in truly educative experiences how these work in practice.

Attention to the Long-Range View

My interpretation of creating an educative experience includes giving careful attention to the long-range view of the subject matter. A teacher not only must see how today's lesson content fits with tomorrow's but also with the knowledge structure of which it is a part. Teachers can plan each educative experience, leading to increasingly mature and complete understandings on the part of students, only with an accurate and comprehensive understanding of the whole subject. The trick is to select, as part of any given educative experience, the next level of content or subject matter that will allow them to build on past experience (even if but a short distance) toward attaining the fullest understanding of the subject as a whole.

Dewey (1938/1988) admits that the "orderly development toward expansion and organization of subject-matter through growth of experience" had not received much attention by many teachers (p. 49). He (1938/1988) adds, "Always bear in mind, however, that intellectual organization is not an end in itself but is the means by which social relations, distinctively human ties and bonds, may be understood and more intelligently ordered" (p. 57). In other words, remember that even full knowledge of a subject is to be used in the service of good living, not for its own sake. How often is that being ignored today in the frantic effort to seek high test scores and mastery of bits and pieces of knowledge!

Significance to Previous Experience

Another prerequisite for creating an appropriate educative experience is to know the content and significance of the students' previous experiences related to ongoing curriculum aims and objectives. This entails careful assessment and observation of where students are in their learning. Moreover, because every student may be at a different point on the road to full understanding, a variety of next steps must be built into the subsequent educative experience. To put it bluntly, there may be no single version of an educative experience that can serve an entire class if differences in what each student needs are detected. At that point, I recommend considering the creation of individualized educative experiences for each student. Or, try creating a broad sort of educative experience—such as a project—within which each student's next step can be addressed.

For each educative experience in which students are invited to engage, teachers need to guide students by giving directions on how they should function. For instance, students will need to bring (through written or oral methods or both) what they know (or think they know) about the subject. Then, they will need to confront the next level of subject matter (through teacher talk, texts, or other media) and ask themselves, "Do I understand this in light of my personal knowledge? Does it fit in or contradict? Will I incorporate it, hold it in suspension, or do more inquiry?" At that point, students again will need to articulate their understanding (through writing or perhaps orally or both).

Guidance also must be given to students about the actual thought processes in which they engage. With regular use, students can learn what is involved in this "continuous process of reconstruction of experience," as Dewey (1938/1988, p. 59) labels it, and they can come to see that all their education involves "the progressive development of what is already experienced into a fuller and richer and also more organized form, a form that gradually approximates that in which subject-matter is presented to the skilled, mature person" (Dewey 1938/1988, p. 48).

Reference

Dewey, J. (1988). Experience and education. In J. A. Boydston (Ed.), *John Dewey: The later works, 1925–1953: Vol. 13. 1938–1939* (pp. 1–62). Carbondale: Southern Illinois University Press. (Original work published 1938)

48

THE TEACHER-ARTIST

George Willis

> *Until the artist is satisfied in perception with what he is doing, he continues shaping and reshaping. The making comes to an end when its result is experienced as good— and that experience comes not by mere intellectual and outside judgment but in direct perception. An artist, in comparison with his fellows, is one who is not only especially gifted in powers of execution but in unusual sensitivity to the qualities of things. This sensitivity also directs his doings and makings.*
>
> *—Art as Experience,* Later Works 10: 56

Despite the deep philosophic ideas John Dewey discusses throughout his writings and the careful, scholarly tone he invariably takes, his philosophy can be described as "naturalistic"—that is, his primary concern is not with abstract matters but with how people actually cope with the basic problems of living. In this sense, he is like a conscientious parent, always reminding us about situations we have lived through that we did not quite understand at the time, always hoping that we will not need his reminders in the future.

The passage cited is not an exception. In it, he insists that you, as a teacher, are an artist. Furthermore, you must remember that each of your students is an artist, too. This observation may not be one you made as you embarked on your teaching career—especially given the emphasis American society now places on technological solutions to all problems, even educational ones—but it is an observation that Dewey insists you make. And he is right to insist. You are not an artist because

Dewey says you are but because artistry is at the heart of what being a thoughtful teacher is all about. Indeed, artistry is an essential part of all thoughtful, moral living.

Aesthetic Experience

Dewey insists again and again in his writings that teachers as artists are necessarily reflective practitioners—constantly sizing up the multitude of newly arising situations in their classrooms, seeking and weighing appropriate evidence, making value judgments, and taking practical actions. As a teacher, you want to do all this well. But how?

Though Dewey often uses the word *science* to describe the public side of reflection, he makes clear (especially in his later writings, such as the passage cited) that the private side, rooted in personal experience, is more important. Reflective teaching is primarily aesthetic; any utilitarian concerns about what specifics students may or may not have learned, however important, are secondary. You, as a teacher, are inevitably a teacher-artist. You can become a better teacher-artist only through deepening your own aesthetic experience, refining your ability to perceive that which is not obvious, and acting on your perceptions in creative ways that help others to perceive the world anew, more clearly and more intensely.

And how is all this done? As the old joke puts it, the lost musician, carrying a violin case, constantly glancing at his watch, and frantically scurrying along mid-Manhattan streets, finally asks a passerby, "Can you tell me how to get to Carnegie Hall?" The reply: "Practice, practice, practice."

Direct Perceptions

You still may find all this difficult to believe. After all, aren't teachers teachers because they help students learn what they need to know? Of course! Except, as Dewey often points out, no one can say with certainty exactly what any one person— let alone everyone—needs to lead a personally fulfilling and socially useful life. Therefore, teachers must rely on their direct perceptions of what goes on in their classrooms to make their own choices about what activities to suggest to students and about how to shape the environment within which each student lives. There is simply no other way to discern the intensely personal reactions of students.

The process is ongoing. It can come to a halt (and then only temporarily— unlike many other forms of art) only when the teacher-artist stops to reflect on it. Remembering that *good* is both an aesthetic and an ethical term, the teacher can stop and say about what is going on in his or her classroom, "I feel this to be good. I believe this to be good. I will try in the future to create something even better, but for the moment this will do."

The Creative Process

Furthermore, you must not lose sight of the fact that your students, too, are artists. What goes on in your classroom is not solely your creation. You must, therefore, involve your students in the creative process, the perceiving, the doing, the shaping, the reshaping—all that goes into making the classroom what it is. There are many ways to do this. You can work out many artistic techniques in your own classroom. You and other teacher-artists in your school, or even throughout the world, can work out and share specifics. Such sharing has been going on for years, and it is now easier than ever. Your students will be glad to help, especially when they understand that their own doings and makings are valued artistic endeavors.

So, as Dewey reminds us, perception heightens sensitivity. Sensitivity heightens awareness. Awareness increases attention to not only what is, but to all the possibilities of what can be. In our present era, one that denigrates the essential aesthetic and moral value of teaching, persevere in what Dewey and all perceptive teachers know to be true. Don't let your identity as a teacher-artist be taken away from you.

Reference

Dewey, J. (1987). Art as experience. In J. A. Boydston (Ed.), *John Dewey: The later works, 1925–1953: Vol. 10. 1934* (pp. 1–352). Carbondale: Southern Illinois University Press. (Original work published 1934)

49

"OF ALL AFFAIRS, COMMUNICATION IS THE MOST WONDERFUL"

Gert Biesta

> *Of all affairs, communication is the most wonderful. That things should be able to pass from the plane of external pushing and pulling to that of revealing themselves to man, and thereby to themselves; and that the fruit of communication should be participation, sharing, is a wonder by the side of which transubstantiation pales.*
>
> —*Experience and Nature*, Later Works 1: 132

Over the years, John Dewey's philosophy has been characterized in a number of different ways. Some have called it a *naturalistic* philosophy, highlighting the influence of evolutionary thinking on Dewey's ideas. Others have stressed the value Dewey places on the *scientific method,* albeit that Dewey sees it as a method of judgment intended to make our actions more intelligent and not as a method that would generate certain knowledge. Yet for me, Dewey's philosophy is first and foremost a philosophy of *communication* or, as I have put it elsewhere (Biesta, 1995), a philosophy of *communicative action.*

When Dewey (1925/1981) writes in *Experience and Nature,* "Of all affairs, communication is the most wonderful" (p.132), it is not because he has found a new topic to philosophize about but because he has come to the conclusion that language, mind, consciousness, meaning, rationality, logic, and truth—all those things that philosophers over the centuries have considered to be part of the natural make-up of human beings—only come into existence through and as a result of communication. "When communication occurs," Dewey writes, "all natural events are subject to reconsideration and revision; they are re-adapted to meet the requirements of conversation, whether it be public discourse or that preliminary discourse termed thinking" (p. 132). And, in a slightly more daring passage:

> That things should be able to pass from the plane of external pushing and pulling to that of revealing themselves to man, and thereby to themselves; and that the fruit of communication should be participation, sharing, is a wonder by the side of which transubstantiation pales. (p. 132)

Dewey is well aware that putting communication at the very center of his philosophy means that he has to think differently about the process of communication itself. He can no longer rely on the idea—still so common in our day—that communication "acts as a mechanical go-between to convey observations and ideas that have prior and independent existence" (p. 134), that is, that communication is nothing but the transportation of information from A to B. In *Experience and Nature,* Dewey unfolds an understanding of communication in thoroughly *practical* terms, that is, "as the establishment of cooperation in an activity in which there are partners, and in which the activity of each is modified and regulated by partnership" (p. 141). This leads him to define communication as the process in which "something is literally *made common* [emphasis added] in at least two different centres of behavior" (p. 141).

Although *Experience and Nature* is the book in which Dewey develops his ideas about communication in much philosophical detail, it is actually in *Democracy and Education* (1916/1980) that he articulates these ideas for the first time (Biesta, 2006). That this is so is significant for two reasons. On the one hand it shows that it was only when Dewey has to reflect upon the fundamental "mechanism" of the educational process that he comes to develop his theory of communication. On the other hand, it makes clear that for Dewey communication—as a thoroughly practical and creative process of making something in common—is the fundamental way in which education "operates."

Although Dewey (1916/1980) does write that "education consists primarily in transmission through communication" (p. 12), he hastens to add that this is not a process of "direct contagion" or "literal inculcation" (p. 14) but rather one "of sharing experience till it becomes a common possession" (p. 12). This means that participation is central to educational communication. For Dewey, participation is neither about physical proximity nor about the situation in which all work toward a common end. It is only when all "are cognizant of the common end and all [are] interested in it" that there is real participation, and it is only this kind of participation "which modifies the disposition of both parties who undertake it" (p. 12) so that things and sounds come to have "the same value for both with respect to carrying on a common pursuit." (p. 19). Along these lines, Dewey suggests a crucial difference between *education* and *training*. Training is about those situations in which those who learn do not really share in the use to which their actions are put, which means that they are not real partners in a shared activity. Education, on the other hand, is about those situations in which one really shares in a common activity and really has an interest in its accomplishment.

Does any of this matter for what goes on in our classrooms? I think it does. Dewey's ideas help us to see the limits of the idea that education is all about the transmission of information from teachers (or textbooks or the Internet) to students. Although transmission may be a worthwhile *goal* of education—there are, after all, important things to learn in school—the transmission metaphor falls short as an account of how information can be given by teachers and received by students. With Dewey we can see that we gain access to meanings—in the widest sense of the word—through participation. After all, what things (in the widest sense of the word, including gestures and sounds) mean is not to be found in the things themselves—the meaning of a traffic light is not hidden somewhere deep down inside the traffic light—but can only be found in the social practices in which the things are being used. It is only when students participate in such practices—and here we might add, when students are *allowed* to participate— that they gain access to the vast stock of meanings that make up human culture. Although we can learn a lot by doing—that is, by experimenting and undergoing the consequences of our experimentations—it is only when we do things *with others,* when we participate, that we transcend our individual meaning making and become connected, both as receivers and as creators, to the ever-ongoing process of meaning making called *culture.* The crucial role of participation also highlights that education, unlike training, always involves students as subjects of their own action and thinking and not just as objects to be molded by teachers (or, even worse, by abstract standardized programs of instruction). Dewey thus helps us to see that any education worthy of its name is a real encounter between human beings—an encounter full of possibilities and radically open toward the future. In this way, Dewey's claim that of all affairs communication is the most wonderful may help us to retain a sense of wonder about the miraculous things that do happen every day in our classrooms.

References

Biesta, G. J. J. (1995). Pragmatism as a pedagogy of communicative action. In J. Garrison (Ed.), *The new scholarship on Dewey* (pp. 105–122). Norwell, MA: Kluwer Academic.

Biesta, G. J. J. (2006). "Of all affairs, communication is the most wonderful": The communicative turn in Dewey's *Democracy and Education*. In D. T. Hansen (Ed.), *John Dewey and our educational prospect: A critical engagement with Dewey's* Democracy and Education (pp. 23–37). Albany: State University of New York Press.

Dewey, J. (1980). Democracy and education. In J. A. Boydston (Ed.), *John Dewey: The middle works, 1899–1924: Vol. 9. 1916* (pp. 1–370). Carbondale: Southern Illinois University Press. (Original work published 1916)

Dewey, J. (1981). Experience and nature. In J. A. Boydston (Ed.), *John Dewey: The later works, 1925–1953: Vol. 1. 1925* (pp. 1–326). Carbondale: Southern Illinois University Press. (Original work published 1925)

PART VI
Inquiry and Education

INQUIRY AND EDUCATION: A WAY OF SEEING THE WORLD

Donna Adair Breault

What is inquiry? Dewey has a great deal to say regarding this question. Throughout his writings, he makes numerous references to, and offers many characterizations of, inquiry. In *A Common Faith* (1933/1986), he calls it "an unseen power . . . of the ideal" (p. 18). In *How We Think* (1910/1978), he speaks of the inquiry process as one in which we enter a contract as thinkers, as something that culminates and is ultimately woven into a "coherent fabric" (p. 245). In that same book, Dewey (1910/1978) talks about the need to be playful when it comes to inquiring so that we can achieve a "largeness and imaginativeness of vision" (p. 290). In *The Quest for Certainty* (1929/1984), Dewey helps us to understand that through the inquiry process, *knowledge* becomes a verb, something active and used for some purpose, by comparing it with the work a tool does rather than the tool itself.

Dewey also spends a great deal of time and attention letting us know what inquiry is *not*. In *The Quest for Certainty* (1929/1984), he warns that inquiry should be "the last thing to be picked up casually and clung to rigidly" (p. 222). Again and again, he argues that inquiry is not stagnant. It involves an active and purposeful process. In *How We Think* (1910/1978), for example, he cautions us that thinking is not just a matter of storing past memories as if in some "antiseptic refrigerator" (p. 264) but involves using our past experiences and understandings for a purpose. Similarly, in *Democracy and Education* (1916/1980), he admonishes that we should not fill our heads like a scrapbook with facts that do not lead to solving real problems.

Not Spectators

In essence, we are not spectators. Learning involves active and purposeful engage-ment. This is a very different view of knowledge than more traditional views. It means that we are part of the meaning-making process. We cannot separate ourselves from what is known. Knowledge is not a bunch of "stuff" out there to be acquired, transmitted, and maintained. Instead, *knowledge* is a verb. It is an active and continually evolving process. Inquiry, according to Dewey, encapsulates that process of coming to know. With this image in mind, it is important to explore why it is important to promote inquiry within the classroom. I offer three such reasons.

First, if you make inquiry a focus of your work as a teacher, you become empowered. You have a voice in what happens in your classroom. This is not to say that you can ignore the curriculum and policy mandates that are part of your system, but it does mean that you can filter those mandates through a belief system and determine the best means through which you act as a teacher. Now more than ever, with No Child Left Behind creating such dreadful circumstances in our schools, you need to empower yourself through inquiry.

Think about it. You make more decisions as a teacher than almost any other person in any other profession. On what do you base those decisions? Tradition? Do you do something because it's what your teachers did when you were in school? Do you do something because it's what you saw your supervising teacher do when you were student teaching? Do you do something because you were taught to do it that way through a prescriptive in-service? Maybe it's just the way you've always done it, and if it isn't broken, why change it? Do you make choices based on convenience? Is it the easiest way to do something? Does it take less time to do it that way? Do you do something for lack of alternatives? Maybe you don't know any other way to do it. If you make inquiry a priority in your professional life, you do something because you believe it to be the best practice based on your beliefs and your understanding of teaching and learning. That is what makes you a professional. That is what keeps you excited about your job.

Second, if you make inquiry a priority in your classroom, you will empower others— namely, your students. Imagine that you have on a pair of sunglasses. While wearing those glasses, you see things around you differently. Likewise, to inquire is to see the world differently. Inquiry is not an external skill that can be trained, imitated, or prescribed; it is an inherent capacity each person possesses. You may have to learn how to use it, how to recognize it, understand the need to value it, give yourself permission to explore it—but it is there. The degree to which you engage in inquiry will significantly impact your life as a teacher, and the degree to which you promote it in your classroom will significantly impact the lives of your students. I believe that the manner in which our world is changing makes it absolutely necessary for our students to think critically, and that won't happen unless teachers can think critically. Inquiry has to become a culture within each classroom. It has to be a way of seeing the world.

Finally, we must make inquiry the focus of our work in education because it is the sole means through which we will achieve reform in schools. Think of all the reform efforts that have failed over the years. Like the pendulum-swinging metaphor, most reforms fail because they are imposed in a prescriptive manner, followed half-heartedly—and dismissed too readily. As long as we continue to blindly follow prescriptive efforts, nothing in education will change. Cuban (1993) looked at 7,000 profiles of classrooms from previous studies and observations spanning 1890 to 1990. In his study, Cuban noted few changes in the way teachers taught. Most of the instruction was teacher centered. Passive learning—teacher-centered learning—will continue to dominate classrooms where reflection or inquiry is not the professional focus of the teacher. Until we make a lifelong commitment to inquiry, things will not change.

Images of Inquiry

Think again about the sunglasses. Let them represent your ability to inquire. Some of you will be comfortable wearing these glasses and probably will keep them on most, if not all, of the time. For some, wearing them may not be natural and may be difficult. You may start out wearing them for only small amounts of time and for only specific situations. As you mature as a professional, you may find yourself able to wear them more and more. Also consider the tint of the glasses. It will be different for everyone. For some, the tint may be a bit rosy. For others, it will be darker— particularly those who find themselves wrestling with issues of power and justice.

Have you ever had your eyes examined by a doctor and endured one of those large machines they put in front of your face? Think about that process. The eye doctor makes slight changes in the lens strengths and then asks, "Is it better this way or that?" The process is what you will do as a reflective practitioner. You will play around with images of inquiry to determine which "fits" and allows you to see things more clearly. To this end, the editors of this volume hope that the images of inquiry offered by the contributors in this section help you to refine your own image and help you to see its place within your work.

References

Cuban, L. (1993). *How teachers taught: Constancy and change in American classrooms, 1890– 1990* (2nd ed.). New York, NY: Teachers College Press.

Dewey, J. (1978). How we think. In J. A. Boydston (Ed.), *John Dewey: The middle works, 1899–1924: Vol. 6. 1910–1911* (pp. 177–356). Carbondale: Southern Illinois University Press. (Original work published 1910)

Dewey, J. (1980). Democracy and education. In J. A. Boydston (Ed.), *John Dewey: The middle works, 1899–1924: Vol. 9. 1916* (pp. 1–370). Carbondale: Southern Illinois University Press. (Original work published 1916)

Dewey, J. (1984). The quest for certainty. In J. A. Boydston (Ed.), *John Dewey: The later works, 1925–1953: Vol. 4. 1929* (pp. 1–250). Carbondale: Southern Illinois University Press. (Original work published 1929)

Dewey, J. (1986). A common faith. In J. A. Boydston (Ed.), *John Dewey: The later works, 1925–1953: Vol. 9. 1933–1934* (pp. 1–58). Carbondale: Southern Illinois University Press. (Original work published 1933)

50

THE POWER OF AN IDEAL

Jim Garrison

> *An unseen power controlling our destiny becomes the power of an ideal. . . . The artist, scientist, citizen, parent, as far as they are actuated by the spirit of their callings, are controlled by the unseen. For all endeavor for the better is moved by faith in what is possible, not by adherence to the actual.*
>
> —*A Common Faith*, Later Works 9: 17

Many teachers experience their choice to enter teaching in the etymological sense of *vocation* that derives from *vocare*, a calling. If you are among those who entered teaching because you experienced a call to serve, perhaps you felt possessed by something unseen, difficult to name, and beyond your capacity to control or even fully comprehend. The word *religion* derives from a root that means being bound or tied to a particular way of life. At the start of your career, you felt bound to your calling, to the particular way of life that is teaching. Do you still?

The Spirituality of Teaching

Whether committed to formal religion or not, you may have a sense of religious wonder, a natural piety toward the infinite plenitude of existence and your place in it. This attitude is born of passion, guided by imagination, and sustained by intelligent faith in possibility. It is a source of wisdom lying beyond knowledge of ideas and facts alone. That is why even those who have taught for many years without losing the call often still find it difficult to articulate their spiritual sense of teaching.

We may think of spirituality as an intimate, dynamic, and harmonious union with the universe that sustains us, wherein our creative acts matter. Dewey considers every individual an active participant in an unfinished and unfinishable universe rather than a spectator of a complete or completable creation. Our senses do not engender universal unity and harmony unaided. Such unity is not a fact of existence; indeed, there is a great deal of evidence to the contrary. This unity lies beyond the actual state of affairs in our world as we find it today, or in any other day, in the history of humankind. Unity is an unseen ideal, discerned only by emotion and imagination, of a possible cosmos beyond the chaos of our actual everyday affairs. For those who feel called and whose faith sustains them, imaginary ideals take possession of them with a power they cannot resist. For those with courage to believe and the passion to pursue things unseen, along with the honesty to accept what their intelligently guided inquiry discloses, the age of revelation is not past. Initially, such a powerful spiritual ideal seems far beyond the call to teach, but it is not.

The death of a single living creature is a greater loss to the universe than the collapse of a whole galaxy lacking living beings. And the procreation of a child is a grander act of creation than the constitution of lifeless worlds. When teachers connect and care for such divine beings and help awaken in them the light of learning, they bring into existence a radiance that outshines the brightest sun. Such care and creation has wonderful spiritual qualities.

Caring and Creativity

Teachers enter teaching and remain for two principal reasons. First, they seek to care for their students, connect with them, and help them learn and grow. Some are not even afraid to say they love their students. Second, they seek creative autonomy. Nothing known to us is more precious than intimate relations with other human beings, nor is anything more miraculous than contributing to creating a life worth living for others and ourselves. Therein reside the spiritual values of the call to teach even when it remains hidden beneath the daily details of busy classroom lives. This spirituality gives the most profound meaning to the simplest acts of teaching. Immaculate moments are always waiting to shine through the clouds.

The busyness demanded by the bureaucratic forces of unreflective accountability does much to extinguish creativity and connection in teaching and thereby cancels the spiritual values that call and sustain teachers. Instead of honoring the numinous, technocrats reduce everything to numbers. They do not see students and teachers as unique human beings that must achieve a unique destiny to make unique contributions to a free and democratic community. Instead, they reduce students and teachers to calculable ciphers in the economic production function.

The powers that control our destiny demand that we adhere to the actual conditions of material existence rather than demonstrate faith in unseen possibilities. Confronted with such conditions, many teachers burn out and leave. Only those of you who have the imagination to comprehend the possible beyond the actual, the faith in things unseen, and who answer your calling wisely will find the values and courage you need to sustain yourself. You are among those teachers who abide in the place to which you were called while finding intimate, harmonious, and creative union with the larger whole of which you are a part. You are among those who realize the meaningful ideals of the spirit instead of the materialistic ideals of mammon.

Reference

Dewey, J. (1986). A common faith. In J. A. Boydston (Ed.), *John Dewey: The later works, 1925–1953: Vol. 9. 1933–1934* (pp. 1–58). Carbondale: Southern Illinois University Press. (Original work published 1933)

51

DOGMA, DEMOCRACY, AND EDUCATION

William G. Wraga

> *Men still want the crutch of dogma, of beliefs fixed by authority, to relieve them of the trouble of thinking and the responsibility of directing their activity by thought. They tend to confine their own thinking to a consideration of which one among the rival systems of dogma they will accept. Hence the schools are better adapted, as John Stuart Mill said, to make disciples than inquirers.*
>
> —*Democracy and Education*, Middle Works 9: 349

Dewey makes this statement in the context of a consideration of the implications of theories of knowledge for education. Specifically, he is concerned that the experimental method is too exclusively associated with scientific and technical branches of knowledge and insufficiently recognized as a way to inform other kinds of thinking, including "the forming and testing of ideas in social and moral matters" (Dewey 1916/1980, p. 349). Dewey expresses concern that schooling has been dominated by "literary, dialectic, and authoritative methods of forming beliefs" (p. 350), beliefs that are rarely if ever tested against logic and evidence and rather were accepted uncritically and blindly.

Freedoms of Thought and Action

For Dewey, this form of education is antithetical to democracy because it militates against freedom of thought and therefore against the integrity of the individual. For Dewey, in a democracy, the individual enjoys control over his or her future experience. Dewey maintains that the popular democratic value of freedom of action is meaningful only when accompanied by freedom of thought. Exercised together, these two freedoms would result in intelligent action. Through intelligent action, individuals best control subsequent experience. For Dewey, all ideas are subject to analysis and to the ultimate test of practical action. Because dogma involves allegiance to unquestioned intellectual authority, it restricts the free play of intelligence, thereby undermining intelligent action.

Obviously, the frame of mind that Dewey advocates is difficult to cultivate in most people. Most individuals at least attempt to inform their actions with thinking. Yet few of us possess the intellectual courage to submit our most cherished beliefs to reconsideration. For pragmatists like Dewey, even the idea of democracy is subject to continual reevaluation. Contrary to the accusations of many of his critics, Dewey advocates an intellectual education for all future citizens, an education in which students do not merely contemplate big ideas but one in which they develop the habit of subjecting all ideas to the test of logic and evidence and in which they develop the capacity to apply their intelligence to the resolution of practical problems.

The Dogma of Ideas

How often does this Deweyan form of intellectual citizenship education occur in schools and colleges? From Mill's time to the present, the expectation in many college classrooms is that students will kowtow to the pet theories of the professor. Let us label this practice "the dogma of ideas." Have you seen this kind of dogma in your educational experience? What effect did it have on you? On your classmates? On the attitude and actions of the instructor?

The Dogma of Information

The situation is different in school classrooms, where the emphasis is less on ideas and more on information. Here, typically, teachers deliver prepackaged parcels of facts to students who effectively return them unopened. Opportunities for critical evaluation of ideas or opinions are rare. Inundated with factoids to regurgitate, pupils have little use or even time for the kind of reflection Dewey advocates. Here, the ideas and facts are not tested for truthfulness and usefulness, but students are tested on their uncritical acceptance of the facts as true. Let us call this "the dogma of information." Have you witnessed the dogma of information? How did pupils respond?

The dogma of ideas or the dogma of information—either way, the effect is the same: The teacher postures as an authoritative source of truth. Students are left with the impression that authority figures are absolute in their posses-sion of truth; students learn that the received wisdom from the powers that be is to be left unquestioned. This effect not only contradicts Dewey's concep-tion of democracy but also the constitutional principles of balance of powers and checks and balances: The people are to serve as a check against the offi-cial powers that be. In short, education in dogma is both anti-intellectual and antidemocratic.

Promoting Independent Thinking

As students, we teachers have no doubt been subject to both the dogma of ideas and the dogma of information. But what can a teacher do to avoid reproducing these kinds of experiences in his or her classroom? Here are several classroom practices that either directly or indirectly can promote the kind of independent thinking that Dewey champions. As a teacher, you can convey implicitly to stu-dents that authority figures do not necessarily possess authoritative truth; you can do this simply by admitting when you do not know an answer to a student ques-tion and by acknowledging when you are mistaken about some matter. Similarly, you can solicit input from students about resolving some classroom difficulty. Routine implementation of these admittedly deceptively simple practices will likely convey implicitly to students a notion of authority consistent with demo-cratic values.

Opportunities for you to foster the kinds of thinking habits that Dewey advocates are plentiful but also depart from the norm in many classrooms, especially in this age when high-stakes testing dominates. Such opportunities range from planning for students to apply subject-related knowledge, skills, and concepts to an evaluation of truth claims (such as news reports related to the subjects you teach), to directly teaching critical thinking skills, to explic-itly discussing the issue of dogma in democracy and in education. In the best scenario, you would structure classroom experiences so that students could examine ideas against logic and evidence from all sides. Enact practices like these, and your students will be less likely to end up as disciples and more likely to become inquirers.

Reference

Dewey, J. (1980). Democracy and education. In J. A. Boydston (Ed.), *John Dewey: The middle works, 1899–1924: Vol. 9. 1916* (pp. 1–370). Carbondale: Southern Illinois University Press. (Original work published 1916)

A portrait inscribed by Dewey.
Special Collections Research Center, Morris Library, Southern Illinois University Carbondale. Used with Permission.

This portrait, inscribed "With love," was taken in the 1930s.
Special Collections Research Center, Morris Library, Southern Illinois University Carbondale. Used with Permission. Photo by Blackstone Studios.

This photo was published in *Saturday Review* in 1949.
Special Collections Research Center, Morris Library, Southern Illinois University Carbondale. Used with Permission. Photo by Sylvia Salmie.

Dewey is shown here seated reading a book.
Special Collections Research Center, Morris Library, Southern Illinois University Carbondale. Used with Permission. Copyright Pix Publishing, Inc. Photo by Eric Schaal.

John Dewey is surrounded by children for his 90th birthday at the Waldorf Astoria Hotel, October 20, 1949. Among the youngsters are Cricket Rogers, Susan Rogers, Johnny Dewey Jr., and Adrienne Dewey.
Photo by Alexander Archer. Courtesy of Craig Kridel.

Hotel Imperial

R. W. FARR, Manager

Knoxville, Tenn. July 1 1904
Friday—

My dear Janey and Lucy & Gordon

52

THE ROLE OF INTELLIGENCE IN THE CREATION OF ART

Elliot W. Eisner

> *Any idea that ignores the necessary role of intelligence in the production of works of art is based upon identification of thinking with use of one special kind of material, verbal signs and words. To think effectively in terms of relations of qualities is as severe a demand upon thought as to think in terms of symbols, verbal and mathematical. Indeed, since words are easily manipulated in mechanical ways, the production of a work of genuine art probably demands more intelligence than does most of the so-called thinking that goes on among those who pride themselves on being "intellectuals."*
> —*Art as Experience*, Later Works 10: 52

The foregoing quotation from Dewey's *Art as Experience* (1934/1987) has profound implications for the ways in which we conceptualize mind and its engine, intelligence. For Dewey, intelligence is not a quantity of something one possesses but the qualities of a process intended to realize some worthwhile aim. The concept of intelligence as a process undermines a view that conceives of intelligence as something that is physical, an entity genetically conferred, something that can be discovered, mapped, and measured.

The qualification that intelligence must be directed toward worthwhile ends is also of consequence; it emphasizes the point that mere cleverness, canniness, and shrewdness that leads to nefarious conduct is not, and cannot be, a mark of intelligence because it neglects the larger consequence to which nefarious modes of thinking ultimately lead. Put most simply, burglars, as Dewey reminds us in *Experience and Education* (1938/1988), do not function as intelligent beings.

Qualities of Intelligence

The association of intelligence with the process of creating art is one that is seldom explored by those studying intelligence. Intelligence, as Dewey suggests, is typically believed to be situated in the use of words and numbers. Consider both the SAT and the Graduate Record Examination as examples of instruments that, among other things, attempt to assess the intellectual ability of students and their readiness for college or graduate school. The abilities to create images in sound and in sight are not included in the data that are used to make judgments about college admission.

The implicit message is that being smart means being smart with words and numbers. Thus, what Dewey gives us is a reconceptualization of intelligence, one that not only emphasizes its process features, one that not only points out its connection to moral considerations, but also one that expands the concept of intelligence so that it includes the selection and organization of qualities as well as the selection and use of symbols, verbal and mathematical.

Smart in Different Ways

Dewey advances this view in 1934, well before conceptions of multiple intelligences and other efforts to diversify the concept emerge in the psychological and educational literature. Dewey recognizes that people are smart in different ways—some in social situations, others in theoretical matters, still others in the arena of the arts.

The implications of this view for school practice are enormous. If we took his views seriously at a practical level, we would be acknowledging the significance of intelligence in all of its varieties and we would be providing opportunities in school for their cultivation. At the moment, individuals smart in ways that schools neglect do not gain opportunities to secure a place in the sun. Our views of human intelligence are limited by comparison, despite the fact that Dewey's ideas on this matter are almost three quarters of a century old.

Ultimately, educational equity requires opportunities for students to follow their bliss, to pursue the realization of their talents, to develop the forms of thought and human intelligence for which they have a special affinity. Dewey provides an early frame of reference for thinking about such matters. It remains for those of us in education to muster the will and the energy to shape educational policies and to structure schools so that the ideals Dewey expresses can be realized in the lives that students lead.

References

Dewey, J. (1987). Art as experience. In J. A. Boydston (Ed.), *John Dewey: The later works, 1925–1953: Vol. 10. 1934* (pp. 1–352). Carbondale: Southern Illinois University Press. (Original work published 1934)

Dewey, J. (1988). Experience and education. In J. A. Boydston (Ed.), *John Dewey: The later works, 1925–1953: Vol. 13. 1938–1939* (pp. 1–62). Carbondale: Southern Illinois University Press. (Original work published 1938)

53

IMAGINATION OF IDEAL ENDS

Craig A. Cunningham

> *Imagination of ideal ends pertinent to actual conditions represents the fruition of a disciplined mind.*
>
> —*A Common Faith,* Later Works 9: 35

In *A Common Faith* (1933/1986), Dewey describes his naturalized conception of God as the active union, or unification, of the actual and the ideal. Although such a union has its mystical or spiritual aspects, for Dewey the most ubiquitous and consequently interesting instances of the union of the actual and the ideal occur in everyday situations involving the application of intelligence to solving practical problems. Such an application of intelligence is, for Dewey, the ultimate expression of the human mind.

Dewey's project in *A Common Faith* is to develop a conception of God that could transcend the specific differences of religions or sects and show that religious experience is a universal element of all human experiences. Religions tend to emphasize what distinguishes them from other religions, resulting in further divisions and separations in an already-divided humanity. Dewey believes that an understanding of the *common* aspects of all religious experiences could help overcome these separations. Although his project ultimately fails—because the particularities of each religious tradition cannot simply be ignored by the followers of that tradition, and because Dewey's reconstruction misses key aspects of what many consider to be the most essential aspects of religion—the book has value as a guide to the ways that ideals and actual conditions interact in myriad situations.

Desirable Ends

Every uncertain situation in life, Dewey suggests, contains a wide range of possible outcomes or endings. (Dewey calls these simply "ends.") Some of these outcomes are desirable, whereas others are not. Desirable ends are those that fulfill the needs or wants of the people involved. The most desirable ends are those that fulfill more needs or more wants for more people. An *ideal end* is an outcome that resolves a situation such that all possible good is realized while any possible negative consequences are avoided. Once an ideal end is chosen, the ideal can be used as a tool for guiding decision making toward the goal of realizing that end. Thus, ideals are tools for solving problems.

The process of selecting a particular end as *ideal* is a process of inquiry or deliberation, in which various possible solutions to a problem or uncertainty are considered. Each possible outcome is examined to determine both how it could be realized and what would be the results if it ensued. Remember that these outcomes don't *exist* initially in any concrete sense. Rather, they are present only in the *imagination*. But imagination should not be dismissed as mere flights of fancy or escape from reality. Rather, imagination is a means for solving problems, especially if it pays attention to real or actual conditions while envisioning ends that are really possible or desirable.

Pertinence

Dewey provides a single word that gives us a clue to the relation of ideal ends to actual conditions: *pertinent*. What is it that makes an ideal end pertinent to actual conditions? The word does not imply a direct causal link between the ideal ends and the conditions. Pertinence is not a straightforward criterion that can be turned into a formula and simply applied in multiple situations. The *Shorter Oxford English Dictionary on Historical Principles* (2002) defines *pertinent* as: "Appropriate, suitable in nature or character; relating to the matter in hand, relevant; to the point; apposite." The words *suitable* and *appropriate* seem to be key synonyms.

How does a person know whether a possible outcome, or end, is "pertinent" to actual conditions? Dewey tells us that it takes a "disciplined mind" to imagine ends that are pertinent to actual conditions. This phrase has two related meanings. A "disciplined" mind is one that has been trained to think effectively, presumably through practice in thinking in a wide variety of situations. But "disciplined" also implies that a mind has acquired the concepts and techniques of one or more disciplines in the academic sense: science, history, art, or mathematics. A "disciplined" mind is better able to imagine suitable or appropriate ideal ends because a disciplined mind is better able to think clearly and to apply a wide range of knowledge and concepts in new situations. A disciplined mind doesn't waste time with impossible or undesirable outcomes but focuses on those ends that are both possible and desirable. A disciplined mind, in other words, is one that uses imagination effectively and efficiently in the choice of suitable solutions to problems.

A simple hypothetical example might help to clarify this process. Suppose that you are driving down the highway at night, in winter, and you get a flat tire. Immediately you are plunged into an uncertain situation. Should you keep driving on the flat tire and hope that you reach a gas station before you destroy the wheel of your car? Should you get out your jack and install the spare? Or should you use your cell phone to call for help? Someone who lacks a disciplined mind may simply panic and fail to consider actual conditions. A more mature or disciplined person will be able to set aside the emotions of fear and panic and focus on reality.

Suppose for a moment that you do not have a cell phone, but you have a spare and a jack in the trunk. However, when you try to loosen the lug nuts on the flat, you discover that the lug nuts will not move. This is certainly a "pertinent" condition! A person who understands physics may know that more leverage can be applied with a longer lug wrench. Or, you may realize that the lug nuts may be rusted in place and that you need a spray lubricant to loosen the nuts. Or, the problem may be that the lug wrench is missing, and the situation involves a choice between trying to flag down passersby or trying to drive to a gas station. Each option presents various difficulties. A knowledge of the geographical area may help you to know whether it is safe to stand outside the car waving your arms.

Imagination

The importance of this idea for teachers is the strong connection it makes between disciplining the mind—teaching it to think and to know—and the imagination. Rather than seeing imagination as the opposite of thought, Dewey suggests that imagination is a key aspect of creative and successful thinking.

Teachers themselves are problem solvers, often working in uncertain situations with multiple goals. In any given situation, what is the best possible outcome? Suppose that a new mainstreamed student with special learning challenges is placed in your classroom. Part of the teacher's job is to work with the parents and resource staff to identify reasonable educational goals for the student. Without imagination, such goals may be limited or unmotivating to the student. Without discipline, such goals may be unrealistic or may fail to take account of available resources. Imagination that pays attention to real conditions (without being completely beholden to changeable conditions) is most likely to result in the formation of goals that are realistic but also inspiring.

References

Dewey, J. (1986). A common faith. In J. A. Boydston (Ed.), *John Dewey: The later works, 1925–1953: Vol. 9. 1933–1934* (pp. 1–58). Carbondale: Southern Illinois University Press. (Original work published 1933)
Shorter Oxford English Dictionary on Historical Principles (5th ed.). (2002). *Pertinent*. Oxford: Oxford University Press.

54

THE TEACHER AS THEORIST AND LOVER

Greg Seals

> *Theory is in the end, as has been well said, the most practical of all things, because this widening of range of attention beyond nearby purpose and desire eventually results in the creation of wider and farther-reaching purposes.*
> —*The Sources of a Science of Education*, Later Works 5: 8

Love, any number of sages would like us to believe, is the most impractical of matters. Love has been compared variously, and by and large unfavorably, with a sweet young dream; a frailty of mind; a purplish wound; and, to paraphrase the Scottish poet James Hogg, "a dizziness that will not let poor bodies go about their bizziness." But anyone who has experienced love knows differently, and better. Over the course of love, we come to recognize the fact that it is love that puts us in touch with what is real, clarifies mind and purpose, contributes to a wholeness and soundness of soul, and establishes equilibrium in the progress of our lives.

As it is with love, so it is with theory. Theory makes it possible for us to interact with the world on more intimate terms. Theories connect isolated facts, as Dewey argues (1929/1984), into a system, a science:

> The practitioner who knows the system and its laws is evidently in possession of a powerful instrument for observing and interpreting what goes on before him. This intellectual tool affects his attitudes and modes of response in what he does. Because the range of understanding is deepened and widened he can take into account remote consequences which were originally hidden from view and hence ignored in his actions. Greater continuity is introduced; he does not isolate situations and deal with them in separation as he was compelled to do when ignorant of connecting principles. At the same time, his practical dealings become more flexible. Seeing more relations he sees more possibilities, more opportunities. He is emancipated from the need of following tradition and

special precedents. His ability to judge being enriched, he has a wider range of alternatives to select from in dealing with individual situations. (p. 11)

In possession of a theory, simple, stagnant *seeing* becomes superabundant, superlatively significant *seeing as*. Ordinary things take on beautiful shapes and wondrous forms they did not possess prior to their appearance in the light shed by the theory. The practitioner with a theory begins to recognize the value and importance of experimenting with, and even romancing, ideas.

Through the Lens of a Theory

Applied more specifically to education, Dewey's idea takes the teacher with a theory to be entirely changed in his or her attitudes and intentions, professional habits of inquiry, observations, and interpretations. Looking at schooling through the lens of a theory enables educators to recognize new problems, devise new procedures, and diversify their understanding and approach to their practical, pedagogical tasks. Ideational interaction with the world of schooling takes on a freer, even flirtatious form for the teacher who is also a theorist of education. What is more, the world, when treated in this manner, magically it would seem, learns to reciprocate in kind.

Loving What You Do

Because he or she has a theory, the scientist, like the lover, is able to see everywhere signs of his or her beloved. If this is true, then the conclusion is obvious. Dewey's apparent paradox about theory being ultimately the most practical of all things is easily resolved by realizing a perfectly clear truth. Having a theory about what you are doing is a way of loving what you do. The difference to everyday action between loving what you do and not loving what you do is so great that it seems entirely correct to say that Dewey is right. There may, after all, be no matter of greater possible practical importance than theory.

Reference

Dewey, J. (1984). The sources of a science of education. In J. A. Boydston (Ed.), *John Dewey: The later works, 1925–1953: Vol. 5. 1929–1930* (pp. 1–40). Carbondale: Southern Illinois University Press. (Original work published 1929)

55

AUTONOMOUS EDUCATION

Free to Determine Its Own Ends

Larry A. Hickman

> *Until educators get the independence and courage to insist that educational aims are to be formed as well as executed within the educative process, they will not come to consciousness of their own function. Others will then have no great respect for educators because educators do not respect their own social place and work.*
> —*The Sources of a Science of Education*, Later Works 5: 38

These two sentences are among the most important that Dewey wrote. They occupy a place at the heart of one of his most important statements about education. Even so, they are in some ways quite surprising—almost absurd, as he would later say—because they contain implicit warnings against several widely accepted ideas.

Implicit Warnings

First, we should not allow social conditions to determine our educational values and practices. When educational values and practices fall prey to ideological constraints, whether political or religious, they inevitably fail. When educational values and practices are called on to reflect community values, they risk default. And when educational values and practices are subsumed to the demands of industry and commerce, they have lost their bearings. Society is a product of education; it does not furnish a standard for educational values and practices.

Second, we should not think that educational values and practices can be determined solely by educational researchers. Educational research can furnish many useful tools by which many educational values and practices can be reconfigured to meet changed and changing conditions. Educational research can provide teachers with inspiration to get through difficult times in the classroom by offering fresh perspectives on old problems. And educational research can help us as teachers think more clearly about our work by locating specific issues in a broader context. But educational research only can provide tools; it cannot determine the specifics of how they are to be used.

Third, and perhaps most surprisingly, we should not think that educational values and practices are determined by us as teachers. As teachers, it is proper and even inevitable that we bring our own ideals and methods to the classroom. But also important is that our ideals and methods be refined and reconfigured by means of the educative process. As teachers, we may be at the heart of the educational process, but we are not the process itself.

Fourth, and finally, the tests we administer to our students must be carefully designed so that they do not interfere with or supplant the educative process. We must remember that IQ tests and other standardized tests tend to focus on only one of many variables to the exclusion of others that may be of equal or greater importance. The educative process demands that a broad range of factors be taken into account. It is easy to forget that tests are by their very nature theoretical exercises; they must not be taken as indicating something final, but only as a source of data for further investigation.

Educational Values and Practices

In short, what Dewey calls the *educative process* determines educational values and practices. The norms of education cannot be conveyed in "cookbook" fashion or in books of lists. They emerge, instead, as teachers interact with students in the process of learning. Education—the educative process—is autonomous, Dewey reminds us. In a robust democracy, it must be free to determine its own ends.

These are complex ideas. They conflict with accepted wisdom and practice, and they are extremely challenging to implement. The influences of social conditions, educational research, the backgrounds and interests of teachers, and standardized testing are often so strong that looking beyond these factors to focus on the educative process itself is difficult. Nevertheless, only by maintaining such a focus can social conditions, educational research, our efforts as teachers, and educational testing enjoy continued reconstruction and renewal.

Reference

Dewey, J. (1984). The sources of a science of education. In J. A. Boydston (Ed.), *John Dewey: The later works, 1925–1953: Vol. 5. 1929–1930* (pp. 1–40). Carbondale: Southern Illinois University Press. (Original work published 1929)

EDITORS AND CONTRIBUTORS

Editors

Donna Adair Breault is department head of Childhood Education and Family Studies at Missouri State University. Her research involves Dewey's theory of inquiry and how it can inform curriculum studies, organizational theory, and faculty development. Her recent work includes two books: *Professional Development Schools: Researching Lessons from the Field* (co-author Rick Breault, Rowman & Littlefield, 2012) and *The Red Light in the Ivory Tower: Contexts and Implications for Entrepreneurial Education* (co-author David M. Callejo-Pérez, Peter Lang, 2012).

Rick Breault is director of the Southwest Regional Professional Development Center. Among his research interests are professional development schools, teacher self-study, and preservice teacher thinking. He was selected in 2013 as a Fulbright Scholar to the Republic of Moldova. Recent publications include "Power and Perspective: The Discourse of PDS Literature" in *The Asian-Pacific Journal of Teacher Education* (upcoming) and "'She was great, but . . .': Examining Preservice Recollections of Favorite and Most Effective Teachers" in *The Professional Educator* (in press).

Contributors

Louise Anderson Allen is a professor of educational leadership at South Carolina State University. She is the author of *A Bluestocking in Charleston: The Life and Career of Laura Bragg* (University of South Carolina Press, 2001) and coauthor of *Turning Points in Curriculum: A Contemporary American Memoir,* 2nd ed. (Pearson, 2006).

Maggie Allison has been a teacher and principal at the middle school level as well as a college instructor of English and education at the graduate and undergraduate levels.

She is pursuing her doctoral degree at West Virginia University while concurrently teaching and conducting action research at a private school in Wheeling, West Virginia.

William Ayers is a school reform activist, distinguished professor of education, and senior university scholar at the University of Illinois at Chicago (retired). His interests focus on the political and cultural contexts of schooling, as well as the meaning and ethical purposes of teachers, students, and families.

Louise M. Berman, whose field is curriculum studies, resides in Washington, DC, and is a professor emerita, University of Maryland, College Park. Her graduate degrees are from Teachers College, Columbia University, where Dewey's presence had a continuing impact on students and programs.

Gert Biesta is professor of educational theory and policy at the University of Luxembourg and editor-in-chief of the journal *Studies in Philosophy and Education*. He writes on the theory and philosophy of education, and educational and social research, with a particular interest in questions of democracy and democratization. His latest book is *The Beautiful Risk of Education* (Paradigm Publishers, 2013).

Robert Boostrom is a professor at the University of Southern Indiana where he teaches courses in the philosophy and history of education. His is the co-editor (with Hugh Sockett) of *A Moral Critique of Contemporary Education* (National Society for the Study of Education Yearbook, 2013) and, since 1997, has been an associate editor of the *Journal of Curriculum Studies.*

Deron Boyles is a professor in the Social Foundations of Education program at Georgia State University. His books include *American Education and Corporations: The Free Market Goes to School* (Garland, 1998) and *Schools or Markets? Commercialism, Privatization, and School-Business Partnerships* (L. Erlbaum Associates, 2005).

Robert V. Bullough, Jr. is professor of teacher education, Brigham Young University, and emeritus professor of educational studies, University of Utah. Since 1999, he has been director of research at the Center for the Improvement of Teacher Education and Schooling. Among his publications is *Uncertain Lives: Children of Promise, Teachers of Hope* (Teachers College Press, 2001).

David M. Callejo-Pérez is the Carl A. Gerstacker Endowed Chair in Education at Saginaw Valley State University in Michigan and the chair of the Human Subjects Institutional Review Board. He has authored three books on civil rights in the South and schools in the inner city and higher education, as well as co-edited five others.

Craig A. Cunningham is an associate professor in the Department of Integrated Studies in Teaching, Technology, and Inquiry at National-Louis University in

Chicago. His research interests include Dewey's metaphysics and theory of moral education, as well as the use of technology to improve teaching and learning.

Laura Dawes is a PhD student at Walden University, where she is studying educational policy. She earned her bachelor's and master's degrees in middle childhood education from the University of Cincinnati and has four years of teaching experience, three in Ohio and one in Virginia.

Audrey M. Dentith is an associate professor of adult learning and development and educational leadership at Lesley University in Cambridge, Massachusetts. Her research and scholarship explores intersections between interdisciplinary curriculum, equity, and ecology.

Sebastián Díaz is the associate vice president for marketing analytics at American Public University System. His research interests include assessment, research methodology, informatics, and knowledge management.

Elliot W. Eisner is the Lee Jacks Professor of Education and professor of art at Stanford University. His work has focused on the arts' contributions to young people's educational development. He is author of *The Arts and the Creation of Mind* (Yale University Press, 2002).

Stephen M. Fishman teaches in the Philosophy Department at the University of North Carolina–Charlotte. His study of student learning in his own classroom has resulted in several publications, including *John Dewey and the Challenge of Classroom Practice* (Teachers College Press, 1998), coauthored with Lucille McCarthy.

David J. Flinders teaches at Indiana University in the areas of secondary education and curriculum foundations. His publications include *Responsive Teaching* (with C. A. Bowers, Teachers College Press, 1990), *Theory and Concepts in Qualitative Research* (with G. E. Mills, Teachers College Press, 1993), and *The Curriculum Studies Reader,* 4th ed. (with S. J. Thornton, Routledge, 2012).

Jim Garrison is a professor of philosophy of education at Virginia Tech in Blacksburg. He is the author of *Teaching, Learning, and Loving* (RoutledgeFalmer, 2004), a book he coedited with Daniel Liston. He is a past president of the Philosophy of Education Society.

Walter S. Gershon is an assistant professor in the School of Teaching, Learning and Curriculum Studies at Kent State University. His scholarship focuses on questions of equity, as well as ways in which educational actors construct meaning through processes of sensation and signification.

Lisa Goeken-Galliart is a sixth-grade teacher in Bloomington-Normal, Illinois, and a part-time instructor in the Curriculum and Instruction Department at Illinois State University.

Jesse Goodman is a professor of education and American studies at Indiana University, co-director of a master's-level elementary teacher education program, and former chair of the doctoral curriculum studies program. He also is a co-director of the Harmony Education Center.

Kyle Greenwalt is an assistant professor in the Department of Teacher Education at Michigan State University. He is interested in the study of curriculum through the lenses of lived experience and performative identity. Like John Dewey, he enjoys walking in the woods with his children, as well as Spartan basketball.

Chara Haeussler Bohan is an associate professor in the School of Education at Baylor University, Waco, Texas. Her research interests include education history, social studies education, and women's studies. She is the author of *Go to the Sources: Lucy Maynard Salmon and the Teaching of History* (Peter Lang, 2004).

James G. Henderson is professor of curriculum studies at Kent State University. He has authored, co-authored, and co-edited five books on the topics of reflective teaching, curriculum leadership, curriculum wisdom, and curriculum critique, and is currently completing a book on the study of democratic practical wisdom.

Randy Hewitt is an assistant professor of educational studies at the University of Central Florida. His research interests include pragmatism, critical theory, the reproduction of social class, and democratic education.

Larry A. Hickman is director of the Center for Dewey Studies and professor of philosophy at Southern Illinois University–Carbondale. He is author or editor of numerous books on Dewey, including *John Dewey Between Pragmatism and Constructivism,* 3rd ed. (Fordham University Press, 2009) and *Pragmatism as Post-Postmodernism: Lessons from John Dewey,* 3rd ed. (Fordham University Press, 2007).

Peter S. Hlebowitsh is the dean of the College of Education at the University of Alabama. He has helped to direct several State Department–sponsored civic education reform projects in Central and Eastern Europe. He is the author of *Designing the School Curriculum* (Pearson, 2005).

Patrick M. Jenlink is professor of doctoral studies in the Department of Secondary Education and Educational Leadership at Stephen F. Austin State University. His published books include *Dewey's Democracy and Education Revisited* (Rowman & Littlefield, 2009) and *Leading for Democracy* (Rowman & Littlefield, 2012).

Matthew Keeler is a master's student in philosophy at Texas Tech University where he studies philosophy of mind, philosophy of cognitive science, and early modern philosophy. Prior to his graduate work, he was a pre-K teacher in Decatur, Georgia.

Thomas E. Kelly is an associate professor of education at John Carroll University where he coordinates the Adolescent and Young Adult Licensure Program. His scholarly interests focus on the meaning, promise, and challenges of critical democratic pedagogy.

M. Frances Klein is professor emeritus of the University of Southern California. She has been an educational researcher and frequent presenter at educational conferences. Her research and publication areas include curriculum theory, translating theory into practice, curriculum practices, and classroom practice.

Craig Kridel is professor of educational foundations and research and director of the McKissick Museum of Education at the University of South Carolina. He serves on the John Dewey Society Advisory Board. His research interests include progressive education, biography, and documentary editing.

Margaret Macintyre Latta is a professor of curriculum theory at the University of British Columbia Okanagan, Canada. In her scholarship, she studies and pursues John Dewey's assertion that within aesthetic experience is a learning approach and direction.

Dan Marshall is retired professor of education from Penn State University. As a member of the College of Education's Educational Leadership Program, he taught courses in curriculum studies and secondary teacher education. His research interests include curriculum studies and various schooling issues.

Jonathan T. Martin is a course mentor in general education at Western Governors University where he mentors undergraduate students in mathematics courses in an online learning environment. He is also currently a curriculum & instruction doctoral student at West Virginia University with a research interest in social and equity issues in mathematics education.

Christy M. Moroye is an assistant professor of educational foundations and curriculum studies at the University of Northern Colorado, Greeley. Her research interests include aesthetic and ecological perspectives of curriculum and teaching. She is the associate editor for *Curriculum and Teaching Dialogue*.

Robert C. Morris is professor of curriculum studies at the University of West Georgia. He is the counselor for the College's Omicron Omega Chapter of

Kappa Delta Pi. His current research interests are related to leadership activities for curricular and instructional change.

George W. Noblit is a professor and head of the PhD program in the School of Education, University of North Carolina–Chapel Hill. He specializes in the sociology of knowledge, school reform, critical race studies, anthropology of education, and qualitative research methods.

John M. Novak is professor of education at Brock University, St. Catharines, Ontario, Canada, and former president of the Society of Professors of Education. Among his books are *Inviting Educational Leadership* (Pearson, 2002) and *Inviting School Success,* 4th ed. (with William W. Purkey, Wadsworth, 2005).

Linda O'Neill is an associate professor in foundations of education at Northern Illinois University where she teaches undergraduate and graduate courses in philosophy of education and educational policy. Her research interests include pragmatism, hermeneutics, and philosophical analysis of educational policy.

William A. Reid was visiting professor of curriculum and instruction, University of Texas at Austin before he retired. He is author of a number of works on curriculum history and deliberative theory, including *Curriculum as Institution and Practice* (L. Erlbaum Associates, 1999).

A. G. Rud is distinguished professor in the Department of Teaching and Learning at Washington State University. His areas of research include philosophy of education and the moral dimensions of teaching, learning, and leading. His most recent book is an edited volume with Jim Garrison, *Teaching with Reverence: Reviving an Ancient Virtue for Today's Schools* (Palgrave Macmillan, 2012).

William H. Schubert is professor of education and chair of curriculum and instruction at the University of Illinois–Chicago. A former president of the John Dewey Society, he has served as vice president of the American Educational Research Association and, in 2004, received AERA's Lifetime Achievement Award in Curriculum Studies.

Greg Seals teaches social foundations of education at the College of Staten Island, City University of New York. His main scholarly loves are the metaphysics of education, the philosophy of John Dewey, and school desegregation.

Paul Shaker, who began his career as a humanities teacher, served as professor and dean of education at six institutions. He retired from his most recent position at Simon Fraser University of British Columbia. As a Fulbright senior scholar, he has studied and worked in Japan, Saudi Arabia, and Kuwait.

Edmund C. Short is professor of education emeritus, The Pennsylvania State University, and is currently faculty associate, University of Central Florida. He is founding editor of the *Journal of Curriculum and Supervision* and editor of *Forms of Curriculum Inquiry* (State University of New York Press, 1991).

Sam F. Stack, Jr. is professor of social and cultural foundations at West Virginia University. He is author of *Elsie Ripley Clapp (1879–1965): Her Life and the Community School* (Peter Lang, 2004) and co-author with Doug Simpson of *Teachers, Leaders, and Schools: Essays by John Dewey* (Southern Illinois University Press, 2010).

Daniel Tanner is former president of the John Dewey Society and professor in the Graduate School of Education, Rutgers University, New Brunswick, New Jersey.

Barbara J. Thayer-Bacon teaches undergraduate and graduate courses on philosophy and history of education, social philosophy, and cultural diversity. Her primary research areas are philosophy of education, pragmatism, feminist theory and pedagogy, and cultural studies in education.

Alexander David Tuel is a third-year doctoral candidate at West Virginia University. He currently works at Garrett College, a small community college in western Maryland.

P. Bruce Uhrmacher is professor of education at the Morgridge College of Education, University of Denver. His research focuses on aesthetic education, alternative schools, and educational environments. He is the editor of *Curriculum and Teaching Dialogue* and faculty advisor to the Aesthetic Education Institute of Colorado.

Gary Weilbacher is an assistant professor of curriculum and instruction at Illinois State University. He taught middle school for 11 years in Madison, Wisconsin. His research interests include curriculum integration, multicultural education, and youth culture.

Ron W. Wilhelm, professor in the Department of Teacher Education and Administration at the University of North Texas, teaches courses in multicultural education, curriculum implementation and evaluation, and qualitative research methods. He has served as counselor for the Alpha Iota Chapter of Kappa Delta Pi since 1992.

George Willis is a professor of education at the University of Rhode Island. He has been a member of the executive board of the John Dewey Society and a co-chair of the Society's Lectures Commission.

William G. Wraga is professor of educational administration and policy, University of Georgia. He teaches and researches in the areas of curriculum theory, development, history, and policy. He is author of *Progressive Pioneer: Alexander James Inglis (1879–1924) and American Secondary Education* (Peter Lang, 2007) and *Democracy's High School* (University Press of America, 1994).

TRANSCRIPT OF PERSONAL LETTER

A handwritten version of this personal letter from John Dewey appears on page 199 of this volume.

My dear Janey and Lucy & Gordon

Your good nice letters came this morning, and as they were written Tuesday you can see how far it is to where I am. This country isn't the mountains, but it is all hills—the funniest kind of hills too. They aren't arranged at all. They just start up everywhere and they are mostly all round so which ever way you go, it is first down & then up, or else first up & then down. The main street is a ridge that only goes down on two sides for a while, but everything else is just knobs & bumps. Maybe ~~Miss Bolli will~~ Gordon will remember Miss Bolli who lived with the Thomases ~~[that over mrs.]~~ the year we lived next to the Thomases.[1] Well she lives here & yesterday she & her mother took me to drive—a very pretty drive along the river which is lined with bluffs & beautiful hills & woods everywhere. The passion vine was in bloom & grows wild by the side of the road just as woodbine does in the Adirondack.

I am sorry to hear about the wasps; just about 12 years ago there were a lot & Fred & Evelyn took their turns getting "fat" then. I am glad Pine Tree Ledge is still there & I hope it wont slip off downhill before we get back from Europe.

Papa sends you lots of love. Thank Mary for writing for you.

ooooo xxxxx +++++

Daddy

---

[1] Calvin Thomas and John Dewey were in Ann Arbor at the University of Michigan together.

INDEX

Note: Page numbers in italics indicate photographs.